The Software Vectorization Handbook

Applying Multimedia Extensions for
Maximum Performance

Aart J. C. Bik

INTEL
PRESS

ISBN 0-9743649-2-4

Publisher: Rich Bowles
Editor: David J. Clark
Managing Editor: David B. Spencer
Content Manager: Stuart Goldstein
Text Design, Graphics, and Composition: Wasser Studios
Cover Art: Ted Cyrek Designs

Library of Congress Cataloging in Publication Data:

Printed in the United States of America

10 9 8 7 6 5 4 3 2 1

First printing, June 2004

For Renu and Karina

Contents

Preface

The growing popularity of multimedia extensions has renewed interest in vectorizing compilers. This book provides a detailed presentation of compiler optimizations that convert sequential code into a form that exploits multimedia extensions. The presentation focuses on the C programming language and multimedia extensions to the Intel® architecture, although most conversion methods easily generalize to other imperative programming languages and multimedia instruction sets. The presented optimizations have been incorporated in the Intel® C++ and Fortran compilers that support automatic vectorization for the Intel MMX™ technology and streaming-SIMD extensions for IA-32 processors, and the Intel Wireless MMX technology for the Intel XScale® microarchitecture. As such, the book addresses an audience such as compiler engineers and programmers of scientific, engineering, and multimedia applications who have an interest in improving software performance by means of multimedia extensions.

Many people have made this book possible. I would like to thank all members of the Intel Compiler Lab and Intel Nizhny Novgorod Lab numerics team. In particular, I would like to thank Richard Wirt, Jonathan Khazam, William Savage, and Kevin J. Smith for giving me the opportunity to write this book; Milind Girkar for skillfully managing IA-32 compiler development; Xinmin Tian for his inspiring work ethics; and Kevin B. Smith for teaching me much about compiler engineering. Other knowledgeable engineers I had the privilege of working closely with are Seth Abraham, Zia Ansari, Robert Cox, Robert Geva, Paul Grey, Mohammad Haghighat, Alexander Isaev, Michael Julier, Wei Li, Christopher Lishka, Knud Kirkegaard, David Kreitzer, Andrey Naraikin, John Ng, Hideki Saito, Dale Schouten, David Sehr, Craig Stoller, and Ernesto Su.

A special thanks to my evaluators and reviewers, Fabian Breg, Robert van Engelen, Milind Girkar, Gerard Harbers, Sam Larsen, Jitendra Maheshwari, Andrey Naraikin, Ramesh Peri, Hideki Saito, Greg Smith, Kevin B. Smith, and Xinmin Tian for providing valuable feedback on early drafts of the book.

The people of Intel Press have been very helpful during the writing process. In particular, I would like to thank my managing editor David Spencer, content manager Stuart Goldstein, and editor David Clark for their kind and professional guidance during all stages of the publishing process.

Finally, I would like to thank my parents for their love and support during my "temporary" visit to the USA and my wife Renu and daughter Karina for their love and patience while this book was written.

Aart J.C. Bik

Santa Clara, 2004

http://www.aartbik.com/

Chapter 1

Introduction

Computer designers have always looked for mechanisms to improve the performance of computer systems. At the technological level, the speed and packaging densities of circuits have been enhanced substantially over the years. In 1978, for example, the Intel® 8086 processor was introduced with a maximum clock frequency of 8 megahertz and with 29,000 transistors on a die. The Pentium® 4 processor, on the other hand, was introduced in 2000 at a clock frequency of 1.5 gigahertz and with 42 million transistors on a die. The physical limitations of the speed of electronic components has led to a search for other mechanisms to improve performance. This chapter briefly reviews acceleration mechanisms at the architectural level.

Architectural Acceleration Mechanisms

At the architectural level, many advances have been made that achieve one of the following two objectives (Flynn 1995; Hennessy and Patterson 1990; Hockney and Jesshope 1981; Jordan and Alaghband 2003; Kumar et al. 1994; Mano 1993; Quinn 1987 and 1994; Sima, Fountain, and Kacsuk 1997; van de Goor 1989):

- Decrease *latency*, the time from start to completion of an operation.
- Increase *bandwidth*, the width and rate of operations.

Architectural advances that provide direct hardware implementations of expensive, frequently-executed operations have reduced execution latency. On the other hand, memory latency has been improved at the architectural level with larger register files, multiple register sets, and caches—high-speed memory buffers placed between the processor and main memory to exploit the spatial and temporal locality of reference exhibited by most programs. Architectural advances that enhance the execution bandwidth or memory bandwidth can usually be classified as one of the following two forms of parallelism: *pipelining* and *replication*.

Pipelining and Replication

Pipelining subdivides the execution of an operation into several stages to enable the simultaneous execution of different stages for a stream of operations. This subdivision allows each subsequent operation to enter the pipeline as soon as the previous operation has exited the first stage, like the construction of automobiles in an assembly line. Once all stages of the pipeline are filled in this manner, a new result becomes available after every unit of time it takes to complete the slowest stage. Replication, on the other hand, simply duplicates hardware resources to enable the simultaneous execution of different operations.

Figure 1.1 illustrates the two acceleration mechanisms. Suppose that an operation that takes three clock cycles to complete is executed many times—o_1, o_2, o_3, etc. The sequential implementation I-seq produces one new result at every third clock cycle. The pipelined implementation I-pipe subdivides execution of the operation into three separate stages of one clock cycle and produces a new result at every clock cycle once all stages of the pipeline are filled. Alternatively, replicating hardware resources three times yields a parallel implementation, I-repl, that produces three new results at every third clock cycle.

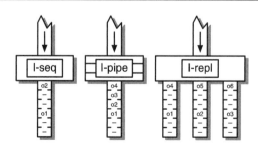

Figure 1.1   Pipelining versus Replication

As can be seen in the performance graph in Figure 1.2, after six clock cycles, pipelining and replication increase the number of results from two to four and six, respectively. After twelve clock cycles, the number of results increases from four to ten and twelve, respectively.

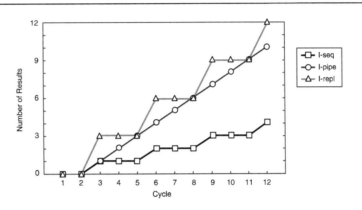

Figure 1.2   Performance of Pipelining versus Replication

Speedup

The *speedup* that results from using an acceleration mechanism is defined as

$$S = \frac{T}{T_a}$$

where T and T_a denote, respectively, the original and accelerated execution time in clock cycles or seconds. This ratio provides an important measure for the quality of acceleration, where $S > 1$ indicates speedup, $S = 1$ indicates no change, and $S < 1$ indicates slowdown (Dowd and Severance 1998, Hennessy and Patterson 1990, Jordan and Alaghband 2003, Kumar et al. 1994, Lewis 1994, Mano 1993, and Quinn 1987). In the example above, the speedup for obtaining three results with three-stage pipelining and three-way replication is 9/5 and 9/3, respectively, which indicates that the accelerated versions execute three operations 1.8 times faster and 3 times faster than the sequential version. Even though exploiting p-way parallelism theoretically bounds the speedup as $S \leq p$, sometimes secondary effects are responsible for a slightly larger speedup. This phenomenon is known as superlinear speedup.

A Quick Tour of Parallel Architectures

Pipelining and replication appear at different architectural levels and in various forms. The introduction of wider data paths and multiple memory paths are examples of using replication to improve memory bandwidth. Similarly, memory interleaving is a form of pipelining that subdivides the memory system into a number of banks that can quickly service consecutive memory references. Common architectures that use parallelism in the form of pipelining and/or replication to enhance execution bandwidth can be classified as shown in Figure 1.3 (Hennessy and Patterson 1990; Sima, Fountain, and Kacsuk 1997).

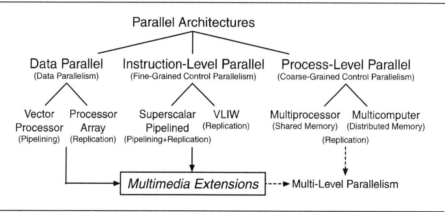

Figure 1.3   Classification of Parallel Architectures

The classification of parallel architectures, briefly discussed in the next sections, provides a context in which to place a recent architectural trend to enhance execution bandwidth: the multimedia extensions.

Data Parallel Architectures

Since the early days of supercomputing, there have been architectural advances that utilize data parallelism to improve execution bandwidth. *Data parallelism* arises in many numerical, floating-point intensive applications in science or engineering, where each operation is applied to multiple elements in a data set, usually a vector or a matrix. As a result, such applications exhibit independent, regular, recurring access patterns and operations that can execute in parallel. Using either pipelining or replication to utilize data parallelism gives rise to two different classes of data parallel architectures.

The pipelined *vector processors*, such as the Cray 1 (Russel 1978), provide an instruction set that operates on vectors rather than scalars. During the execution of vector instructions, vectors of data elements stream directly from memory or vector registers to pipelined functional units and back—possibly optimized with *chaining*, where results that exit the last stage of one pipeline directly enter the first stage of a second pipeline. Because all operations in a vector instruction are independent, the functional units can use deep pipelines in which short stages allow for high clock frequencies. Moreover, since one single vector instruction defines many operations, vector processors have low instruction bandwidth requirements, while fetching a unit stride vector from memory works well with memory interleaving.

The translation of sequential code into vector instructions is referred to as *vectorization*. To illustrate this kind of translation, consider the following Fortran DO loop that sequentially adds 64 elements of arrays A and B into array C.

```
      REAL A(64), B(64), C(64)
      ...
      DO 10 I = 1, 64
        C(I) = A(I) + B(I)
 10   CONTINUE
```

Since all iterations perform independent operations, the sequential loop as a whole can be mapped onto only a few vector instructions, as illustrated below with a pseudo vector-assembly language.

```
MOVE    VL,  #64        ; set vector length to 64
VLOAD   VR0, A          ; load  VL elements from A      into VR0
VLOAD   VR1, B          ; load  VL elements from B      into VR1
VADD    VR2, VR1, VR0   ; add   VL elements from VR0/1 into VR2
VSTORE  C,   VR2        ; store VL elements from VR2    into C
```

During execution of the VADD instruction, two vectors stream from vector registers VR0 and VR1 through a pipelined adder back into a third vector register VR2, as shown in Figure 1.4. Once all stages of the pipeline are filled, this accelerated execution mechanism produces one new result at every clock cycle.

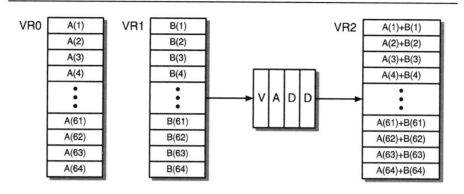

Figure 1.4   The VADD Instruction

Because rewriting a large sequential application into vector instructions by hand is time consuming, successfully using the full potential of vector processors strongly depends on the ability of a compiler to do this translation with little or no assistance from the programmer. A compiler that can automatically detect opportunities to exploit vector instructions in sequential code is called a *vectorizing compiler*. Over the years, compiling for vector processors, with a traditional emphasis on Fortran programs, has become one of the more mature areas of compiling for parallel architectures.

The *processor arrays*, such as the Maspar MP-1 (Blank 1990), utilize data parallelism by means of replication. These massively parallel supercomputers fit the single-instruction-multiple-data (SIMD) paradigm (Flynn 1966), because a single control unit dispatches instructions to an ensemble of simple processing elements that apply each of these instructions synchronously to different data elements. Rewriting sequential code into a form that exploits this kind of lock-step parallelism is usually also referred to as vectorization, although the translation has the added complexity of efficiently dealing with the private memories of processing elements and the interconnection network.

Instruction-Level Parallel Architectures

Architectures that exploit *fine-grained control parallelism* between individual instructions to enhance execution bandwidth can be classified into two common kinds of instruction-level parallel architectures.

The first kind uses instruction pipelining to subdivide the execution of each machine instruction into a number of stages, traditionally something like an instruction fetch, an instruction decode, an operand fetch, an instruction execute, and a store back. Because short stages allow for high clock frequencies, recent trends favor deeper instruction pipelines. Instruction pipelining is commonly combined with replication, which gives rise to *superscalar pipelined architectures.* The Pentium processor, for example, was introduced in 1993 as the first member of the Intel architecture family featuring two five-stage pipelines, named the U pipe and the V pipe, that together are able to execute two instructions per clock cycle. Members of the P6 family—the Pentium Pro, Pentium II, and Pentium III processors—are three-way superscalar pipelined architectures that use 12-stage pipelines with out-of-order execution. The Pentium 4 processor even uses 20-stage pipelines.

The second kind of instruction-level parallel architecture is formed by the *very long instruction word* or *VLIW architectures,* where a very long instruction word controls usually 5 to 30 replicated execution units. Because all operations in one instruction must be independent, VLIW architectures pose a heavier burden on the compiler for efficient code generation than today's superscalar architectures, where hazards between subsequent instructions are resolved in hardware. A recent derivative of the VLIW architecture is the Itanium® processor, where *explicit parallel instruction computing* (EPIC) technology provides the capability to execute multiple instructions simultaneously.

Process-Level Parallel Architectures

Architectures that exploit *coarse-grained control parallelism* in constructs like loops, functions, or complete programs are called process-level parallel architectures. Such architectures replicate complete asynchronously executing processors to enhance execution bandwidth and, hence, fit the multiple-instruction-multiple-data (MIMD) paradigm (Flynn 1966). As illustrated in Figure 1.5, the memory organization further subdivides these architectures into *multicomputers*, also called distributed memory or message-passing architectures, and *multiprocessors*, or shared memory architectures. In a multicomputer, each processor has its own local memory; access to remote memory requires explicit message passing over the interconnection network, which is typically a ring, tree, mesh, or hypercube. A multiprocessor, on the other hand, uses a shared memory address space for the processors and typically a bus, crossbar switch, or multistage network as an interconnection network.

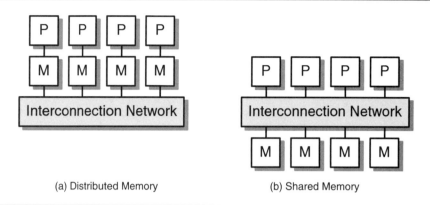

(a) Distributed Memory   (b) Shared Memory

Figure 1.5   Process-Level Parallel Architectures

Process-level parallel architectures once belonged to the domain of expensive supercomputers. The reduced cost of processor manufacturing has enabled the use of these architectures in mainstream computing as well. Scientific institutes use clusters of PCs as cheaper alternatives to distributed memory supercomputers. Furthermore, desktop computers with two or four processors and a shared memory are quite common nowadays. A related architectural advancement is the Hyper-Threading Technology (HT Technology) (Intel 2003), in which a single physical processor consists of several logical processors that are able to execute different processes in parallel. Unlike a multiprocessor, however, some core resources of the physical processor are shared among the logical processors.

Multimedia Extensions

Prompted by the growing popularity of multimedia applications, a recent architectural trend uses multimedia extensions to enhance execution bandwidth. These extensions follow the SIMD paradigm by exploiting *wide* data paths and functional units as *replicated* functional units that simultaneously operate on narrow data paths of *packed data elements*— relatively short vectors that reside in memory or registers. Because a single multimedia instruction applies one operation to multiple data elements in parallel, such instruction sets provide a new way to utilize data parallelism at instruction level. As such, multimedia extensions borrow concepts from both the instruction-level parallel architectures and the data parallel architectures as shown in Figure 1.3. When incorporated in process-level parallel architectures, multimedia extensions also enable exploiting multilevel parallelism—both fine-grained and coarse-grained control parallelism.

Although different vendors support various families of multimedia instruction sets (Slingerland and Smith 2000), each with its own unique characteristics, the underlying concepts are quite similar. This book focuses on multimedia extensions to the Intel architecture, briefly described below.

MMX™ Technology

The 64-bit Intel MMX technology became available on the Pentium processor and Pentium II processor (Bhargava et al. 1998; Bistry et al. 1997; Booth 1997; Greene 1997; Intel 1997, 2003b, and 2003c; Lempeg, Peleg, and Weiser 1997; Peleg and Weiser 1996). This technology consists of the following extensions to the Intel architecture:

- Eight 64-bit registers: mm0 through mm7
- Four 64-bit integer data types:
  - 8 packed bytes (8 x 8-bit)
  - 4 packed words (4 x 16-bit)
  - 2 packed doublewords (2 x 32-bit)
  - 1 quadword (1 x 64-bit)
- Instructions that operate on the 64-bit data types

As illustrated in Figure 1.6, the eight 64-bit registers are equivalent to the lower part of the data register stack R0 through R7 of the floating-point unit (FPU). This aliasing keeps the MMX technology transparent to the operating system, because instructions that save and restore the FPU state during a context switch also save and restore the registers of the MMX technology. Unfortunately, this implies that MMX instructions and FPU code cannot easily be mixed at the instruction level. Each FPU code section should be exited with an empty FPU stack, and instruction emms must be used after each MMX instruction section to empty the tag register. All other MMX instructions fill the entire tag register and clear the top-of-stack (TOS) field in the status register, which causes subsequent FPU instructions to produce unexpected results.

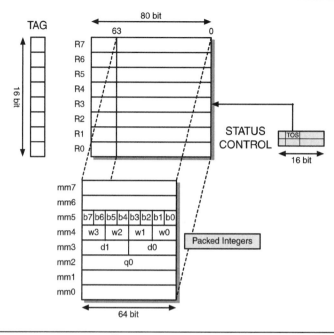

Figure 1.6 The 64-bit MMX™ Technology

The MMX technology supports data movement, arithmetic, logical, comparison, conversion, and shift instructions that operate on the 64-bit integer data types. Some of the arithmetic instructions process the packed data elements using conventional *wrap-around arithmetic,* where individual results that exceed the corresponding data type range wrap around by truncating the results to the least significant bits. Other arithmetic instructions use *saturation arithmetic,* where individual results that would wrap around are clipped to an appropriate data type range limit. For example, the four-way SIMD parallel instruction `paddw` `mm0, mm1` adds four individual words in the source operand `mm1` to four individual words in the destination operand `mm0` using wrap-around arithmetic, as illustrated in the following table:

mm0	0xfffc	0xfffd	0xfffe	0xffff
mm1	0x0001	0x0001	0x0001	0x0001
mm0	0xfffd	0xfffe	0xffff	0x0000

On the other hand, the four-way SIMD parallel instruction `paddusw` `mm0, mm1` uses saturation arithmetic to add four unsigned words, where individual data elements that would wrap around are clipped to the maximum unsigned word value `0xffff`, or 65,535 in decimal, as can be seen below. No interaction, such as carry, exists between the individual data elements.

mm0	0xfffc	0xfffd	0xfffe	0xffff
mm1	0x0001	0x0001	0x0001	0x0001
mm0	0xfffd	0xfffe	0xffff	0xffff

Streaming-SIMD Extensions

Support for instructions on packed single-precision floating-point numbers was first introduced by the Pentium III processor with the 128-bit streaming-SIMD extensions, or SSE (Intel 2003b and 2003c; Raman, Pentkovski, and Keshava 2000; Thakkar and Huff 1999). The Pentium 4 processor further extended this support with the 128-bit SSE2 (Hinton et al. 2001; Intel 2003b and 2003c), featuring instructions on packed double-precision floating-point numbers and integers, while the Pentium 4 processor with HT Technology introduced the 128-bit SSE3 with some additional support for complex numbers (Intel 2003b and 2003c; Smith, Bik, and Tian 2004). These technologies together extend the Intel architecture as follows:

■ Eight 128-bit registers: xmm0 through xmm7

■ Two 128-bit floating-point and five 128-bit integer data types:
 – 4 packed single-precision floating-point numbers (4 x 32-bit)
 – 2 packed double-precision floating-point numbers (2 x 64-bit)
 – 16 packed bytes (16 x 8-bit)
 – 8 packed words (8 x 16-bit)
 – 4 packed doublewords (4 x 32-bit)
 – 2 packed quadwords (2 x 64-bit)
 – 1 double quadword (1 x 128-bit)

■ Instructions that operate on the 128-bit data types

The eight 128-bit registers together with control and status register MXCSR, shown in Figure 1.7, form an extension to the state of the Intel architecture. This state must be explicitly saved and restored by the operating system during a context switch.

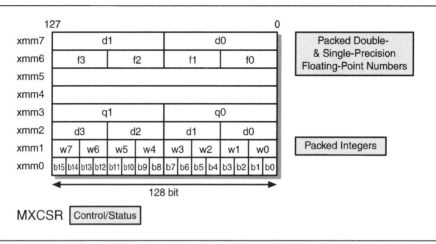

Figure 1.7   The 128-bit Streaming-SIMD Extensions

The SSE/SSE2/SSE3 instructions can be grouped in data movement, arithmetic, logical, comparison, conversion, shift, shuffle, and unpack instructions that operate on the 128-bit data types, and some cacheability control, prefetch, and state-management instructions. The integer instructions are mostly extensions of the MMX technology to the wider data format. The floating-point arithmetic instructions perform IEEE 754-compliant operations on packed floating-point single-precision and double-precision numbers. For instance, as illustrated below, the four-way SIMD parallel instruction addps xmm0, xmm1 adds the individual single-precision floating-point numbers in the source operand xmm1 to the individual single-precision floating-point numbers in the destination operand xmm0.

xmm0	72.0	20.0	25.3	11.1
xmm1	12.1	11.1	10.6	44.3
xmm0	84.1	31.1	35.9	55.4

Intra-Register Vectorization

Converting sequential code into a form that exploits a multimedia instruction set strongly resembles vectorization for data parallel architectures. Multimedia extensions, however, utilize data parallelism at a more fine-grained level than data parallel architectures. Figure 1.8 contrasts the level of data parallelism exploited by a typical vector processor against the level exploited by the MMX technology. In the former, a vector of 64-bit operands streams from a vector register (VR0) to a pipelined functional unit to allow *vertical parallelism* in applying an operation to different data elements. In the latter, a single 64-bit operand streams from a multimedia register (mm0) into the functional unit to allow *horizontal parallelism* in applying an operation to packed data elements. To emphasize this difference, this book will sometimes use the term *intra-register vectorization* to refer specifically to the conversion of sequential code into a form that utilizes multimedia extensions to exploit data parallelism. Similar terminology found in the literature is SWAR, or SIMD within a register (Fisher and Dietz 1998); SLP, or *super*word level parallelism (Larsen 2000; Larsen and Amarasinghe 2000; Shin, Chame, and Hall 2003); or, conversely, *sub*word parallelism (Krall and Lelait 2000; Lee 1996; Pryanishnikov, Krall, and Horspool 2003; Sreraman and Govindarajan 2000); and mini-vector instructions (Skadron et al. 2001).

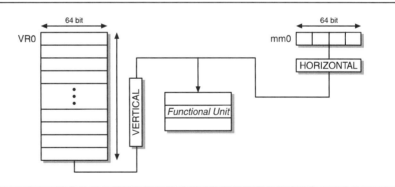

Figure 1.8   Vertical Parallelism versus Horizontal Parallelism

Intra-register vectorization is illustrated with the following saturation example, written in C programming language:

```c
unsigned short x[N], y[N], z[N];

void sat(int n) {
  int i;
  for (i = 0; i < n; i++) {
    int t = x[i] + y[i];
    z[i] = (t <= 65535) ? t : 65535;
  }
}
```

The for statement in this example can be mapped onto a loop with only a few multimedia instructions, as shown below. Do not worry if this conversion is not clear, it will be thoroughly revisited in later chapters.

```asm
     xor     eax,    eax      ; i = 0
L:   movdqa  xmm0,   x[eax]   ; load  8 words from x
     paddusw xmm0,   y[eax]   ; add   8 words from y and saturate
     movdqa  z[eax], xmm0     ; store 8 words into z
     add     eax,    16       ; increment 8x2
     cmp     eax,    ecx      ;
     jb      L                ; looping logic (iterates n/8 times)
                              ; followed by cleanup loop
```

Because the multimedia instructions exploit eight-way SIMD parallelism, this vector loop only iterates n/8 times. A sequential cleanup loop deals with iterations that remain if n is not a multiple of eight. Figure 1.9 plots the speedup of the vector version compared to a sequential version on a 3-gigahertz Pentium 4 processor for increasing values of n—based on execution times that were obtained by running the function sat() repeatedly and dividing the total run time accordingly. Up to a maximum of eight iterations, all work must be performed by the cleanup loop, and no speedup is achieved. After that, the vector version exhibits speedup, with local maxima for workloads where n is a multiple of eight and a local minimum for workloads where n is one less than a multiple of eight. For larger values of n, exploiting eight-way SIMD parallelism combined with branch overhead reduction for both the conditional expression and looping logic even yields superlinear speedup, where the vector version with saturation arithmetic is 10 times faster than the sequential version with conventional wrap-around arithmetic and conditional flow.

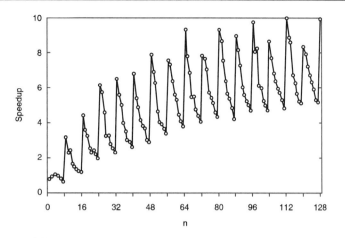

Figure 1.9   Saturation Speedup—3-Gigahertz Pentium® 4 Processor

Intra-register vectorization can be done *explicitly* by the programmer with intrinsics, inline assembly, or data parallel language extensions such as the SWAR-C language supported by the Scc compiler (Fisher and Dietz 1998) that provides a portable programming model for a variety of multimedia extensions, or the data parallel Pascal dialect supported by the Vector Pascal compiler (Cockshott and Renfrew 2002). Alternatively, this conversion can be done *implicitly* by a vectorizing compiler that automatically detects opportunities to exploit multimedia instructions in the original sequential code. Although the explicit approaches can be very effective, letting a compiler automatically do at least parts of the intra-register vectorization has some definite advantages.

First, automatic vectorization has been well studied in the context of data parallel architectures, and techniques to convert sequential code into vector instructions are described in detail in the literature (Allen and Kennedy 1987; Banerjee 1988, 1993, 1994, and 1997; Dongarra et al. 1991; Kuck 1978; Levesque and Williamson 1991; Neves 1984; Padua and Wolfe 1986; Polychronopoulos 1988; Wolfe 1988, 1989, and 1996; Zima and Chapman 1990). Many of these techniques are directly applicable to converting sequential code into multimedia instructions. Second, the use of a vectorizing compiler is less prone to error, simplifies the task of the programmer, and enables the vectorization of existing software. Use of a compiler also avoids potentially huge investments that would be required to rewrite this code into a form that exploits multimedia instructions.

Finally, the implicit approach is more flexible. One sequential program can be mapped to many vectorized versions that are tailored to peculiarities of different target architectures such as available multimedia extensions, cache-line size, or relative cost of instructions. This approach also allows future-generation vectorizing compilers to take advantage of new multimedia extensions.

This book gives a detailed account of the methods that are used by the Intel C++ and Fortran compilers to exploit multimedia extensions, with a focus on the streaming-SIMD extensions and the C programming language. Preliminaries on the instruction set, the C programming language, and data dependence analysis are given in Chapters 2 through 4. Readers who are already familiar with these topics can skim this material or jump directly to Chapters 5 through 8, which discuss intra-register vectorization in detail. Finally, Chapter 9 shows how to use the Intel compilers to exploit multimedia extensions effectively with a minimum of engineering efforts.

Chapter 2

Instruction Set Preliminaries

The 128-bit streaming-SIMD extensions extend the Intel architecture with eight 128-bit registers xmm0 through xmm7, a few 128-bit integer and floating-point data types, and instructions that operate on these data types. The instruction set features data movement, arithmetic, logical, comparison, and conversion instructions that are based on the SIMD paradigm. In addition, shift, shuffle, and unpack instructions transfer individual data elements into the appropriate position; cacheability control and prefetch instructions help to minimize cache pollution for non-temporal data and prefetch data before its actual use; and state management instructions operate on the new multimedia state.

This chapter summarizes the SSE/SSE2/SSE3 instruction set and provides a short description of the Intel NetBurst® microarchitecture as background for performance discussions in subsequent chapters. A detailed description of all aspects of the Intel architecture can be found in the Intel documentation (Intel 2003b, 2003c, and 2003d).

Instruction Set Summary

In the following description of the instruction set, instructions and possible suffixes are listed separately. For example, instruction pavg with suffix set [b,w] actually gives rise to two instructions pavgb and pavgw. Integer instructions use suffixes b for byte, or 8-bit; w for word, or 16-bit;

d for doubleword, or 32-bit; q for quadword, or 64-bit; and dq for double quadword, or 128-bit. Floating-point instructions use suffixes ss and ps for scalar and packed single-precision, or 32-bit, and sd and pd for scalar and packed double-precision, or 64-bit, respectively. Other suffixes are explained where used.

Instruction Format

The SSE/SSE2/SSE3 instructions typically use the format

```
<instruction> xmm, xmm/m128
```

where the destination operand xmm denotes one of the eight 128-bit registers, and the source operand xmm/m128 denotes either one of the eight 128-bit registers or a 128-bit memory location defined by any of the allowable addressing modes. Most floating-point instructions operate in two modes: *packed mode*—suffixes ps and pd—where an operation is applied to all individual data elements, or *scalar mode*—suffixes ss and sd—where an operation is applied only to the lower data elements. In scalar mode, the instructions follow a slightly different format where the memory operand is either m32 or m64 to denote a 32-bit memory operand or 64-bit memory operand, respectively. Some instructions take an 8-bit immediate operand, denoted by imm8, or a 32-bit register operand, denoted by r32.[1]

Packed Data Elements

Most SSE/SSE2/SSE3 instructions operate on 128-bit data types that are packed data elements, although a few instructions also operate on the full double quadword. Table 2.1 summarizes how packed data elements can be interpreted, where vl denotes the *vector length*—the number of data elements packed together, and P denotes the *precision*—the number of bits per data element.

---

[1] Formats that use the old style 64-bit operands of MMX™ instructions are not included in this summary.

Table 2.1 Interpretations of Packed Data Elements

Packed Data Type	vl	P	Data Type Range
signed bytes	16	8	-2^7 to 2^7-1
unsigned bytes	16	8	0 to 2^8-1
signed words	8	16	-2^{15} to $2^{15}-1$
unsigned words	8	16	0 to 2^{16}
signed doublewords	4	32	-2^{31} to $2^{31}-1$
unsigned doublewords	4	32	0 to $2^{32}-1$
signed quadwords	2	64	-2^{63} to $2^{63}-1$
unsigned quadwords	2	64	0 to $2^{64}-1$
single-precision fps	4	32	2^{-126} to 2^{127}
double-precision fps	2	64	2^{-1022} to 2^{1023}

Packed bytes, words, doublewords, and quadwords can be interpreted as signed integers using the two's complement encoding or as unsigned integers using the ordinary binary encoding. The finite precision gives rise to a data type range for each individual value, shown in the last column of Table 2.1. Packed single-precision and double-precision floating-point numbers use IEEE 754-compliant finite precision formats (Intel 2003b, Chapter 4) to represent real numbers with the listed approximate *normalized* data type range for each individual value. Note that tiny values are represented by denormalized numbers.

Data Movement Instructions

Table 2.2 lists instructions that can be used to move data from a memory location into a register—load, move data from a register into a memory location—store, or move data between two registers.

Table 2.2 Data Movement Instructions

Instruction	Suffix	Description
movdqa		move double quadword aligned
movdqu		move double quadword unaligned
mova	[ps,pd]	move floating-point aligned
movu	[ps,pd]	move floating-point unaligned
movhl	[ps]	move packed floating-point high to low
movlh	[ps]	move packed floating-point low to high
movh	[ps,pd]	move high packed floating-point
movl	[ps,pd]	move low packed floating-point
mov	[d,q,ss,sd]	move scalar data
lddqu		load double quadword unaligned
mov<d/sh/sl>dup		move and duplicate

Instructions that move a double quadword between a 128-bit register and a memory location that is 16-byte aligned are movdqa, movaps, and movapd for packed integers, single-precision floating-point numbers, and double-precision floating-point numbers, respectively. These aligned data movement instructions also transfer a double quadword between two 128-bit registers. An aligned data movement instruction cannot be used for a memory location that is not 16-byte aligned, because this use results in a program fault. If the memory location is unaligned, or has an unknown alignment, one of the less efficient instructions movdqu, movups, or movupd must be used. Likewise, only a memory location that is 16-byte aligned can appear directly as an m128 operand in instructions other than unaligned data movement instructions. Unaligned memory operands must first be loaded into a 128-bit register, as illustrated in Table 2.3 for a 128-bit memory operand [esp].

Table 2.3 Loading Memory Operands into a 128-bit Register

unaligned (or unknown):	16-byte aligned:
movups xmm1, [esp] addps xmm0, xmm1	addps xmm0, [esp]

All data movement instructions adhere to the *little endian order* of the Intel architecture, where the bytes of a data type appear from the least significant byte in the lowest memory address up to the most significant byte in the highest memory address. As a result, packed data elements that are moved between a memory location at address a and a 128-bit register xmm0 appear right-to-left in this register, as illustrated in Figure 2.1, for packed words—which are 8 x 16-bit. Word w_0 at address a resides in bits 0 through 15 of xmm0, word w_1 at address $a + 2$ resides in bits 16 through 31 of xmm0, etc.

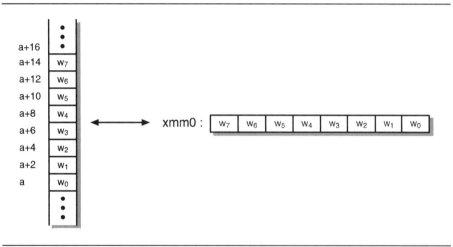

Figure 2.1   Little Endian Order

The data movement instructions movhlps and movlhps move the two higher/lower single-precision floating-point numbers of the source operand into the two lower/higher single-precision floating-point numbers of the destination operand, as illustrated below for movhlps xmm0, xmm1.

xmm0	a_3	a_2	a_2	a_0
xmm1	b_3	b_2	b_1	b_0
xmm0	a_3	a_2	b_3	b_2

Instructions movhpd and movlpd move a double-precision floating-point number between the higher or lower part of a 128-bit register and a 64-bit memory location. If data is loaded from memory into one part of a 128-bit register, the other part of the register remains unaffected.

Instructions `movhps` and `movlps` can be used similarly to move two single-precision floating-point numbers between a 128-bit register and a 64-bit memory location, as illustrated in Figure 2.2, where *a* denotes the address of the memory operand and "–" is used to indicate a data element that does not participate in the operation.

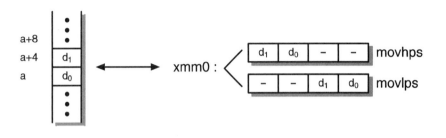

Figure 2.2   Instructions `movhps` and `movlps`

A doubleword can be moved between a 32-bit register or memory operand and the lower part of a 128-bit register using one of the formats

```
movd  xmm, r32/m32
movd  r32/m32, xmm
```

where the higher 96-bit part is cleared when a 128-bit register is used as destination. Likewise, a quadword can be moved between a 64-bit memory operand or lower part of a 128-bit register and the lower part of a 128-bit register using one of the formats

```
movq  xmm, xmm/m64
movq  xmm/m64, xmm
```

where the higher 64-bit part is cleared when a 128-bit register is used as destination of a load. A single-precision or double-precision floating-point scalar is moved similarly using the instructions `movss` and `movsd`, respectively. Again, the higher part is cleared for a load operation, as illustrated in Figure 2.3 for loading a single-precision floating-point number from a memory location at address *a*.

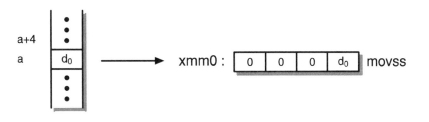

Figure 2.3   Instruction `movss`

The remaining data movement instructions in Table 2.2 were introduced in SSE3. Instruction `lddqu` provides an alternative way of loading a double quadword from an unaligned memory location into a 128-bit register. This instruction is particularly useful when the unaligned load is likely to cross a cache line.

Instruction `movddup` duplicates a quadword of the source operand into the destination operand, as illustrated below for `movddup xmm0, xmm1`.

xmm0	a_1	a_0
xmm1	b_1	b_0
xmm0	b_0	b_0

Instructions `movshdup` or `movsldup` duplicate the doublewords at, respectively, high positions 1/3 or low positions 0/2 into the destination operand, as illustrated below for `movshdup xmm0, xmm1`.

xmm0	a_3	a_2	a_1	a_0
xmm1	b_3	b_2	b_1	b_0
xmm0	b_3	b_3	b_1	b_1

Table 2.4 shows data movement instructions that are useful for accessing particular parts of a 128-bit register directly. Instructions `pextrw` and `pinsrw` move a word directly from and into a 128-bit register. The format

```
pextrw r32, xmm, imm8
```

extracts one of the eight words specified by the three least significant bits of the 8-bit immediate operand from the 128-bit source register and moves it to the lower half of the 32-bit destination register. The higher half of the destination register is cleared.

Table 2.4   Data Movement Instructions

Instruction	Suffix	Description
pextr	[w]	extract word
pinsr	[w]	insert word
pmovmsk	[b]	move mask
movmsk	[ps, pd]	move mask

Likewise, the format

```
pinsrw xmm, r32, imm8
```

can be used to insert the word from the lower half of the 32-bit source register into one of the eight words of the 128-bit destination register that is specified by the three least significant bits of the 8-bit immediate operand. All other words in the destination register remain unaffected, as illustrated below for pinsrw xmm0, eax, 1.

eax								w
xmm1	a_7	a_6	a_5	a_4	a_3	a_2	a_1	a_0
xmm0	a_7	a_6	a_5	a_4	a_3	a_2	w	a_0

The move-mask instructions pmovmskb, movmskps, and movmskpd take the format

```
[p]movmsk[b,ps,pd] r32, xmm
```

and construct a 16-bit, 4-bit, and 2-bit mask from the most significant bits of the packed bytes, packed single-precision floating-point numbers, and packed double-precision floating-point numbers in the 128-bit source register, respectively, and save this mask in the 32-bit destination register.

For instance, if the binary contents of register xmm0 are of the form

xmm0	1 . . .	1 . . .	1 . . .	0 . . .

then executing movmskps eax, xmm0 yields the 4-bit mask 1110 in register eax; the higher 28-bit part is cleared. These instructions are typically used to compress a 128-bit bit mask generated by a SIMD comparison instruction into a general-purpose register.

Arithmetic Instructions

Table 2.5 shows instructions for integer arithmetic. The first two instructions provide wrap-around addition and subtraction for packed bytes, words, doublewords, and quadwords, and can be interpreted as both signed and unsigned.

Table 2.5   Integer Arithmetic Instructions

Instruction	Suffix	Description
padd	[b,w,d,q]	packed addition (signed and unsigned)
psub	[b,w,d,q]	packed subtraction (signed and unsigned)
padds	[b,w]	packed addition with saturation (signed)
paddus	[b,w]	packed addition with saturation (unsigned)
psubs	[b,w]	packed subtraction with saturation (signed)
psubus	[b,w]	packed subtraction with saturation (unsigned)
pmins	[w]	packed minimum (signed)
pminu	[b]	packed minimum (unsigned)
pmaxs	[w]	packed maximum (signed)
pmaxu	[b]	packed maximum (unsigned)

For example, the four-way SIMD parallel instruction psubd xmm0, xmm1 subtracts four doublewords in the source operand xmm1 from four doublewords in the destination operand xmm0, as illustrated in the following table:

xmm0	a_3	a_2	a_1	a_0
xmm1	b_3	b_2	b_1	b_0
xmm0	$a_3 - b_3$	$a_2 - b_3$	$a_1 - b_1$	$a_0 - b_0$

Furthermore, additions and subtractions with saturation are supported for packed signed and unsigned bytes and words, where individual results that would wrap around are clipped to the appropriate data type range limit, as shown in Table 2.1. Minimum and maximum operations are supported with instructions for packed signed words and packed unsigned bytes.

The floating-point arithmetic instructions shown in Table 2.6 support addition, division, minimum, maximum, multiplication, square root, subtraction, and two operations to approximate a single-precision reciprocal or reciprocal square root, where accuracy $|\varepsilon| \leq 1.5 \cdot 2^{-12}$ is guaranteed for the approximation error ε. Floating-point arithmetic can run in *IEEE 754-compliant mode* for applications that rely on precise and portable computations, or in *flush-to-zero mode* for high performance applications that are less sensitive to precision. This latter mode, enabled with bit 15 of register MXCSR, provides faster underflow handling at the expense of a slight precision loss.

Table 2.6   Floating-Point Arithmetic Instructions

Instruction	Suffix	Description
add	[ss,ps,sd,pd]	addition
div	[ss,ps,sd,pd]	division
min	[ss,ps,sd,pd]	minimum
max	[ss,ps,sd,pd]	maximum
mul	[ss,ps,sd,pd]	multiplication
sqrt	[ss,ps,sd,pd]	square root
sub	[ss,ps,sd,pd]	subtraction
rcp	[ss,ps]	approximated reciprocal
rsqrt	[ss,ps]	approximated reciprocal square root

The suffix determines whether the instruction is performed in either packed mode or scalar mode for single-precision or double-precision floating-point numbers. For example, the four-way SIMD parallel instruction mulps xmm0, xmm1 operates in packed mode by multiplying four single-precision floating-point numbers in the source operand xmm1 with four single-precision floating-point numbers in the destination operand xmm0, as shown in the following table:

xmm0	a_3	a_2	a_1	a_0
xmm1	b_3	b_2	b_1	b_0
xmm0	$a_3 \cdot b_3$	$a_2 \cdot b_2$	$a_1 \cdot b_1$	$a_0 \cdot b_0$

In contrast, instruction mulss xmm0, xmm1 operates in scalar mode by multiplying only the lower data elements a_0 and b_0. All other data elements in the destination operand remain unaffected, as shown in the following table:

xmm0	a_3	a_2	a_1	a_0
xmm1	b_3	b_2	b_1	b_0
xmm0	a_3	a_2	a_1	$a_0 \cdot b_0$

Idiomatic arithmetic instructions are listed in Table 2.7. Instructions `pavgb` and `pavgw` compute the average of unsigned packed bytes or words as

$$a_i := (a_i + b_i + 1) >> 1$$

using one additional bit of precision to compute each individual result. Instruction `pmullw` multiplies signed or unsigned packed words and stores the 16 least significant bits of the 32-bit results as packed words in the destination operand. Instructions `pmulhw` and `pmulhuw` can be used similarly to store the 16 most significant bits of the 32-bit results as packed words, although here a distinction between signed and unsigned operands must be made. Instruction `psadbw` computes the sums of absolute differences

$$s_0 := \sum_{i=0}^{7} |a_i - b_i| \quad \text{and} \quad s_1 := \sum_{i=8}^{15} |a_i - b_i|$$

of the packed bytes and stores the 16-bit sums s_0 and s_1 back in *word* zero and four of the destination operand; hence, the suffix bw. All other words are cleared. Instruction `pmaddwd xmm0, xmm1` multiplies signed packed words and stores the 16-bit sums of pair-wise results as packed *double-words* in the destination operand `xmm0`; hence, the suffix wd, as illustrated in the following table:

xmm0	a_7	a_6	a_5	a_4	a_3	a_2	a_1	a_0
xmm1	b_7	b_6	b_5	b_4	b_3	b_2	b_1	b_0
xmm0	$a_7 \cdot b_7 + a_6 \cdot b_6$		$a_5 \cdot b_5 + a_4 \cdot b_4$		$a_3 \cdot b_3 + a_2 \cdot b_2$		$a_1 \cdot b_1 + a_0 \cdot b_0$	

Table 2.7 Idiomatic Arithmetic Instructions

Instruction	Suffix	Description
pavg	[b,w]	packed average with rounding (unsigned)
pmulh	[w]	packed multiplication high (signed)
pmulhu	[w]	packed multiplication high (unsigned)
pmull	[w]	packed multiplication low (signed and unsigned)
psad	[bw]	packed sum of absolute differences (unsigned)
pmadd	[wd]	packed multiplication and addition (signed)
addsub	[ps,pd]	floating-point addition/subtraction
hadd	[ps,pd]	floating-point horizontal addition
hsub	[ps,pd]	floating-point horizontal subtraction

The floating-point instructions `addsubps`, `addsubpd`, `haddps`, `haddpd`, `hsubps`, and `hsubpd` were introduced by SSE3 and can only be used in packed mode. The first two instructions alternate subtracting and adding packed data elements, as illustrated in the following table, for `addsubps xmm0, xmm1`.

xmm0	a_3	a_2	a_1	a_0
xmm1	b_3	b_2	b_1	b_0
xmm0	$a_3 + b_3$	$a_2 - b_2$	$a_1 + b_1$	$a_0 - b_0$

The other two instructions add the packed data elements horizontally. Instruction `haddpd xmm0, xmm1` adds the two double-precision floating-point numbers in the source operand `xmm1` and destination operand `xmm0` separately, as illustrated in the following table:

xmm0	a_1	a_0
xmm1	b_1	b_0
xmm0	$b_1 + b_0$	$a_1 + a_0$

Likewise, instruction `haddps xmm0, xmm1` computes separate sums of pairs of single-precision floating-point numbers in the source operand `xmm1` and destination operand `xmm0`, as shown in the following table:

xmm0	a_3	a_2	a_1	a_0
xmm1	b_3	b_2	b_1	b_0
xmm0	$b_3 + b_2$	$b_1 + b_0$	$a_3 + a_2$	$a_1 + a_0$

Logical Instructions

The bitwise logical instructions in Table 2.8 apply the AND, AND-NOT (which inverts the destination before applying the AND), OR, and XOR operation to full double quadwords.

Table 2.8   Logical Instructions

Instruction	Suffix	Description
pand		bitwise logical AND
pandn		bitwise logical AND-NOT
por		bitwise logical OR
pxor		bitwise logical XOR
and	[ps,pd]	bitwise logical AND
andn	[ps,pd]	bitwise logical AND-NOT
or	[ps,pd]	bitwise logical OR
xor	[ps,pd]	bitwise logical XOR

As an example, the impact of instruction `pand xmm0, xmm1` on some sample bits is illustrated in the following table:

xmm0	110001100010011 ... 0010000100000111
xmm1	100000100010001 ... 0010010001001111
xmm0	100000100010001 ... 0010000000000111

Logical instructions are frequently applied to the bit mask that is generated by a comparison instruction to implement conditional operations without the use of explicit branches, as discussed in the next section.

Comparison Instructions

The instructions in Table 2.9 compare packed data elements in the destination operand with packed data elements in the source operand using the relation defined by the comparison code <cc> and set each individual data element in the destination operand to all-ones if the comparison is true, or to all-zeros otherwise. The instructions do not set status flags. Instead, the resulting bit mask is typically used by subsequent logical instructions to select the data elements that satisfy a certain condition.

Table 2.9 Comparison Instructions

Instruction	Suffix	Description
pcmp<cc>	[b,w,d]	packed compare
cmp<cc>	[ss,ps,sd,pd]	floating-point compare

The format `pcmp<cc>` supports comparisons of packed bytes, words, or doublewords for the comparison codes `eq` or equal, applicable to signed and unsigned operands alike, and `gt` or greater-than for signed operands.

The impact of instruction `pcmpeqd xmm0, xmm1` on some sample values is shown in the following table:

xmm0	11	0	105	110
xmm1	11	20	100	334
xmm0	0xffffffff	0x00000000	0x00000000	0x00000000

In this example, hexadecimal numbers provide a notational convenience for the resulting bit masks.

$$0xffffffff = \underbrace{111111...111111}_{32} \quad 0x00000000 = \underbrace{000000...000000}_{32}$$

Format cmp<cc> supports comparisons of single-precision and double-precision floating-point numbers for the comparison codes eq—equal; lt—less-than; le—less-than-or-equal; unord—unordered; neq—not-equal; nlt—not-less-than; nle—not-less-than-or-equal; and ord—ordered. The instructions are supported in either packed mode, which generates a full double quadword bit mask, or in scalar mode, which generates a bit mask for the lower data element, leaving all other parts of the destination operand unaffected.

Relations that are not directly supported in hardware require straightforward software emulations. Although most assemblers support the pseudo instructions formed by concatenating a comparison code and suffix, the actual format of the floating-point comparison instruction is

cmp<suffix> xmm, xmm/m128, imm8

where the third operand imm8 denotes the following 8-bit encoding of the comparison code:

$0 \equiv \text{eq}$ $1 \equiv \text{lt}$ $2 \equiv \text{le}$ $3 \equiv \text{unord}$

$4 \equiv \text{neq}$ $5 \equiv \text{nlt}$ $6 \equiv \text{nle}$ $7 \equiv \text{ord}$

Conversion Instructions

Conversion instructions are listed in Table 2.10. The pack instructions convert packed data elements into packed data elements with narrower precision while saturating the individual data elements to the appropriate data type range limit.

Table 2.10 Conversion Instructions

Instruction	Suffix	Description
packss	[wb, dw]	pack with saturation (signed)
packus	[wb]	pack with saturation (unsigned)
cvt<s2d>		conversion
cvtt<s2d>		conversion with truncation

The instruction `packsswb` converts eight signed words from the source operand and eight signed words from the destination operand into sixteen signed *bytes* in the destination operand; hence, the suffix wb. Word values that are greater or less than the range of a signed byte are saturated to the maximum signed byte value $2^7 - 1$ or minimum signed byte value -2^7, respectively. The instructions `packuswb` and `packssdw` similarly convert signed words into unsigned bytes—hence, the suffix wb again—and signed doublewords into signed words—hence, the suffix dw, respectively. The impact of instruction `packssdw xmm0, xmm1`, for example, is illustrated below, where d^{sw} denotes the result of saturating d into a signed word.

xmm0		a_3			a_3			a_1			a_0	
xmm1		b_3			b_3			b_1			b_0	
xmm0	b_3^{sw}	b_2^{sw}	b_1^{sw}	b_0^{sw}	a_3^{sw}	a_2^{sw}	a_1^{sw}	a_0^{sw}

Other conversion instructions use the format `cvt<s2d>` for a conversion code `<s2d>`. The following conversion codes define a conversion between signed integers and floating-point numbers, where `cvtpd2dq` clears the two higher doublewords in the destination operand.

> dq2pd ≡ two *lower* signed doublewords to two double-precision FP
>
> pd2dq ≡ two double-precision FP to two *lower* signed doublewords
>
> dq2ps ≡ four signed doublewords to four single-precision FP
>
> ps2dq ≡ four single-precision FP to four signed doublewords

The *rounding mode* for conversions from floating-point numbers to signed integers is specified in bits 13 and 14 of the control and status register `MXCSR` as follows.

$$\begin{cases} 00 & \textit{round to nearest} \\ 01 & \textit{round to } -\infty \\ 10 & \textit{round to } +\infty \\ 11 & \textit{round to zero (truncate)} \end{cases}$$

Alternatively, rounding with truncation can be defined with the instruction `cvtt<s2d>` and one of the following conversion codes. Again, the two higher doublewords are cleared for instruction `cvttpd2dq`.

> pd2dq ≡ two double-precision FP to two *lower* signed doublewords
>
> ps2dq ≡ four single-precision FP to four signed doublewords

Conversions between single-precision and double-precision floating-point numbers are defined by combining `cvt<s2d>` with one of the conversion codes shown below, where instruction `cvtpd2ps` clears the two higher single-precision floating-point numbers. The instructions `cvtsd2ss` and `cvtss2sd` operate in scalar mode.

> pd2ps ≡ two double-precision FP to two *lower* single-precision FP
>
> ps2pd ≡ two *lower* single-precision FP to two double-precision FP
>
> sd2ss ≡ one double-precision FP to one single-precision FP
>
> ss2sd ≡ one single-precision FP to one double-precision FP

The instruction set further features a number of conversion instructions with 32-bit operands and old-style 64-bit operands of MMX instructions. The full set of conversion codes can be found in the instruction set reference (Intel 2003c).

Shift Instructions

The shift instructions shown in Table 2.11 support logical shifts on packed words, doublewords, quadwords, and even the full double quadword, as well as arithmetic shifts on packed words and doublewords; byte shifts are not supported at all. In the default format of the packed shift instructions, the full lower 64-bit part of the 128-bit register or memory source operand specifies the shift factor in *bits*. Alternatively, the format

```
<instruction> xmm, imm8
```

can be used to define the shift factor as an 8-bit immediate operand. For the double quadword shift instructions, this is the only format supported, where the immediate operand now defines the shift factor in *bytes*.

Table 2.11 Shift Instructions

Instruction	Suffix	Description
psll	[w,d,q,dq]	shift left logical (zero in)
psra	[w,d]	shift right arithmetic (sign in)
psrl	[w,d,q,dq]	shift right logical (zero in)

Logical shift instructions shift the bits of each of the individual packed data elements to either the left or right, filling the empty bits with zeros. The arithmetic shift instructions shift the bits of each of the packed data elements to the right, filling the empty bits with the original value of the sign bit of each packed data element. Shift factors that exceed the precision of the data elements result in either all-zeros or all-ones data elements. Logically shifting left by n bits effectively multiplies the packed signed or unsigned data elements by 2^n. Likewise, logically shifting right by n bits divides packed unsigned data elements by 2^n. Arithmetically shifting right by n bits divides packed signed data elements by 2^n using round to $-\infty$, unlike the more common signed division that uses round to zero.

Shuffle Instructions

The shuffle instructions shown in Table 2.11 provide some essential functionality for rearranging data. Instruction `pshufw` was introduced in SSE to rearrange packed words in old style 64-bit operands of MMX instructions. Similar functionality was introduced in SSE2 for doublewords with the instruction `pshufd` that takes the format

```
pshufd xmm, xmm/m128, imm8
```

where bits $2 \cdot i$ and $2 \cdot i + 1$ of the 8-bit immediate operand provide a 2-bit encoding of which of the four packed doublewords in the source operand is stored in doubleword i of the destination operand. The instruction `pshufd xmm0, xmm1, 240`, for example, shuffles that data as shown in the following table. Note that 240 in decimal is 11110000 in binary.

xmm0	a_3	a_2	a_1	a_0
xmm1	b_3	b_2	b_1	b_0
xmm0	b_3	b_3	b_0	b_0

Table 2.12 Shuffle Instructions

Instruction	Suffix	Description
pshuf	[w,d]	packed shuffle
pshufh	[w]	packed shuffle high
pshufl	[w]	packed shuffle low
shuf	[ps,pd]	shuffle

Instructions `pshufhw` and `pshuflw` provide similar functionality to shuffle the higher and lower words, respectively, copying the non-shuffled part directly from the source operand into the destination operand, as illustrated in the following table for `pshufhw xmm0, xmm1, 0`.

xmm0	a_7	a_6	a_5	a_4	a_3	a_2	a_1	a_0
xmm1	b_7	b_6	b_5	b_4	b_3	b_2	b_1	b_0
xmm0	b_4	b_4	b_4	b_4	b_3	b_2	b_1	b_0

The floating-point shuffle instructions `shufps` and `shufpd` use a 2-bit and 1-bit encoding to select from the packed single-precision and double-precision floating-point numbers, respectively. In this case, higher data elements are taken from the source operand and lower data elements from the destination operand. This data shuffling is illustrated in the following table for instruction `shufps xmm0, xmm1, 240`.

xmm0	a_3	a_2	a_1	a_0
xmm1	b_3	b_2	b_1	b_0
xmm0	b_3	b_3	a_0	a_0

Unpack Instructions

Another set of data-rearranging instructions is provided with the unpack instructions of Table 2.13. These instructions interleave the lower or higher packed data elements from the source and destination operand. The interleaving done by instruction `punpckhwd xmm0,xmm1`, for instance, is shown in the following table:

xmm0	a_7	a_6	a_5	a_4	a_3	a_2	a_1	a_0
xmm1	b_7	b_6	b_5	b_4	b_3	b_2	b_1	b_0
xmm0	b_7	a_7	b_6	a_6	b_5	a_5	b_4	a_4

Table 2.13 Unpack Instructions

Instruction	Suffix	Description
punpckh	[bw,wd,dq,qdq]	unpack high
punpckl	[bw,wd,dq,qdq]	unpack low
unpckh	[ps,pd]	unpack high
unpckl	[ps,pd]	unpack low

If the source operand consists of all zeros, this instruction effectively implements a zero extension of the packed data elements in the destination operand; hence, the suffixes bw, wd, dq, and qdq. The floating-point unpack instructions perform a similar interleaving on packed floating-point numbers.

Under certain circumstances, unpack, shuffle, and certain data movement instructions perform the same data rearrangement, as illustrated below. Since the latency of instructions varies among processors, these equivalences can be used to optimize data-rearranging instruction sequences for particular target architectures.

```
shufps xmm0, xmm1, 68    ≡  movlhps  xmm0, xmm1
shufps xmm0, xmm0, 80    ≡  unpcklps xmm0, xmm0
shufps xmm0, xmm0, 160   ≡  movsldup xmm0, xmm0
shufps xmm0, xmm0, 230   ≡  movshdup xmm0, xmm0
shufps xmm0, xmm0, 238   ≡  movhlps  xmm0, xmm0
shufps xmm0, xmm0, 250   ≡  unpckhps xmm0, xmm0
shufpd xmm0, xmm0, 0     ≡  movddup  xmm0, xmm0
shufpd xmm0, xmm1, 0     ≡  unpcklpd xmm0, xmm1
shufpd xmm0, xmm1, 3     ≡  unpckhpd xmm0, xmm1
```

For example, since on the Pentium 4 processor the latency of shufps and movlhps is six clock cycles versus four clock cycles (Intel 2003a), a peephole optimizer could replace each shufps xmm0, xmm1, 68 with movlhps xmm0, xmm1 to reduce latency. As the latency of each instruction changes with architectural improvements, the peephole optimizer will favor different instruction sequences for a given data rearrangement.

Cacheability Control and Prefetch Instructions

The cacheability control instructions listed in Table 2.14 can improve the manipulation of *streaming data*—non-temporal data that is referenced once and not reused in the immediate future. The instructions movntps, movntpd, and movntdq store a double quadword from a 128-bit register into an aligned memory location, while minimizing pollution in the memory hierarchy with a non-temporal buffer. Instruction movntq similarly stores a quadword from old style 64-bit operands of MMX instructions. These non-temporal data movement instructions are sometimes referred to as streaming stores.

Table 2.14 Cacheability Control and Prefetch Instructions

Instruction	Suffix	Description
`movnt`	`[ps,pd,q,dq]`	move aligned non-temporal
`prefetch<hint>`		prefetch with hint

The prefetch instructions take the format

`prefetch<hint> m8`

to preload the cache line containing the byte defined by memory address `m8` into the memory hierarchy without actually stalling the processor. The locality hint `<hint>` may be one of `t0`, `t1`, `t2`, or `nta` to specify pre-fetching into, respectively, the L1/L2/L3 cache, the L2/L3 cache, the L3 cache, and a non-temporal buffer useful for read-once data. Locality hints do not affect the actual semantics of a program. Hardware implementations may even ignore the hints.

State Management Instructions

This instruction set summary concludes with the state management instructions shown in Table 2.15. The instructions `fxsave` and `fxrstor` save and restore the FPU/MMX and SSE/SSE2/SSE3 state to and from a memory area defined by a single operand. These instructions are typically used only by operating system software to implement a context switch. For more information on this topic, see Intel (2003d).

Table 2.15 State Management Instructions

Instruction	Description
`fxrstor`	restore state
`fxsave`	save state
`ldmxcsr`	load control and status word
`stmxcsr`	store control and status word

The instructions `ldmxcsr` and `stmxcsr` take the format

`<ld/st>mxcsr m32`

to load or store the control and status register MXCSR from or to the 32-bit memory operand `m32`. These two instructions can be used to set modes or to examine status flags. The format of the control and status register MXCSR is illustrated in Figure 2.4, where bit 15 controls the flush-to-zero mode for floating-point arithmetic and bits 13 and 14 define the rounding mode of conversion instructions.

Figure 2.4   Format of the Control and Status Register MXCSR

Bit 6 controls the denormals-are-zero mode that was introduced in later models of the Pentium 4 processor to improve the performance of applications that are less sensitive to precision. In this mode, denormal source operands are converted to zero before any computations are performed. More details on MXCSR can be found in Intel (2003b).

The Intel NetBurst® Microarchitecture

The Pentium 4 processor is the first processor based on the Intel Net-Burst microarchitecture (Hinton et al. 2001), which allows processors to operate at significantly higher clock frequencies than earlier generation IA-32 processors. The two major components of this microarchitecture are formed by the execution logic and the memory hierarchy, both briefly described in this section.

Execution Logic

Instructions are executed in three stages, as illustrated in Figure 2.5. First, in the *in-order* front end, instructions are fetched, decoded, and broken up into smaller, simpler operations called micro-operations, or μ-ops. The μ-ops are stored in an advanced form of instruction cache, called the *trace cache*. Once decoded instructions are stored in this cache, subsequent execution of these instructions is done without fetching and decoding overhead. Highly accurate *branch prediction* is used to speculate from what memory addresses new instructions have to be fetched. As long as all guesses are correct, fetching and decoding of instructions proceeds without interruption. If the direction of a branch is mispredicted, however, the processor must discard the results of all mispredicted instructions before executing instructions along the actually taken path.

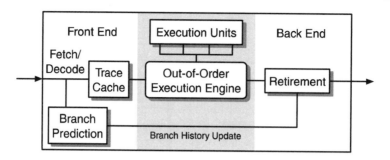

Figure 2.5   Simplified Diagram of the Intel NetBurst® Microarchitecture

The second stage is formed by the *out-of-order* execution engine, which attempts to execute as many μ-ops as possible in each clock cycle, even if this violates the original program order. Ready μ-ops are dispatched through four dispatch ports to the execution units, where the μ-ops are actually executed. Two execution unit dispatch ports, called port 0 and port 1, can dispatch up to two μ-ops per clock cycle. Two other dispatch ports, called the load and store port, can dispatch one ready load-and-store operation per clock cycle. Effectively utilizing all available ports is essential for obtaining high performance. To save on die size and to lower power consumption, the FP execution units support only half the multimedia data format, which implies that each 128-bit packed floating-point addition or multiplication takes two clock cycles. So, even if the processor is kept busy by interleaving independent packed floating-point additions and multiplications, this hardware restriction currently limits the theoretical peak performance of a 3-gigahertz Pentium 4 processor to 6 GFLOPS for single-precision and 3 GFLOPS for double-precision floating-point computations, respectively. Future architectural enhancements, however, can be expected to further replicate execution units to match the wider data formats.

The final retirement stage reorders the results of all completed μ-ops back to the original program order and updates the branch history of the branch prediction logic. Up to three μ-ops per clock cycle can retire in this back end. A store may take many clock cycles before appearing in cache or memory, because committing to permanent machine state is only safe after the store operation has retired. To avoid long stalls for subsequent load operations, the out-of-order execution engine uses store buffers to allow load operations to use the results of pending store operations before these stores actually retire. This *store-to-load forwarding* is possible if a load operation requests a same-sized or smaller data item from the same memory address as used by a pending store operation. If the load operation uses a different memory address or if the load operation requests more bytes than stored by the pending store operation, store-to-load forwarding cannot occur. The instruction sequence shown below, for instance, fails to forward the 16-byte store into the second subsequent 4-byte load.

```
movdqa [esp], xmm0      ; store 16 bytes into stack
mov     eax,   [esp]    ; forwarding enabled
mov     ecx,   [esp+12] ; forwarding disabled
```

Due to the large performance penalty of missed store-to-load forwarding, compilers should attempt to avoid generating store-load combinations that fail to forward.

Memory Hierarchy

Memory hierarchies, designed to reduce memory latency, are based on the principle of locality of reference. This principle states that in a short time interval, a program tends to reference the same data items several times—temporal locality—and tends to reference data items near previously referenced data items—spatial locality.

Figure 2.6 illustrates a typical memory hierarchy for the Intel NetBurst microarchitecture, where both the storage capacity and access time increases with distance from the processor. Nearest to the processor are the registers, trace cache for μ-ops and L1 cache for data, with a capacity of 12 Kμ-ops and 8 kilobytes, respectively. The unified L2 cache is used for instructions and data and has a capacity of 256 kilobytes or more. Storage that is farther away from the processor consists of an optional L3 cache and main memory, which have typical capacities of, respectively, 512 kilobytes and 128 megabytes or more. The L1 cache is organized as a four-way set associative cache (Hennessy and Patterson 1990, Chapter 8) with a cache line size of 64 bytes (128 cache lines × 64 bytes = 8 kilobytes).

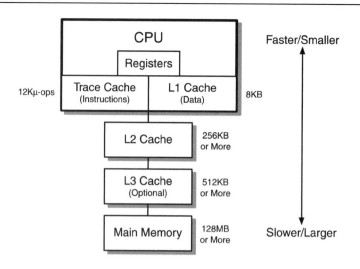

Figure 2.6   Simplified Diagram of the Memory Hierarchy

When the processor references a data item that is not in cache, a *cache miss* occurs, and a 64-byte aligned chunk of memory that contains the requested data item is loaded into the cache line, thereby possibly replacing previously loaded data items. The L2 cache is furthermore assisted by *hardware prefetching* that, based on the history of cache misses, tries to detect and prefetch independent streams of data in a program. The prefetching logic attempts to stay ahead of currently accessed memory locations while also trying to minimize the amount of unwanted data that is moved into the cache. When the processor references a data item that is already in cache, a *cache hit* occurs, which means that the data item can be accessed without touching slower storage in the memory hierarchy. Not surprisingly, therefore, improving cache usage is an important objective for effective optimization.

Chapter 3

Language Preliminaries

The methods presented in this book to translate sequential code into multimedia instructions are applicable to any imperative programming language like Ada, C, C++, Java[†], Fortran, or Pascal. This book, however, focuses on the automatic intra-register vectorization of C programs, although a discussion on simplifications or complications arising in other languages is occasionally included. Therefore, this chapter briefly reviews some preliminaries of the C programming language.

The C Programming Language

Since its introduction in the seventies, the C programming language (Kernighan and Ritchie 1988) has become very popular. Although often deemed a language suited only for operating system or compiler software, C has been used in many other domains as well. The lasting popularity and the vast amounts of existing software written in C motivated its choice as the primary programming language in this book.

Data Types

There are only a few basic data types in C. For notational convenience, the following type definitions are used as shorthand for all possible combinations of qualifiers and basic integer data types.

```
typedef unsigned char       u8;
typedef signed   char       s8;
typedef unsigned short      u16;
typedef signed   short      s16;
typedef unsigned int        u32;
typedef signed   int        s32;
typedef unsigned long long  u64;
typedef signed   long long  s64;
```

Although the C standard allows some freedom for the precision of integer data types, this book simply assumes an 8-bit, 16-bit, 32-bit, and 64-bit precision for char, short, int, and long long, respectively, as suggested by the names shown above. The qualifier signed or unsigned defines whether bit patterns are interpreted as signed integers using two's complement encoding or as unsigned integers using ordinary binary encoding. The fixed precision implies that each data type

$$t \in \{u8, s8, u16, s16, u32, s32, u64, s64\}$$

has a finite data type range, denoted by the set V_t. Data type s8, for example, has the data type range $V_{s8} = \{-128, \ldots, 127\}$. In addition, the following type definitions are used as shorthand for the two basic single-precision and double-precision floating-point data types that represent real numbers. This book assumes a 32-bit and 64-bit precision for these data types.

```
typedef float  f32;
typedef double f64;
```

Derived data types are constructed recursively from other data types by declaring arrays []; pointers *; structures struct; unions union; and functions (). Arrays are stored in row-major order (Aho, Sethi, and Ullman 1986), which means that an array like

```
s32 x[3][2];
```

that is stored at address a has the data layout in memory as illustrated in Figure 3.1.

a+24	⋮
a+20	x [2] [1]
a+16	x [2] [0]
a+12	x [1] [1]
a+8	x [1] [0]
a+4	x [0] [1]
a	x [0] [0]
	⋮

Figure 3.1   Row-Major Order

To simplify programming with complex numbers, the C99 standard (ISO 1999) extended the basic data types of the C programming language with two built-in single-precision and double-precision complex data types. The type definitions shown below are used as shorthand for these new data types.

```
typedef float  _Complex c32;
typedef double _Complex c64;
```

As suggested by the names, this book assumes 32-bit and 64-bit precision for the real part and the imaginary part of a single-precision and double-precision complex data type, respectively, where the real part appears lower in memory. For example, a single-precision complex array like

```
c32 c[N];
```

that is stored at address a has the data layout illustrated in Figure 3.2, where $c_r[i]$ and $c_i[i]$ denote the real part and imaginary part of the complex element $c[i]$, respectively.

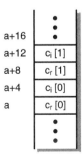

a+16	⋮
a+12	$c_i[1]$
a+8	$c_r[1]$
a+4	$c_i[0]$
a	$c_r[0]$
	⋮

Figure 3.2   Data Layout of Single-Precision Complex Array

Expressions

Expressions in C are formed by primary expressions such as variables and constants as well as operators applied to other expressions. Table 3.1 shows some important operators. For all operators, the C standard defines type conversion rules that bring all operands into a common type before applying the operator. Table 3.2 summarizes the usual arithmetic conversions (Kernighan and Ritchie 1988) for binary operators by defining this common type in terms of the data types of the two operands, where $T_N = \{\texttt{u8}, \texttt{s8}, \texttt{u16}, \texttt{s16}\}$ is used as shorthand for all narrow precision integer data types. Converting into a floating-point data type simply yields the closest value that can be represented. An unsigned integer data type is converted into a wider precision integer data type with zero extension.

Table 3.1   Important Operators

	Binary	Unary
Arithmetic	+ – * / %	–
Bitwise	& | ^ << >>	~
Equality	== !=	
Logical	&& ||	!
Relational	< <= > >=	

As an example, Figure 3.3. illustrates converting the bit pattern for the value 255 with data type u32 into either u32 or s32.

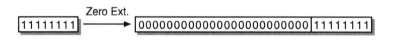

Figure 3.3   Zero Extension

Table 3.2 The Usual Arithmetic Conversions

	T_N	u32	s32	u64	s64	f32	f64
T_N	s32	u32	s32	u64	s64	f32	f64
u32	u32	u32	u32	u64	s64	f32	f64
s32	s32	u32	s32	u64	s64	f32	f64
u64	u64	u64	u64	u64	u64	f32	f64
s64	s64	s64	s64	u64	s64	f32	f64
f32	f32	f32	f32	f32	f32	f32	f64
f64	f64	f64	f64	f64	f64	f64	f64

A signed integer data type, on the other hand, is converted into any wider precision integer data type with sign extension. The bit pattern for the value −1 with data type s8, for instance, is converted into either u32 or s32 as illustrated in Figure 3.4, where the resulting bit pattern is interpreted either as 4,294,967,295 or −1 again, respectively.

Figure 3.4 Sign Extension

For clarity, this book sometimes makes implicit type conversions that arise from the usual arithmetic conversions explicit in the program text. Cast operators and a subscript for the operator denote the resulting data type, as illustrated in the following example for an expression (x+y)+1.0, where variables x and y have data types u32 and s8, respectively.

$$((f64)(x +_{u32} ((u32) y))) +_{f64} 1.0$$

The resulting data type eventually determines the kind of machine instruction that has to be used to implement the operator. For example, the 32-bit relational operators $>=_{s32}$ and $>=_{u32}$ must be implemented with machine instructions that use the conditional codes ge—signed greater or equal and ae—unsigned above or equal, respectively. In contrast, both the 32-bit additive operators $+_{u32}$ and $+_{s32}$ can be implemented with the machine instruction add. Instead, the outcome is merely defined by the interpretation of bit patterns after wrap-around arithmetic, where the most significant bits of results that would require more than 32 bits are simply truncated.

Consider, for example, the following two additions:

```
0xffffffff          0x7fffffff
0x00000001 +        0x00000001 +
───────────         ───────────
0x00000000          0x80000000
```

The first addition gives rise to an unsigned wrap-around interpretation

$$4{,}294{,}967{,}295 + 1 = 0$$

or signed interpretation $-1 + 1 = 0$. The second addition has an unsigned interpretation

$$2{,}147{,}483{,}647 + 1 = 2{,}147{,}483{,}648$$

or the following signed wrap-around interpretation:

$$2{,}147{,}483{,}647 + 1 = -2{,}147{,}483{,}648$$

Other important operators in C are the indirection or de-reference operator `*`; the subscript operator where `a[i]` is equivalent to `*(a+i)`; structure reference `.`; the arrow operator where `x->y` is the same as `(*x).y`; the unary address operator `&`; and the ternary conditional operator `?:`. Furthermore, although assignment operators, such as `=`, and function calls can be used anywhere in an expression, most compilers internally represent such operators as separate statements. Likewise, other than in loop control expressions, this book usually makes the effects of pre/post increment/decrement operators, namely `++` and `--`, explicit by means of assignment statements to keep the evaluation of expressions free of unexpected side effects.

Statements

The C programming language supports various statements. Expression statements are usually assignment statements or function calls. An assignment statement that uses the assignment operator `=` as follows

S: `lhs = rhs;`

evaluates the value of the *right-hand side* and assigns this value to the *left-hand side*. A label such as *S* is often associated with statements for easy reference in the accompanying text. Other assignment operators provide a convenient shorthand for a combination of operators; for example, `x+=y` is equivalent to `x=x+y` for an expression `x` that is free of side effects.

A function call like

```
void f(s32 x, s32 y) {
    /* function body */
}

...

f(a,b);   /* function call */
```

first assigns the values of the *actual arguments*—a and b—to the *formal arguments*—x and y—and then transfers control into the function body of function f(). The call by the value-parameter passing mechanism of C implies that changes to the formal arguments do not alter the actual arguments. Note that the call by the reference-parameter passing mechanism can still be implemented in C using pointer arguments.

The C programming language also supports if and switch statements for selection, goto, continue, break, and return statements for transfer of control, and the while, do-while, and for statements for iteration. The following statement

```
for (e1; e2; e3) /* loop body */
```

first evaluates the initialization expression e1. Subsequently, while expression e2 evaluates to a nonzero value, the loop body is executed followed by evaluation of expression e3. The statement is semantically equivalent to the following while statement.

```
e1;
while (e2) {
   /* loop body */
   e3;
}
```

Many compiler optimizations specifically target loops that are implemented by means of the iteration statements, since that is usually where most execution time is spent.

Loop and Idiom Recognition

Compilers benefit from recognizing loops and conditional constructs that are particularly amenable to analysis and optimization, as further explained in this section.

Well-Behaved Loops

The `for` statement is an important construct to define iteration. Because the C standard does not impose many restrictions on the loop control expressions, it is desirable to define when such statements behave more analogous to Fortran `DO` loops and Pascal `for` statements. To this effect, a `for` statement of the form that follows is called a *well-behaved loop* (Muchnick 1997, Chapter 14) if loop index `i` iterates from 0 to an upper bound `U` and the loop body can neither alter the value of the loop index or upper bound nor jump outside the loop.

```
for (i = 0; i < U; i++) {
  /* loop body */
}
```

This restricted form makes well-behaved loops amenable to analysis and optimization. Consequently, this book focuses mainly on optimizing well-behaved loops with multimedia extensions, although search loops that iterate until a certain condition on the input data is met are considered in Chapter 7. Loops that use slightly different kinds of loop control can often be converted into well-behaved form with *loop normalization* (Zima and Chapman 1990, pages 174–177). Loops that have been coded alternatively with `while` statements, or a combination of `if` statements and `goto` statements, can often be rewritten into well-behaved form by means of conventional program transformations. An example of such a transformation is shown below, where `_t` denotes a compiler-generated temporary variable. Note that `n` is decremented *after* its value is used in the test.

```
n = 100;                      for (_t = 0; _t < 100; _t++) {
while (n-- > 0) {                 p[99-_t] = 0;
  p[n] = 0;          →           }
}                             n = -1;
```

If a well-behaved loop appears within the loop body of another well-behaved loop, a *nested loop* results. A statement S that is surrounded by d well-behaved loops with loop indices $i_1,...,i_d$ is said to appear at *nesting depth* d, as follows:

```
      for (i₁ = 0; i₁ < U₁; i₁++) {
        ⋱
            for (i_d = 0; i_d < U_d; i_d++) {
S:            ...
            }
        ⋰
      }
```

Executing the loop body for loop index values $i_1 = i_1,...,i_d = i_d$ gives rise to the execution of a *statement instance* of S, denoted by $S(i_1,...,i_d)$. The set of all iteration values $(i_1,...,i_d) \in \mathbb{Z}^d$ for which the loop body is executed is called the *iteration space* $I \subset \mathbb{Z}^d$ of the nested loop. Most loop bounds encountered in practice can be expressed as affine functions of more outer loop indices. Hence, an iteration space can usually be represented by a system of linear inequalities.

Consider, for example, the following code fragment:

```
      for (i₁ = 0; i₁ < 7; i₁++) {
        for (i₂ = 0; i₂ < 100+2*i₁; i₂++) {
S:          a[i₁][i₂] = b[i₂] + 1;
        }
      }
```

The iteration space $I \subset \mathbb{Z}^2$ of this nested loop can be represented by a system of inequalities, as in the following:

$$I = \{(i_1,i_2) \in \mathbb{Z}^2 \mid \begin{pmatrix} -1 & 0 \\ +1 & 0 \\ 0 & -1 \\ -2 & +1 \end{pmatrix} \begin{pmatrix} i_1 \\ i_2 \end{pmatrix} \le \begin{pmatrix} 0 \\ 6 \\ 0 \\ 99 \end{pmatrix} \}$$

The order in which all statement instances $S(i_1, i_2)$ with $(i_1, i_2) \in I$ are executed is exactly defined by the sequential semantics of C:

```
      a[0][0]   = b[0]   + 1;
      a[0][1]   = b[1]   + 1;
            ⋮
      a[6][109] = b[109] + 1;
      a[6][110] = b[110] + 1;
      a[6][111] = b[111] + 1;
```

The execution order can be formalized as follows. Consider a statement S_x at nesting depth d_x of a nested loop with loop indices $i_1,...,i_{d_x}$ and iteration space $I \subset \mathbb{Z}^{d_x}$, and a statement S_y at nesting depth d_y of a nested loop with loop indices $j_1,...,j_{d_y}$ and iteration space $J \subset \mathbb{Z}^{d_y}$, where both statements have $d \le \min(d_x,d_y)$ outer loops in common— $i_k \equiv j_k$ for $1 \le k \le d$. Then, sequential semantics define that statement instance $S_x(i_1,..., i_{d_x})$ with $(i_1,..., i_{d_x}) \in I$ is executed before statement instance $S_y(j_1,..., j_{d_y})$ with $(j_1,..., j_{d_y}) \in J$ if and only if either the former is executed in an earlier iteration of the common loops than the latter, that is, a $1 \leq k \leq d$ exists such that

$$i_1 = j_1 \wedge \ldots \wedge i_{k-1} = j_{k-1} \wedge i_k < j_k$$

or both statement instances are executed in the same iteration of the common loops, but the former appears lexically before the latter, that is

$$i_1 = j_1 \wedge \ldots \wedge i_d = j_d \wedge x < y$$

under the assumption that statement labels reflect the relative textual position in the program. Consider, for example, the following fragment, where statements S_1, S_2, and S_3 appear at nesting depth $d_1 = 0$, $d_2 = 2$, and $d_3 = 1$, respectively.

```
S₁:    . . .
       for (i₁ = 0; i₁ < 2; i₁++) {
          for (i₂ = 0; i₂ < 3; i₂++) {
S₂:          . . .
          }
S₃:       . . .
       }
```

Because S_1 appears lexically before S_2 and S_3 at nesting depth 0, it has only one trivial statement instance that is executed before all other statement instances. Since S_2 and S_3 have one outer loop in common—the i_1-loop, statement instance $S_2(i_1,i_2)$ is executed before statement instance $S_3(j_1)$ if and only if $i_1 \leq j_1$. Furthermore, $S_2(i_1,i_2)$ is executed before another instance $S_2(j_1,j_2)$ of the same statement if and only if $i_1 < j_1$ or $i_1 = j_1 \wedge i_2 < j_2$. Using similar reasoning for statement instances of S_3 eventually reveals that sequential semantics define the following execution order on all the statement instances in this fragment:

$$S_1 \; ; S_2(0,0) \; ; S_2(0,1); \; S_2(0,2); \; S_3(0); \; S_2(1,0) \; ; S_2(1,1); \; S_2(1,2); \; S_3(1)$$

Idiom Recognition

Although not directly supported in the C programming language, compiler analysis and optimization benefit from internally representing programming constructs that compute a minimum, maximum, or absolute function with explicit operators. In this book, explicit MIN/MAX/ABS operators are denoted as follows where, analogous to other arithmetic operators, the subscript is restricted to $t \in \{u32, s32, u64, s64, f32, f64\}$, since the usual arithmetic conversions require that narrow precision operands are compared in 32-bit precision.

```
MIN_t ( x, y )
MAX_t ( x, y )
ABS_t ( x )
```

These operators can be recognized in two different sorts of programming constructs. First, because external library functions in the standard C library may be expanded into inline code (Plauger 1992), the compiler is permitted to convert the function call abs(x), for example, into the operator $ABS_{s32}(x)$. Second, the compiler uses idiom recognition to convert conditional constructs that implement minimum, maximum, or absolute functions into explicit operators. This idiom recognition is driven by a number of rewriting rules. An example of a rewriting rule that recognizes a MAX operator for unsigned operands in an if statement is shown below, where x_t denotes an arbitrary expression with data type t and identical symbols must be bound to equivalent expressions.

```
if ( x_u32 >_u32 y_u32 ) {
    y_u32 = x_u32;                    →    y_u32 = MAX_u32 ( x_u32, y_u32 );
}
```

Other rewriting rules account for the type of conversions that arise because relational operators on narrow precision operands are always done in 32-bit precision, as in the following, for a MIN operator.

```
if ( ((s32) x_s16) <_s32 ((s32) y_s16) ) {
    y_s16 = x_s16;
}
    →    y_s16 = (s16) MIN_s32 ( ((s32) x_s16), ((s32) y_s16) );
```

A sample rewriting rule that recognizes an ABS operator is as follows:

```
if ( x_s32 >= 0 ) {
    t_s32 = x_s32;
} else {                    →            t_s32 = ABS_s32 ( x_s32 );
    t_s32 = - x_s32;
}
```

Although rewriting rules must deal with all combinations of data types, type conversions, alternative operators, conditional constructs, and with commutative and associative laws, a practical set of rewriting rules can be expressed quite compactly by separating a few general patterns from a number of conditions under which they become applicable (Bik et al. 2002). Representing the conditional operator ?: with explicit if statements further reduces the number of required rewriting rules. By repetitively applying the rewriting rules interleaved with traditional compiler optimizations, this approach can be quite successful in detecting MIN/MAX/ABS operators in user code. For instance, this approach rewrites the following assignment statement:

```
s32 a, b, c;
...
a = (10 < ((b*c > 20) ? 20 : b*c))
        ? ((b*c > 20) ? 20 : b*c) : 10;
```

into the following form:

```
a = MAXs32( MINs32( b*c, 20 ),  10 );
```

The resulting expression is more amenable to subsequent compiler analysis and optimization.

Chapter 4

Data Dependence Theory

A s seen in the previous chapter, an imperative programming language like C imposes a *total order* on the execution of statement instances in a program. Central to exploiting any form of implicit parallelism in a sequential program is the observation that this total order can be relaxed into the *partial order* that is defined by data dependences between statement instances without affecting the semantics of the original program. Data dependences, therefore, provide compilers with essential information on the validity of applying transformations that change the execution order in a program. This chapter defines data dependences and briefly discusses data dependence analysis. A thorough presentation of these topics can be found in the excellent textbooks by Banerjee (Banerjee 1993, 1994, 1997) and Wolfe (Wolfe 1996).

Data Dependences

Data dependences impose essential execution order constraints on the statement instances in a program, as formalized in this section.

Data Dependence Definitions

Suppose that a programmer has written the following two statements in C:

S_1:   a = 100;
S_2:   b = 200;

The sequential semantics of the language pose the following execution order on the statements: first execute statement S_1, which assigns the value 100 to variable a, and then execute statement S_2, which assigns the value 200 to variable b. In this case, however, executing S_2 before S_1 or even executing the statement simultaneously has no effect on the final values of the variables. In contrast, suppose the statement sequence reads as follows.

```
S₁:    a = 100;
S₂:    b = a + 200;
```

The sequential execution order must now be respected to avoid a change in semantics. Swapping the two statements would yield the value 200 for b—assuming an initial value 0 for a—rather than the intended value 300. The difference with the first example is that, in the second case, a read-after-write data dependence exists between statements S_1 and S_2.

This concept can be generalized to statements that appear in well-behaved loops. Consider a statement S_x in a nested loop with loop indices $i_1,...,i_{d_x}$ and statement S_y in a nested loop with loop indices $j_1,...,j_{d_y}$, where both statements have $d \leq \min(d_x,d_y)$ outer loops in common: $i_k \equiv j_k$ for $1 \leq k \leq d$. If sequential semantics define that statement instance $S_x(i_1,...,i_{d_x})$ must be executed before statement instance $S_y(j_1,...,j_{d_y})$, then the following memory-based data dependences between the two statement instances prohibit changing this execution order:

- A *flow dependence*, denoted by $S_x(i_1,...,i_{d_x}) \; \delta \; S_y(j_1,...,j_{d_y})$, occurs if the former instance writes to a memory location that is subsequently read by the latter—read-after-write.

- An *antidependence*, denoted by $S_x(i_1,...,i_{d_x}) \; \delta^a \; S_y(j_1,...,j_{d_y})$, occurs if the former instance reads from a memory location that is subsequently overwritten by the latter—write-after-read.

- An *output dependence*, denoted by $S_x(i_1,...,i_{d_x}) \; \delta^o \; S_y(j_1,...,j_{d_y})$, occurs if the former instance writes to a memory location that is subsequently overwritten by the latter—write-after-write.

Any change in execution order that preserves the partial order defined by the data dependences arising in the original sequential code does not affect the final values appearing in memory and, hence, the semantics of the original program. The necessary execution order on I/O statements is easily preserved within this framework by modeling the effect of such statements with a write to the corresponding file pointer variable.

Data Dependence Terminology

For a data dependence between two statement instances $S_x(i_1,...,i_{dx})$ and $S_y(j_1,...,j_{dy})$ that have d outer loops in common, the *data dependence distance vector* $(\sigma_1,...,\sigma_d)$ defines each component as $\sigma_k = j_k - i_k$. The *data dependence direction vector* $(\rho_1,...,\rho_d)$ defines each component as follows:

$$\rho_k = \begin{cases} < \text{ if } \sigma_k > 0 \\ = \text{ if } \sigma_k = 0 \\ > \text{ if } \sigma_k < 0 \end{cases}$$

A data dependence is *loop-independent* if every ρ_i is =, or *loop-carried* otherwise. Furthermore, for $x < y$, $x > y$ and $x = y$, the data dependence is called *lexically forward, lexically backward,* and a *self-data-dependence,* respectively. Lexically backward and self-data-dependence are always loop-carried, although a loop-independent, self-antidependence is possible by noting that all reads in a statement instance must occur prior to writing the result.

Consider, for example, the following well-behaved loop:

```
        for (i = 0; i < U; i++) {
S₁:       a[i] = b[i];
S₂:       c[i] = c[i+1] + a[i];
        }
```

The data dependences $S_1(i) \; \delta^f \; S_2(i)$ that are caused by writing and reading the same element of array a in each iteration $0 \leq i < U$ have a data dependence distance vector (0) and data dependence direction vector (=). These flow dependences are loop-independent, lexically forward data dependences. The data dependences $S_2(i) \; \delta^a \; S_2(i + 1)$ that are caused by reading an element of array c that is overwritten in the next iteration have a data dependence distance vector (1) and data dependence direction vector (<). These antidependences are loop-carried self-data-dependences.

Data dependences that arise in sequential programs are *plausible* as defined in Table 4.1 for a data dependence direction vector that is positive—first nonequal component is <; zero—all components are =, or loop-independent; or negative—first nonequal component is >.[1] Implausible data dependences are nevertheless useful for solving data dependence problems.

---

[1] Textbooks often define plausibility for nonzero *direction vectors*. The definition that is used here can also classify loop-independent data dependences.

Table 4.1 Plausible and Implausible Data Dependences

	lexically backward	self-data-dependence	lexically forward
positive direction	*plausible*	*plausible*	*plausible*
zero direction	*implausible*	if δ^a: *plausible* if δ^t: *implausible*	*plausible*
negative direction	*implausible*	*implausible*	*implausible*

Data Dependence Graphs

Because data dependences arise between statement *instances,* it is generally infeasible to represent all the data dependences that arise in a program. Therefore, usually only *static data dependences* are recorded by dropping all instance information and instead annotating the data dependence with a data dependence direction vector. For example, the following loop has 10,000 flow dependences $S_1(i)\ \delta\ S_2(i)$ for $0 \leq i < 10,000$ caused by writing and reading an element of array a in the same iteration and 9,999 flow dependences $S_2(i)\ \delta\ S_2(i + 1)$ for $0 \leq i < 9,999$ caused by writing an element of array c that will be read in the next iteration:

```
        for (i = 0; i < 10000; i++) {
S₁:        a[i]    = b[i] * 5;
S₂:        c[i+1] = c[i] + a[i];
        }
```

This large set of data dependences is represented compactly with only two static data dependences:

$$S_1\delta^f_{(=)}S_2 \text{ and } S_2\delta^f_{(<)}S_2$$

Information on static data dependences can be easily represented by a *data dependence graph* $G = (V,E)$, where each vertex $v \in V$ corresponds to a statement and each edge $e \in E$ with $E \subseteq V \times V$ represents one or more static dependences between two statements. Edges can be labeled with more information on the static data dependences, such as type—flow, anti-, or output—and data dependence direction vector. Figure 4.1 shows the actual data dependences in the example given above together with the following data dependence graph representation:

$$G = (\{S_1,S_2\}, \{(S_1,S_2),(S_2,S_2)\})$$

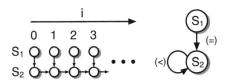

Figure 4.1   Data Dependence Graph

Although a static representation may lose information by lumping all statement instances together, data dependence graphs usually still provide sufficient information on implicit parallelism in a program.

Data Dependence Analysis

Data dependence analysis involves solving the problem of whether two statement instances can refer to the same memory location where at least one of these memory references is a write. Although this problem is undecidable in general, in most practical cases the data dependence problem can be formulated as an integer linear programming problem. However, since these problems are NP-complete (Schrijver 1986, Sedgewick 1988), most compilers trade off some accuracy for efficiency while solving the problem. In any case, the outcome of data dependence analysis must be *conservative*—it is safe to report a data dependence when in reality none exists—but independence must never be reported incorrectly.

Data Dependence Problems

Consider a program fragment with an occurrence of an *n*-dimensional array a at the left-hand side of an assignment statement S_x in a nested loop with loop indices $i_1,...,i_{d_x}$ and iteration space I, and with another occurrence of the same array at the right-hand side of an assignment statement S_y in a nested loop with loop indices $j_1,...,j_{d_y}$ and iteration space J.

S_x: $\mathtt{a}[f_1(\mathtt{i_1}, \ldots, \mathtt{i}_{d_x})] \ldots [f_n(\mathtt{i_1}, \ldots, \mathtt{i}_{d_x})] = \ldots ;$

$$\vdots$$

S_y: $\ldots = \mathtt{a}[g_1(\mathtt{j_1}, \ldots, \mathtt{j}_{d_y})] \ldots [g_n(\mathtt{j_1}, \ldots, \mathtt{j}_{d_y})] ;$

Then, deciding if the two statements can be involved in a flow or antidependence involves solving the problem of whether statement instances of S_x and S_y can reference the same memory location during execution of the program. This data dependence problem is formulated as the following system of equations, Constraints 4.1:

$$
\begin{cases}
f_1\left(i_1,\ldots,i_{d_x}\right) = g_1\left(j_1,\ldots,j_{d_y}\right) \\
\quad\vdots \\
f_n\left(i_1,\ldots,i_{d_x}\right) = g_n\left(j_1,\ldots,j_{d_y}\right)
\end{cases}
$$

Constraints 4.1

Since the subscript functions f_i and g_i are typically affine functions of loop indices, Constraints 4.1 usually forms a system of linear equations. In fact, since solving an under-specified data dependence problem is conservative, non-affine subscript functions can simply be omitted from the system.

The iteration space constraints $(i_1,\ldots,i_{d_x}) \in I$ and $(j_1,\ldots,j_{d_y}) \in J$ give rise to a system of linear inequalities, Constraints 4.2, where, again, non-affine loop bounds can simply be left out to obtain an under-specified data dependence problem.

$$
X\begin{pmatrix} i_1 \\ \vdots \\ i_{d_x} \end{pmatrix} \le \begin{pmatrix} x_1 \\ \vdots \\ x_{d_x} \end{pmatrix} \qquad Y\begin{pmatrix} j_1 \\ \vdots \\ j_{d_y} \end{pmatrix} \le \begin{pmatrix} y_1 \\ \vdots \\ y_{d_y} \end{pmatrix}
$$

Constraints 4.2

Even more constraints arise when testing for a particular data dependence distance or direction vector. For example, if the statements have $d \le \min(d_x, d_y)$ of the outermost loops in common—$i_k \equiv j_k$ for $1 \le k \le d$, then specifically testing for a *flow* dependence between S_x and S_y that is carried by the i_d-loop gives rise to Constraints 4.3, because the write must be executed before the read.

$$\begin{cases} i_1 = j_1, \ldots, i_{d-1} = j_{d-1} \\ i_d < j_d \end{cases}$$

Constraints 4.3

Testing for a similar *anti*dependence requires replacing the latter constraint with $j_d < i_d$. Testing for a flow dependence carried by less than four iterations of the i_d-loop requires $0 < j_d - i_d < 4$ instead. Such constraints are particularly useful to test the validity of vectorization with a particular short vector length, as further explained in Chapter 5.

The systems of linear equations (Constraints 4.1) and linear inequalities (Constraints 4.2) together with any additional constraints (Constraints 4.3) form the *data dependence system* of the data dependence problem. A similar data dependence system results for the reversed situation where the array occurrences appear at the right-hand side of S_x and the left-hand side of S_y, with potential anti- and flow dependences, or for the situation where the array occurrences appear at the left-hand sides of both statements, with potential output dependences.

Data Dependence Solvers

If a data dependence system is provably inconsistent, that is, no solution exists, then the data dependence considered in the data dependence problem cannot exist. In all cases where inconsistency cannot be shown, the tested data dependence is assumed. Most state-of-the-art compilers attack the data dependence system with a series of data dependence solvers that progressively increase in accuracy as well as computational and storage requirements. A detailed survey of data dependence solvers can be found in Wolfe's textbook (Wolfe 1996, Chapter 7). If simple inexpensive solvers fail to prove inconsistency, the compiler resorts to more powerful but potentially expensive solvers, such as those based on Fourier-Motzkin elimination (Dantzig 1963, Dantzig and Eaves 1973, Schrijver 1986, Wolfe 1989). Central to this latter elimination method is the observation that a variable i can be eliminated from a system of linear inequalities by replacing each pair-wise combination of inequalities that define a lower and upper bound for that variable, as expressed below for two integer constants $c_1, c_2 > 0$.

$$\begin{cases} L \le c_1 \cdot i \\ c_2 \cdot i \le U \end{cases} \rightarrow c_2 \cdot L \le c_1 \cdot U$$

After this elimination, which only requires integer arithmetic, another system of inequalities that does not involve the variable i results. For a variable $i \in \mathbb{R}$, the original system is consistent if and only if the resulting system is consistent. On the other hand, for a variable $i \in \mathbb{Z}$, the elimination given above may be inaccurate. For example, eliminating the variable i from the pair of inequalities $16 \le 3 \cdot i$ and $2 \cdot i \le 11$ yields a consistent system $32 \le 33$, whereas the original system has no integer solution for $\lceil \frac{16}{3} \rceil \le i \le \lfloor \frac{11}{2} \rfloor$.[2]

Solving a data dependence problem is illustrated by the following loop, which contains a single assignment statement S:

```
        for (i = 0; i <= 100; i++) {
S:         a[i] = a[i+30] + 1;
        }
```

This assignment statement is involved in a self-flow or antidependence if two statement instances $S(i)$ and $S(j)$ write and read the same element of array a, which can be formulated as the following data dependence problem defined by subscript functions $f(i) = i$ and $g(j) = j + 30$.

$$\begin{cases} i = j + 30 \\ 0 \le i, j \le 100 \end{cases}$$

Specifically testing for a flow or antidependence adds, respectively, either inequality $i < j$ or inequality $j \le i$ to this data dependence system. The latter constraint still includes the possibility of loop-independent self-antidependences. Although such simple data dependence systems, illustrated in Figure 4.2, can easily be handled by the inexpensive solvers alluded to above, the inconsistency of the former system is proven in the following with Fourier-Motzkin elimination. Note that $i < j$ rewrites into $i + 1 \le j$ for integers.

---

[2] Although such simple inaccuracies are easily remedied by tightening the inequalities as shown during each elimination step, the method generally still provides a *conservative* test for data dependence.

$$\begin{cases} i+1 \le j \\ \quad j \le i-30 \end{cases} \rightarrow \; 1 \nleq -30$$

The latter system has several solutions for $j \le i$, although none for $i = j$, which can be summarized with static data dependence

$$S\delta^a_{(<)}S$$

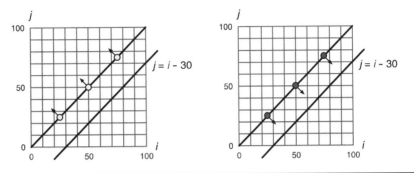

Figure 4.2   Data Dependence Systems

Hierarchical Data Dependence Analysis

A structured method for finding static data dependences between a pair of memory references was proposed by Burke and Cytron (1986). Given a data dependence system defined by only the linear equations (Constraints 4.1) and inequalities (Constraints 4.2), the method first tests for data dependence direction vector

$$\left(\rho_1,\ldots,\rho_d\right) = \left(*,\ldots,*\right)$$

imposing no additional constraints on the system. If independence cannot be proven, one *-component is refined into directions <, =, and >, which gives rise to three new data dependence systems, each of which has one additional constraint in the system (Constraints 4.3). The data dependence hierarchy that arises in this manner is illustrated in Figure 4.3 for $d = 2$.

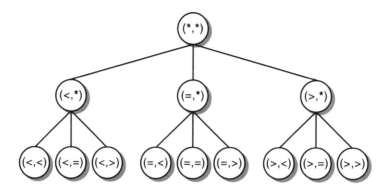

Figure 4.3   Data Dependence Hierarchy

If independence has been proven for a particular data dependence direction vector, this proof effectively prunes all further refinements. On the other hand, if a particular data dependence cannot be further refined but still gives rise to a consistent data dependence system, a flow, anti-, or output dependence with this data dependence direction vector is reported, depending on whether the data dependence is between a write and a read, a read and a write, or two writes, respectively. An implausible data dependence, as shown in Table 4.1, is first reversed into a plausible data dependence by reversing each non-equal component of the data dependence direction vector as $< \leftrightarrow >$, reversing a flow dependence into an antidependence, and vice versa.

This kind of hierarchical data dependence analysis is illustrated with the data dependence problem arising in the following simple program fragment:

```
       for (i₁ = 0; i₁ < U₁; i₁++) {
         for (i₂ = 0; i₂ < U₂; i₂++) {
S₁:         a[i₁][i₂+2] = ...;
S₂:         ... = a[i₁+1][i₂];
         }
       }
```

Simultaneously testing for a potential flow or antidependence between statement instances $S_1(i_1,i_2)$ and $S_2(j_1,j_2)$ gives rise to the following initial data dependence system:

$$\begin{cases} i_1 = j_1 + 1 & 0 \le i_1, j_1 < U_1 \\ i_2 + 2 = j_2 & 0 \le i_2, j_2 < U_2 \end{cases}$$

Since this system is consistent, the data dependence direction vector $(\rho_1, \rho_2) = (*,*)$ is refined into $(<,*)$, $(=,*)$, and $(>,*)$, which gives rise to three new data dependence systems with additional constraints $i_1 < j_1$, $i_1 = j_1$, $i_1 > j_1$, respectively. Since only the system belonging to $(>,*)$ is consistent, the data dependence systems for $(>,<)$, $(>,=)$, and $(>,>)$ are considered, which further adds the constraints $i_2 < j_2$, $i_2 = j_2$, $i_2 > j_2$, respectively. Only the system belonging to the flow dependence

$$S_1 \delta^f_{(>,<)} S_2$$

is consistent. This implausible data dependence, by nature, reverses into the plausible antidependence

$$S_2 \delta^a_{(<,>)} S_1$$

before reporting. Note that this particular case only considers seven systems rather than the nine systems that would have been considered if all possible data dependence direction vectors were tested directly.

Improving Data Dependence Analysis

In the data dependence problems considered so far, memory was accessed through a single variable. In general, however, compilers must be aware of complications that arise due to aliasing—the situation where the same memory locations can be accessed through multiple variables. This situation is best illustrated with the following example:

```
        void copy(u8 *p, u8 *q, s32 n) {
          s32 i;
          for (i = 0; i < n; i++) {
S₁:          p[i] = q[i];
          }
        }
```

Due to pointer arithmetic in C, the pointer variables p and q can be associated with identical or partially overlapping memory regions. This potential aliasing allows for data dependences in all directions, illustrated as follows with three different invocations of the function:

```
u8 x[100];
...
copy(x+1,x,    99);    /*  S₁δᶠ₍<₎S₁   */

copy(x,   x,  100);    /*  S₁δᵃ₍=₎S₁   */

copy(x,   x+1, 99);    /*  S₁δᵃ₍<₎S₁   */
```

Because compilers make conservative assumptions about the possibility of such forms of aliasing in a program, usually inaccurate data dependence information results. The inaccuracy due to assumed data dependences can be remedied, however, with one or all of the following methods: (a) compiler hints, (b) aliasing analysis, and (c) dynamic data dependence analysis.

Compiler Hints for Data Dependences

As an example of the first method, many compilers support the keyword `restrict` that can be used to assert that a pointer variable provides exclusive access to its associated memory region. If function `copy()` is only applied to distinct arrays, for example, this non-aliasing information can be conveyed to the compiler as follows. Note that using such a language extension may require an additional compiler switch, like `-Qrestrict`.

```
        void copy(u8 * restrict p, u8 * restrict q, s32 n) {
          s32 i;
          for (i = 0; i < n; i++) {
S₁:         p[i] = q[i];
          }
        }
```

Even though compiler hints can improve the performance of a program in a relatively simple manner, hints must always be used with care since incorrect usage may ultimately cause an undesired change in semantics. A complete list of data dependence hints that are supported by the Intel C++ and Fortran compilers is given in Chapter 9.

Aliasing Analysis

State-of-the-art compilers perform intraprocedural (within a single function) and interprocedural (between several or all functions in a program) aliasing analysis to gather information on all variables that could potentially provide access to the same memory locations. Simple approaches are based on the observation that only a variable whose address is taken can be associated with a pointer variable.

In the function `copy()`, for instance, neither n nor i can be modified through pointer variables p or q, because the address of these local variables is never taken. More advanced approaches also analyze the way addresses propagate through the whole program. For example, if all calls to `copy()` associate addresses of disjoint data structures to the formal arguments p and q, the compiler can safely discard the possibility of aliasing in this function.

Some programming languages pose further restrictions on aliasing. The Fortran standard, for example, states that as long as an actual argument is associated with more than one formal argument, no modifications to the actual argument may occur. This implies that potential data dependences between array accesses that use different formal array arguments can be safely discarded. Incorporating such language-specific restrictions in the alias analysis substantially improves the accuracy of the data dependences that are eventually reported. A detailed presentation of aliasing analysis can be found in Muchnick's textbook (1997, Chapter 10).

Dynamic Data Dependence Analysis

In situations where the previous methods fail to resolve assumed data dependences, the compiler can resort to *dynamic data dependence analysis,* where the outcome of a run-time test decides between a data dependent and a data independent version of the same code, each of which is subsequently optimized accordingly (Bik et al. 2002; Bik, Girkar, and Haghighat 1999; Callahan, Dongarra, and Levine 1988; Levine, Callahan, and Dongarra 1991; Padua and Wolfe 1986; Wolfe 1996, Chapter 10). A simple overlap test is based on the observation that for two half open intervals

$$\begin{cases} A = [a,b) \\ B = [c,d) \end{cases}$$

where $a,b,c,d \in \mathbb{Z}$ with $a < b$ and $c < d$, the property

$$A \cap B \neq \emptyset \Leftrightarrow a < d \wedge c < b$$

defines a necessary and sufficient condition for overlap between A and B. This observation gives rise to the following method to resolve assumed data dependences in a well-behaved loop. First, for every memory reference in the loop, an approximated address interval of the accessed memory locations is constructed. Some sample address intervals for memory references through pointer s32 *r in a well-behaved loop with index i and upper bound U are shown in Table 4.2.

Table 4.2 Sample Address Intervals for Memory References

Memory Reference	Address Interval	
`*r`	$[r, r + 4)$	
`*(r+i)`	$[r, r + 4 \cdot U)$	
`*(r+i+1)`	$[r + 4, r + 4 \cdot U + 4)$	
`*(r+U-i-1)`	$[r, r + 4 \cdot U)$	(reversed bounds)
`*(r+2*i)`	$[r, r + 8 \cdot U)$	(approximated interval)

Subsequently, for every pair of memory references in the loop that may cause a data dependence, the compiler generates code that tests overlap between the corresponding address intervals using the property described in the previous paragraph. The outcome of these run-time tests determines whether a data dependent or data independent version of the loop is executed.

For the function `copy()` discussed earlier, for example, the assumed data dependences between `*p` and `*q` in the i-loop can be resolved as follows.

S_1:

S'_1:

```
if ((p < q+n) && (q < p+n)) {
    /* data dependent loop */
    for (i = 0; i < n; i++) {
        p[i] = q[i];
    }
} else {
    /* data independent loop */
    for (i = 0; i < n; i++) {
        p[i] = q[i];
    }
}
```

Short-circuit evaluation of the condition ensures that the second loop is executed as soon as data independence has been proven. The compiler can eventually optimize this loop under the safe assumption of data independence. Although generating this kind of multi-version code can be very effective, a potential drawback of dynamic data dependence analysis is that the performance gains obtained by better optimization are outweighed by introducing testing overhead, since potentially every left-hand side memory reference has to be tested against every left-hand and right-hand side memory reference. Therefore, in general it is best to restrict dynamic data dependence analysis to loops with only a few memory references. Furthermore, even though the overlap test provides a convenient way to resolve assumed data dependences for memory references with simple subscripts, other sorts of run-time tests may be required to deal with more complicated situations, where approximated address intervals become too conservative.

Some programming languages pose restrictions on aliasing that can be exploited in the run-time tests. For example, because in the Java programming language (Gosling, Joy, and Steele 1996), reference variables—which effectively are the same as pointer variables in C—are either associated with disjoint or identical memory regions, an overlap test between two pointer variables can simply be done by testing equivalence of the two pointers, as exploited in the Java JIT compiler described in Bik, Girkar, and Haghighat (1999). The loop in function `copy()` could even be vectorized unconditionally in Java, because the memory regions are either disjoint—`p != q`—or equivalent—`p == q`, where the latter case gives rise only to the harmless loop-independent self-data-dependence:

$$S_1 \delta^a_{(=)} S_1$$

Chapter 5

Vectorization Essentials

This chapter provides the essentials of intra-register vectorization. First, because the conversion of sequential code into a form that exploits multimedia extensions changes the order of execution and possibly the precision of operations, conditions that guarantee the validity of vectorization are established. Second, for several basic constructs, effective implementations with the multimedia instructions of streaming-SIMD extensions are given. The focus of this initial discussion is on intra-register vectorization of relatively simple statements in well-behaved innermost loops. More advanced aspects of effective vectorization and the vectorization of straightline code are discussed in Chapters 6 through 8.

Validity of Vectorization

Converting sequential code into multimedia instructions is valid if all data dependences as well as the precision of all final results are preserved, as discussed in this section.

Preserving Data Dependences

Implementing a sequential loop with vector instructions changes the execution order on statement instances, as illustrated in the following example:

```
         for (i = 0; i < U; i++) {
S₁:          lhs₁[i] = rhs₁[i];
                 ⋮
Sₙ:          lhsₙ[i] = rhsₙ[i];
         }
```

Vectorizing this loop consists of *strip-mining* (Wolfe 1996, Zima and Chapman 1990) the iteration space by a vector length vl and replacing all statements in the loop body by corresponding vl-way SIMD parallel instructions. This conversion is sketched in the following with *triplet notation* (Brainerd, Goldberg, and Adams 1990), where $l{:}u{:}s$ denotes the lower bound l, upper bound u, and the stride s of a data parallel operation, and where, for the moment, the assumption is made that vl evenly divides U:

```
         for (i = 0; i < U; i+=vl) {
S₁:          lhs₁[i:i+vl-1:1] = rhs₁[i:i+vl-1:1];

                 ⋮

Sₙ:          lhsₙ[i:i+vl-1:1] = rhsₙ[i:i+vl-1:1];
         }
```

Executing groups of vl statement instances in parallel changes the execution order on statement instances as illustrated in Figure 5.1 for $vl = 4$ and $n = 4$. Because in the original fragment all data dependences between different statement instances are plausible, vectorization preserves loop-independent and loop-carried lexically forward data dependences—directions (1) and (2), but may violate loop-carried self and lexically backward data dependences—directions (3) and (4). Since a lexically backward data dependence not involved in any cycle can be made lexically forward by reordering statements in the loop body, the implication is that only cycles in a data dependence graph can actually prohibit the change in execution order that is inherent to vectorization. Such cycles must be recognized either as a special idiom or otherwise isolated into a separate loop that remains sequential.

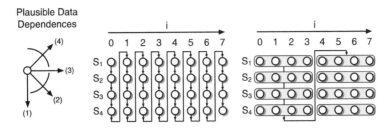

Figure 5.1   Execution Order Before and After Vectorization ($vl = 4$)

These observations give rise to a data dependence-driven approach to vectorization, pioneered by Kuck (1978), and Allen and Kennedy (1987; see also Allen and Kennedy 2002; Wolfe 1989 and 1996; Zima and Chapman 1990). A modified version of their method is given for vectorizing statements $S_1,...,S_n$ at nesting depth d of a nested loop in the following:

1. Construct the *pruned* data dependence graph $G = (V, E)$ for the nested loop, where $V = \{S_1,...,S_n\}$ and $E \subseteq V \times V$ represents all data dependences except:

    (a) Data dependences that are carried by outer loops—the data dependence distance vector $(\sigma_1,...,\sigma_d)$ has at least one component $\sigma_k \neq 0$ for $k < d$.

    (b) Data dependences that are carried by the innermost loop over a distance of at least the vector length—the data dependence distance vector has the form $(0,...,0,\sigma_d)$ for $\sigma_d \geq vl$.

2. Construct the strongly-connected components of G (Tarjan 1972) and subsequently apply *statement reordering* according to a topological sort $SCC_1, ... , SCC_m$ of these strongly-connected components—any ordering where for each $(v,w) \in E$ with v belonging to SCC_i and w belonging to SCC_j, the relation $i \leq j$ holds. Within each strongly-connected component, statements remain in original order, as follows:

    ```
    for (i_d = 0; i < U_d; i++) { SCC_1 ... SCC_m }
    ```

3. If a cyclic SCC_k is not recognized as an idiom that can be vectorized, all statements involved in the data dependence cycle are isolated by means of *loop distribution* (Padua and Wolfe 1986, Wolfe 1996, Zima and Chapman 1990), as follows:

```
for (i_d = 0; i < U_d; i_d++) {   SCC_1   ...   SCC_{k-1}   }
for (i_d = 0; i < U_d; i_d++) {             SCC_k             }
for (i_d = 0; i < U_d; i_d++) {   SCC_{k+1}   ...   SCC_m     }
```

This transformation is valid since all other data dependences have been made lexically forward. Loops with acyclic or idiomatic strongly-connected components are candidates for vectorization. All other loops must remain sequential.

For example, the data dependence graph G for the following loop together with a topological sort of the two strongly-connected components $(\{S_2\}, \varnothing)$ and $(\{S_1, S_3\}, \{(S_1, S_3), (S_3, S_1)\})$ are shown in Figure 5.2.

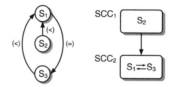

Figure 5.2   Topological Sort of SCCs

```
      for (i = 0; i < U; i++) {
S_1:    a[i]    = c[i] * b[i];
S_2:    b[i+1]  = d[i] - e[i];
S_3:    c[i+1]  = a[i] * e[i];
      }
```

The method described above transforms this loop as follows:

```
      for (i = 0; i < U; i++) {  /* candidate vector loop */
S_2:    b[i+1]  = d[i] - e[i];
      }
      for (i = 0; i < U; i++) {  /* sequential loop */
S_1:    a[i]    = c[i] * b[i];

S_3:    c[i+1]  = a[i] * e[i];

      }
```

In the original loop, instances of S_2 write elements of b before instances of S_1 read them. The combination of statement reordering and loop distribution preserves this behavior. A single lexically backward data dependence can always be made lexically forward in this manner and, for this particular example, yields a candidate vector loop. The other loop remains sequential, since the cyclic strongly-connected component does not belong to any idiom.

In general, pruning step 1(a) can be used because the sequential execution of outer loops guarantees that all corresponding data dependences are preserved. Pruning step 1(b) is typically more useful for multimedia instruction sets with relatively short vector lengths ranging from 2 to 16 than for more traditional pipelined vector processors with much longer vector lengths ranging from 32 to 64K. Note that instead of pruning data dependences with $\sigma_d \geq \text{vl}$ from an already computed data dependence graph, the opposite constraint, $\sigma_d < \text{vl}$, can also already be fed into the data dependence system *during* data dependence analysis, as alluded to in Chapter 4.

Cycles in step 3 that can be recognized as an idiom are as follows:

■ Self-antidependences can be ignored, since vector instructions fetch all right-hand sides before storing back results.

For example, neither $S\overline{\delta}^a_{(=)}S$ nor $S\overline{\delta}^a_{(<)}S$ prevent vectorization of the following loop:

```
        for (i = 0; i < U; i++) {
S:        a[i] = a[i] - a[i+1];
        }
```

■ Self-data-dependences that are caused by scalars can be ignored for the following three constructs—see the section "Scalar Memory References" later in this chapter for details:

(a) Induction variables with induction variable elimination.

(b) Reduction variables by computing partial results.

(c) Private variables with scalar expansion.

In the context of intra-register vectorization, preserving data dependences alone is not sufficient, as explained in the following section.

Preserving Integer Precision

Given the possible interpretations of packed integer data elements shown in Table 2.1, loops in which all memory references have one of the integer data types u8, s8, u16, s16, u32, s32, u64, or s64 are candidates for vectorization by means of SSE/SSE2/SSE3 instructions. For wide data types, this translation usually preserves the required precision of all operations. Take, for example, the following loop that adds two arrays into a third array:

```
/* arrays x, y, and z are 16-byte aligned */
for (i = 0; i < 128; i++) {
  x[i] = y[i] + z[i];
}
```

If all arrays have data type s32, translating this sequential loop into SIMD form preserves the required 32-bit precision of the integer addition.

```
L: movdqa xmm0,   y[eax]  ; load  4 doublewords from y
   paddd  xmm0,   z[eax]  ; add   4 doublewords from z
   movdqa x[eax], xmm0    ; store 4 doublewords into x
   add    eax,    16      ;
   cmp    eax,    512     ;
   jb     L               ; looping logic (iterates 32 times)
```

On the other hand, implicit type conversions appear around operators for narrow data types. If, for instance, all arrays have data type s8, then the usual arithmetic conversions shown in Table 3.2 define that both operands must be promoted into data type s32 before the outcome of a subsequent 32-bit addition is truncated back into data type s8. These type conversions are illustrated in Figure 5.3 and are made explicit in the following program text:

```
for (i = 0; i < 128; i++) {
  x[i] = (s8) ( ((s32) y[i]) +s32 ((s32) z[i]) );
}
```

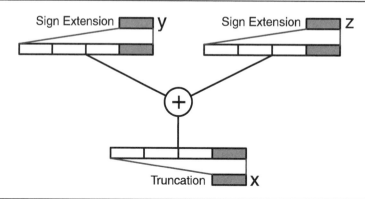

Figure 5.3   Narrow Data Type Addition

Because more significant bits cannot affect less significant bits in an addition, however, translating this sequential loop into the following SIMD form that uses an 8-bit addition with wrap-around arithmetic does not affect the final results that are stored into array x.

```
L: movdqa xmm0,    y[eax]  ; load   16 bytes from y
   paddb  xmm0,    z[eax]  ; add    16 bytes from z
   movdqa x[eax],  xmm0    ; store  16 bytes into x
   add    eax,     16      ;
   cmp    eax,     128     ;
   jb     L                ; looping logic (iterates 8 times)
```

In general, *intra-register vectorization of a loop by means of narrower precision integer operations is valid if higher order bits of intermediate results cannot contribute to the final results that are stored back.* Most arithmetic and bitwise operators satisfy this property. Vectorization cannot proceed, however, if higher order bits may contribute to the final results.

A 32-bit shift-right operator, for instance, cannot generally be vectorized with only 16-bit precision, because higher order bits that are shifted into lower positions could be lost. Relational and equality operators generally also require full precision in order to obtain the correct results; exceptions appear later in this book.

Preserving Floating-Point Precision

The possible interpretations of packed floating-point data elements shown in Table 2.1 reveal that loops in which all memory references have one of the data types f32 and f64 are also candidates for vectorization by means of the SSE/SSE2/SSE3 instructions. Again, this translation often preserves the required precision of all operations. Take, for example, the following loop, which adds a constant to all elements in an array with data type f32:

```
for (i = 0; i < 128; i++) { /* a is 16-byte aligned */
  a[i] = a[i] + 3.14159f;
}
```

Translating this sequential loop into the SIMD form shown in the following code preserves the required 32-bit precision of the floating-point addition:

```
    movaps xmm0,    _const  ; setup 4 floats
L:  movaps xmm1,    a[eax]  ; load  4 floats from a
    addps  xmm1,    xmm0    ; add   4 floats
    movaps a[eax],  xmm1    ; store 4 floats into a
    add    eax,     16      ;
    cmp    eax,     512     ;
    jb     L                ; looping logic (iterates 32 times)
```

If the f is omitted, changing the data type of the literal constant into f64, the usual arithmetic conversion requires that the addition also proceeds in 64-bit precision, as shown explicitly in the following program text:

```
for (i = 0; i < 128; i++) {
  a[i] = (f32) ( ((f64) a[i]) +f64 3.14159 );
}
```

Implementing this code with just the single-precision required for the final results to enable the four-way SIMD parallelism shown above is more acceptable to programmers who require high performance than to programmers who favor precision over performance.

A similar trade-off arises from the fact that many compiler optimizations rely on mathematical equivalences that do not necessarily hold in finite-precision floating-point arithmetic. For example, floating-point arithmetic is not always associative: $(x + y) + z$ is not necessarily the same as $x + (y + z)$. To accommodate a trade-off in both directions, the following two modes are used to control the degree of freedom that the compiler has during intra-register vectorization of loops with floating-point operations.

- ■ The *fp:precision mode* allows only those optimizations that preserve the precise behavior of floating-point operations as defined by the programming language standard.

- ■ The *fp:performance mode* allows optimizations that rely on mathematical equivalences as well as optimizations that modify the precision of floating-point operations into the precision required for the final results if this yields higher performance.

These two modes also determine whether floating-point arithmetic runs in the IEEE 754-compliant mode or the flush-to-zero mode, respectively.

If the fp:performance mode causes a significant difference in the results, this result may be an indication that the algorithm lacks numerical stability and has to be rewritten. If this is not the case, the fp:precision mode can be used to enforce more precise and portable computations. Independent of the used mode, however, programmers should generally not rely on the *exact* outcome of floating-point operations—unlike integer operations, where the outcome of all operations should always be the same.

Vector Code Generation

If vectorization of a sequential loop is valid and deemed profitable by efficiency heuristics, the loop is translated into SSE/SSE2/SSE3 instructions. This section discusses actual vector code generation in more detail.

General Framework

Vectorizing a well-behaved loop

```
for (i = 0; i < U; i++) { B(i); }
```

in which B(i) is used as shorthand for all statements in the loop body consists of generating instructions that implement the following general framework for a vector length vl:

```
           i = 0;
prelude:   if (<run-time-tests>) goto cleanup;
           V = U - (U % vl)
           ...
vector:    for ( ; i < V; i+=vl) { B(i:i+vl-1:1); }
postlude:  ...
cleanup:   for ( ; i < U; i++)   { B(i);            }
exit:
```

The vector loop strip-mines the iteration space by vl and uses vl-way SIMD parallel instructions to implement the loop body, as denoted above with triplet notation. The sequential cleanup loop executes iterations that remain when vl does not evenly divide the trip count or in case the run-time tests enforce complete sequential execution. The prelude and postlude are used to insert instructions that, when required, implement certain pre-processing or post-processing operations for the vector loop. Typical run-time tests that may appear in the prelude include a test for sufficient iterations in case the trip count is not known statically and tests that implement the dynamic data dependence analysis discussed in Chapter 4. Standard compiler optimizations are applied to the resulting code. For example, if no run-time tests are required and U is a constant that is evenly divisible by v1, only the vector code will remain.

This general framework is illustrated with the following example:

```
u8 x[N]; /* 16-byte aligned */

void setx(s32 n) {
  s32 i;
  for (i = 0; i < n; i++) x[i] = 0;
}
```

Intra-register vectorization of the i-loop yields the following code:

```
          xor      edx,      edx      ; i = 0
prelude:  mov      ecx,      [ebx+8]  ; load n
          test     ecx,      ecx      ;
          jle      exit               ; exit loop if n <= 0
          cmp      ecx,      16       ;
          jb       cleanup            ; exit vector loop if n < 16
          mov      eax,      ecx      ;
          and      eax,      15       ;
          neg      eax                ;
          add      eax,      ecx      ;
          pxor     xmm0,     xmm0     ; setup vector zero
vector:   movdqa   x[edx],   xmm0     ; store 16 bytes into x
          add      edx,      16       ;
          cmp      edx,      eax      ;
          jb       vector             ; looping logic
          cmp      edx,      ecx      ;
          jae      exit               ; exit loop if done
cleanup:  mov      x[edx],   0        ; store 1 byte into x
          add      edx,      1        ;
          cmp      edx,      ecx      ;
          jb       cleanup            ; looping logic
exit:
```

The prelude first performs the top test for the loop; if n ≤ 0, it exits directly. Subsequently, if sufficient iterations exist for the vector loop, the vector trip count is computed and a vector register is set to all zeros. The vector loop then executes, possibly followed by the sequential cleanup loop to deal with any remaining iterations. In contrast, suppose that interprocedural constant propagation (Callahan et al. 1986) reveals that n = 16 holds for the formal argument. In this case, the complete loop translates into just two instructions:

```
prelude:  pxor    xmm0, xmm0   ; setup vector zero
vector:     movdqa x,    xmm0   ; store 16 bytes into x
```

For explanation purposes, most examples in this chapter are relatively simple, well-behaved loops with constant trip counts, obvious data dependence graphs, and suitably aligned memory references. Each example typically focuses on only one particular aspect of intra-register vectorization by abstracting from all other implementation details. While reading the examples, however, please keep in mind that effective intra-register vectorization of real-world applications is much more elaborate since unknown trip counts, complex control flow, assumed data dependences, and misalignments all have to be dealt with simultaneously. Such issues are revisited in subsequent chapters.

Vector Data Type Selection

The vector length vl is defined by the number of data elements packed together in the 128-bit data type used to implement the vector loop, henceforth referred to as the *vector data type*. If all memory references in a loop have the same data type—say $s16$—and all operations can be done in corresponding precision ($P = 16$), then selecting a single vector data type is straightforward—packed words—and yields a uniform vector length ($vl = 8$).

The selection of appropriate vector data types for mixed-type loops is more elaborate, however, because the mismatches in data types and possibly even the mismatches in vector lengths must be dealt with in some manner. The general strategy assumed in this book is to try to resolve mixed data types *between* statements with a valid statement reordering and loop distribution, as in the following example:

```
s8  x[N];                          /* select packed doubles */
f64 a[N], b[N];                    for (i = 0; i < N; i++) {
...                                  a[i] += 4.0;
for (i = 0; i < N; i++) {            b[i] *= 2.0;
  a[i] += 4.0;              →      }
  x[i] &= 0x0f;                    /* select packed bytes */
  b[i] *= 2.0;                     for (i = 0; i < N; i++) {
}                                     x[i] &= 0x0f;
                                    }
```

and to restrict mixed data types *within* a statement to constructs that can be implemented efficiently. Hence, unless stated otherwise, the following discussion assumes that the data types of all memory references in a loop give rise to a single vector data type.

Unit-Stride Memory References

A memory reference that incrementally accesses adjacent memory locations in successive iterations of a loop is called a unit-stride memory reference. To vectorize the loading or storing of a unit-stride memory reference, one of the data movement instructions listed in Table 5.1 is applied.

Table 5.1   Data Movement Instructions for Unit-Stride Memory References

	unaligned	aligned
packed integers	movdqu	movdqa
packed floats	movups	movaps
packed doubles	movupd	movapd

As explained in Chapter 2, elements that are moved between a memory location and 128-bit register xmm0 appear right-to-left in this register. Given an array

```
s32 x[4];
```

that is stored at memory address a, loading or storing the four elements into or from register xmm0 adheres to the data layout illustrated in Figure 5.4.

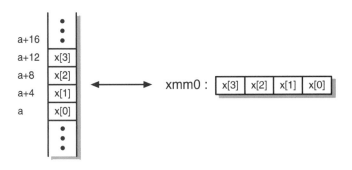

Figure 5.4   Data Layout for a Unit-Stride Memory Reference

Aligned data movement instructions are used for all unit-stride memory references for which the compiler can prove or enforce that the corresponding vector access patterns are 16-byte aligned. Most instructions also allow such memory references to appear directly as memory operand. The less efficient unaligned data movement instructions must be used in all other cases, as illustrated by the following loop:

```
u16 x[65]; /* 16-byte aligned */
...
for (i = 0; i < 64; i++) {
```
S:
```
    x[i] = x[i+1];                    /* Sδᵃ₍<₎S */
}
```

As seen earlier, vector execution preserved the self-antidependences and the loop can be vectorized with packed words as vector data type (vl = 8). The resulting aligned and unaligned access patterns are implemented as follows:

```
L: movdqu xmm0,    x[eax+2]  ; load  8 words from x (unaligned)
   movdqa x[eax],  xmm0      ; store 8 words into x (aligned)
   add    eax,     16        ;
   cmp    eax,     128       ;
   jb     L                  ; looping logic
```

While vectorizing mixed-type loops, some unit-stride memory references may have to be implemented with a narrower data movement instruction or, conversely, with several data movement instructions in order to resolve mismatches in vector lengths, as will become apparent later in this chapter.

Rotating Read-Only Memory References

A memory reference that uses a modulus operator to read cyclically from a series of constants is called a rotating read-only memory reference. This kind of memory reference is illustrated as follows, where M and C denote two compile-time constants:

```
static const u16 primes[] = {
  2, 3, 5, 7, 11, 13, 17, 19
};
...
for (i = 0; i < 64; i++) {
  ... = primes[ (i+C) % M ];
}
```

If M evenly divides the vector length vl of the selected vector data type, intra-register vectorization of a loop with such a construct is straightforward. First, the compiler replicates the appropriate series of constants $\frac{vl}{M}$ times into a rotation vector rot[0:vl-1:1]. Subsequently, this rotation vector is used to implement the read operation in the loop body of the vector loop. If, for instance, M = 4 and C = 2 in the example above, which rotates through the series 5, 7, 2, 3, 5, 7, 2, 3, etc., and the loop is vectorized with packed words (vl = 8), vectorization proceeds as follows:

```
      movdqa xmm0, _const   ; rot[0:7:1] = |3|2|7|5|3|2|7|5|
L: movdqa ...,  xmm0        ; store 8 words
      add    eax,  16        ;
      cmp    eax,  128       ;
      jb     L               ; looping logic
```

Since the iteration space is strip-mined by vl, the rotation vector fits in a single 128-bit register. As another example, if M = 8 and C = 0, the prelude can load the rotation vector directly from the original array as movdqa xmm0, primes. A statically unknown but loop-invariant value of C is dealt with by generating code that constructs the rotation vector at run time. This slightly more complicated situation may also arise after certain compiler transformations, as revisited in subsequent chapters.

Non-Unit-Stride Memory References

A memory reference that accesses different, but not incrementally adjacent memory locations in successive iterations of a loop is called a non-unit-stride memory reference. Array references with non-unit slope affine subscript functions—a[2*i+1], non-affine subscript functions—a[i*i], and indexed subscripts—a[ix[i]], are all examples of non-unit-stride memory references.

Vectorizing a non-unit-stride memory reference requires data rearranging instructions to insert or extract all corresponding data elements. For some vector data types, this data rearrangement is rather straightforward. For example, loading a double-precision floating-point memory reference a[3*i] can be vectorized with only two data movement instructions:

```
L: ...                      ;
     movsd  xmm0, a[eax]     ; |   0      |a[3*i+0]|
     movhpd xmm0, a[eax+24]  ; |a[3*i+3]  |a[3*i+0]|
     add    eax,  48         ;
     ...                     ;
     jb     L                ; looping logic
```

Favoring data movement instruction movsd over movlpd enables register renaming in hardware since false dependences on previous contents of xmm0 are eliminated.

For other vector data types, the data rearrangement may be more elaborate. Vectorizing a load operation of a single-precision floating-point memory reference such as b[3*i], for example, requires additional unpack instructions to move data elements into place.

```
L:  ...                    ;
    movss xmm3, b[eax]    ; |     -    |     -    |     -    |b[3*i+0]|
    movss xmm2, b[eax+12];  |     -    |     -    |     -    |b[3*i+3]|
    movss xmm1, b[eax+24];  |     -    |     -    |     -    |b[3*i+6]|
    movss xmm0, b[eax+36];  |     -    |     -    |     -    |b[3*i+9]|
    unpcklps xmm3, xmm1   ; |     -    |     -    |b[3*i+6]|b[3*i+0]|
    unpcklps xmm2, xmm0   ; |     -    |     -    |b[3*i+9]|b[3*i+3]|
    unpcklps xmm3, xmm2   ; |b[3*i+9]|b[3*i+6]|b[3*i+3]|b[3*i+0]|
    add      eax, 48      ;
    ...                    ;
    jb       L            ; looping logic
```

For all vector data types, similar instruction sequences can be given to load or store a non-unit-stride memory reference in the vector loop. Due to the associated overhead of data rearrangement, however, and the lack of efficient support for gather/scatter operations (Lewis and Simon 1988), in general it is profitable to vectorize only those loops that have relatively few non-unit-stride memory references. If valid, loop distribution can isolate unit-stride memory references from non-unit-stride references to make code more amenable to effective vectorization. The access pattern for reshaping transformations, discussed in Chapter 7, may convert non-unit-stride memory references into unit-stride memory references. Furthermore, although a loop that exclusively uses negative-unit slope memory references, such as c[64-i], can sometimes be handled with *loop reversal* (Allen and Kennedy 2002, Banerjee 1993, Wolfe 1986 and 1996) or otherwise with an appropriate displacement in the data movement instructions (Bik, Girkar, and Haghighat 1999), negative-unit slope memory references are usually implemented as non-unit-stride memory references to obtain a consistent order on all packed data elements.

Scalar Memory References

A memory reference that accesses the same memory location in successive iterations of a loop is called a scalar memory reference. Examples of scalar memory references are scalar variables (x), arrays with loop invariant subscripts (a[3]), and literal constants (3.0). If and how a scalar memory reference can be vectorized depends on whether it implements an induction variable, a reduction variable, or a variable that carries a value that is private to each loop iteration, as further discussed in this section.

Induction Variable Elimination

A scalar that in every iteration of a loop is incremented once by the same loop invariant value—often a constant—is called a *basic induction variable*[1]. As shown below, all preceding and following uses of basic induction variable x can be expressed as an affine function of the loop index i—also a basic induction variable—where a and b denote arbitrary loop invariant expressions.

```
S₁:  x = b;
     for (i = 0; i < U; i++) {
        ...                         ← x ≡ a · i + b
S₂:     x += a;
        ...                         ← x ≡ a · i + (a + b)
     }
```

A scalar that in each iteration of a loop is defined once as an affine function of another induction variable before any use in the loop body is called a *derived induction variable*. As illustrated below, all uses of a derived induction variable z can be expressed as an affine function of the loop index i, given that the other induction variable y—basic or derived—can be expressed as affine function of the loop index at its use in S_3, where c, d, e, and f all denote arbitrary loop invariant expressions:

```
     for (i = 0; i < U; i++) {
        ...                      ← no uses of z
S₃:     z = e * y + f;           ← y ≡ c · i + d
        ...                      ← z ≡ (ec) · i + (ed + f)
     }
```

As a result, every use of a basic or derived induction variable can be replaced by an affine function of the loop index. This, in turn, implies that data dependence cycles caused by induction variables can be removed from a loop with *induction variable elimination*—replacing all uses of induction variables by appropriate affine functions and replacing the induction statements by last value assignments in the

---

[1] Definitions in this section are slightly different from the definitions generally found in the compiler literature (Aho, Sethi, and Ullman 1986; Appel and Ginsburg 1998; Fischer and LeBlanc 1991; Muchnick 1997; Parsons 1992), where induction variable analysis is used to enable optimizations like strength reduction in three-address code (Wolfe 1989, Chapter 6).

postlude of the loop. The last value assignment may be omitted for each induction variable that is not live (Aho, Sethi, and Ullman 1986) upon exiting the loop. Induction variable elimination is illustrated with the following loop:

```
        s32 x = 3, y, i;
        for (i = 0; i < 128; i++) {
S₁:         y = 2*x + 1                    ← x ≡ i + 3
S₂:         x++;
S₃:         u[x] = - y;                    ← x ≡ i + 4, y ≡ 2 · i + 7
        }
```

Replacing all uses of the basic induction variable x and derived induction variable y with appropriate affine functions of the loop index i, followed by replacing the induction statements S_1 and S_2 with last value assignments in the postlude of the loop, yields the following code:

```
        for (i = 0; i < 128; i++) {
S₃:         u[i+4] = -2*i - 7;
        }
S₁':    y = 261; /* omitted if y not live */

S₂':    x = 131; /* omitted if x not live */
```

Loop peeling is used to expose a hidden derived induction in a variable that is first used before being defined as an affine function of another induction variable (Padua and Wolfe 1986, Wolfe 1996, Zima and Chapman 1990). For example, in the following loop, all iterations except the first see the value i-1 in variable j. Consequently, peeling off one iteration exposes a derived induction variable j that can be replaced as follows:

```
                                    u[0] = ... j ... ;
for (i = 0; i < 100; i++) {         for (i = 1; i < 100; i++) {
  u[i] = ... j ... ;        →           j = i-1;
  j = i;                                u[i] = ... j ... ;
}                                   }
```

Applying loop peeling repetitively, in combination with induction variable elimination, may even expose a cascade of hidden derived induction variables that are defined in this manner (Wolfe 1996).

Integer Induction Variables

After induction variable elimination, each resulting induced expression that can be expressed as an affine function a · i + b, where a and b denote arbitrary loop invariant expressions, is vectorized for packed integers as vector data type as follows. To implement the induction, the compiler generates an instruction sequence in the prelude that constructs the following induction and increment vector:

```
ind[0:vl-1:1] = |    ...   | a·2+b | a·1+b | a·0+b |
inc[0:vl-1:1] = |    ...   |  a·vl |  a·vl |  a·vl |
```

If a and b are both statically known constants, this part simply consists of loading two constant vectors into 128-bit registers. Otherwise, the instruction sequence is slightly more elaborate. The initial induction vector is used for the first vector iteration. For subsequent vector iterations, the induction vector is kept up-to-date by adding the increment vector at the end of the vector loop body. For the induced expression -2*i-7 in statement S_3 of the earlier example, this scheme yields the following vector code in case u is a 16-byte aligned array with data type s32:

```
      movdqa xmm0, _const1  ; ind[0:3:1] = |-13|-11| -9| -7|
      movdqa xmm1, _const2  ; inc[0:3:1] = | -8| -8| -8| -8|
L:    movdqa u[eax+16], xmm0; store 4 doublewords into u
      paddd  xmm0, xmm1     ; ind[0:3:1] += inc[0:3:1]
      add    eax, 16        ;
      cmp    eax, 512       ;
      jb     L              ; looping logic
                            ;
      mov    y,   261       ; last value assignment for y
      mov    x,   131       ; last value assignment for x
```

Eliminating a narrow precision integer induction variable requires a cast in the replacing expression to preserve wrap-around arithmetic. In the following loop:

```
T v[N];
u8 x = 253;
for (i = 0; i < N; i++) {
  v[i] = (T) x;
  x++;
}
```

the induction variable x successively takes the following values:

253, 254, 255, 0, 1, 2, ... , 253, 254, 255, 0, 1, 2, ...

This wrap-around behavior is preserved by casting the affine function 253+i that replaces induction variable x into the data type u8:

```
v[i] = (T) x;    →   v[i] = (T) ((u8)(253+i));
```

Most type conversions that arise from eliminating such narrow precision integer induction variables can be vectorized. For more detailed information, see the section "Type Conversions" later in this chapter. If T denotes data type u32, for example, the loop can be vectorized with packed doublewords (vl = 4) after the right-hand side has been rewritten into the expression (253+i)&0xff. The resulting vector code uses the pand instruction to preserve 8-bit wrap-around arithmetic in the induction that is implemented with the paddd instruction. As another example, if T denotes data type u8, the straightforward type conversions disappear and the loop is vectorized with the following initial induction, increment vector, and packed bytes as vector data type (vl = 16):

```
ind[0:15:1] = | 12| 11|  ...  |  1|  0|255|254|253|
inc[0:15:1] = | 16| 16|  ...  | 16| 16| 16| 16| 16|
```

In this case, using the paddb instruction suffices to preserve the 8-bit wrap-around arithmetic.

A wider precision integer induction variable with data types u64 or s64 can be vectorized with a similar scheme if the vector data type has been selected accordingly. The following loop:

```
s64 x;
s64 w[100]; /* 16-byte aligned */
...
for (i = 0; i < 100; i++) {
  w[i] = x;
  x += 4;
}
```

translates into the following vector code that operates on packed quadwords, which also illustrates the slightly more elaborate code sequence required to set up the induction and increment vector in case the initial value of the induction variable is not known statically. In the following code, the assumption is made that the values of x and x+4 have already been moved into register pairs ebx/ecx and edx/edi, respectively:

```
movd       xmm0,    ebx     ; load x from ebx/ecx
movd       xmm3,    ecx     ;
movd       xmm4,    edx     ; load x+4 from edx/edi
```

```
       movd       xmm2,   edi     ;
       punpckldq  xmm0,   xmm3    ;
       punpckldq  xmm4,   xmm2    ;
       punpcklqdq xmm0,   xmm4    ; ind[0:1:1] = |x+4|  x|
       movdqa     xmm1,   _const  ; inc[0:1:1] = |  8|  8|
L:     movdqa     w[eax], xmm0    ; store 2 quadwords into w
       paddq      xmm0,   xmm1    ; ind[0:1:1] += inc[0:1:1]
       add        eax,    16      ;
       cmp        eax,    800     ;
       jb         L               ; looping logic
```

Floating-Point Induction Variables

If a floating-point induction variable has the same or narrower precision as the individual packed floating-point numbers of the selected vector data type, vectorization proceeds as discussed above, using a floating-point induction and increment vector. The following loop:

```
f64 a[100]; /* 16-byte aligned */
f64 b = 3.0;
for (i = 0; i < 100; i++) {
  a[i] = b;                          ← b ≡ 1.5 · i + 3.0
  b += 1.5;
}
```

is vectorized as follows with $vl = 2$:

```
       movapd xmm0,   _const1 ; ind[0:1:1] = | 4.5 | 3.0 |
       movapd xmm1,   _const2 ; inc[0:1:1] = | 3.0 | 3.0 |
L:     movapd a[eax], xmm0    ; store 2 doubles into a
       addpd  xmm0,   xmm1    ; ind[0:1:1] += inc[0:1:1]
       add    eax,    16      ;
       cmp    eax,    800     ;
       jb     L               ; looping logic
```

A single-precision floating-point induction variable is implemented similarly for either packed single-precision or packed double-precision numbers as vector data type. A double-precision floating-point induction variable cannot be vectorized with packed single-precision floating-point numbers as vector data type, however, because that could cause too much precision loss. Since induction variable elimination relies on mathematical equivalences that may not hold in finite floating-point precision, the other cases are only vectorized in the fp:performance mode.

Mixed-Type Induction Variables

Integer induction variables in a loop that is vectorized with packed floating-point numbers as vector data type require extra care to preserve exact integer arithmetic. Generally, this kind of induction is best vectorized with an integer induction and increment vector—as before, accounting for wrap-around arithmetic for narrow precision integer induction variables—followed by an appropriate conversion instruction. For the following fragment:

```
f32 c[100]; /* 16-byte aligned */
s32 g = 0x7fffff00;
for (i = 0; i < 100; i++) {
  c[i] = (f32) g;
  g += 1;
}
```

this approach yields the vector implementation shown here:

```
       movdqa    xmm0,     _const1   ; ind[0:3:1] = |g+3|g+2|g+1| g |
       movdqa    xmm1,     _const2   ; inc[0:3:1] = | 4 | 4 | 4 | 4 |
  L: cvtdq2ps  xmm2,     xmm0      ; convert 4 dwords into 4 floats
       movaps    c[eax],   xmm2      ; store   4 floats into c
       paddd     xmm0,     xmm1      ; ind[0:3:1] += inc[0:3:1]
       add       eax,      16        ;
       cmp       eax,      400       ;
       jb        L                   ; looping logic
```

If the induction had been implemented according to the selected vector data type, the increment ((f32)0x7fffff00)+1.0f would have been lost in single-precision floating-point arithmetic. Consequently, all subsequent values in the induction would remain 2147483392.0f.

If packed double-precision floating-point numbers are selected as vector data type, integer induction can be implemented similarly in the lower two double words of a 128-bit register, followed by the conversion instruction cvtdq2pd. In such cases, however, the integer induction can also be implemented directly in floating-point arithmetic to avoid the overhead of this conversion instruction. A common example of this optimization is shown here:

```
f64 a[100]; /* 16-byte aligned */
...
for (i = 0; i < 100; i++) {
  a[i] = (f64) i;
}
```

Since this integer induction can be directly implemented in double-precision floating-point arithmetic without changing semantics, a conversion instruction can be avoided as follows:

```
      movapd   xmm0,     _const1   ; ind[0:1:1] = | 1.0 | 0.0 |
      movapd   xmm1,     _const2   ; inc[0:1:1] = | 2.0 | 2.0 |
L:    movapd   a[eax],   xmm0      ; store 2 doubles into a
      addpd    xmm0,     xmm1      ; ind[0:1:1] += inc[0:1:1]
      add      eax,      16        ;
      cmp      eax,      800       ;
      jb       L                   ; looping logic
```

Reduction Variables

An operation that computes a single scalar value from a set of values is called a *reduction*. A reduction is typically implemented with a loop that accumulates the result into a scalar memory reference, such as r += $a[i]$; for a sum reduction. Such scalar memory references give rise to data dependence cycles that prohibit straightforward vectorization of the loop. Many common reductions can still exploit fine-grained parallelism, however, by (a) setting up a reduction vector in the prelude, (b) computing partial results into this reduction vector in the vector loop, and, finally (c) combining these partial results into a final scalar value in the postlude. Table 5.2 shows the general form of a sum, product, minimum, maximum, bitwise-AND, and bitwise-OR reduction that uses a reduction variable r, together with an appropriate initialization of the reduction vector.[2]

Table 5.2   Reductions

Reduction	Form	Initial Reduction Vector
sum	r += ...	| 0 | 0 |...| 0 | r |
product	r *= ...	| 1 | 1 |...| 1 | r |
minimum	r = MIN(r, ...)	| r | r |...| r | r |
maximum	r = MAX(r, ...)	| r | r |...| r | r |
bitwise-AND	r &= ...	| r | r |...| r | r |
bitwise-OR	r |= ...	| r | r |...| r | r |

---

[2] Alternative initial reduction vectors that do not depend on the initial value of r can simplify prelude code at the expense of an additional scalar operation in the postlude.

Under this general vectorization scheme, a sum reduction of the array elements of a into an accumulator r

```
for (i = 0; i < U; i++) {
  r += a[i];
}
```

is converted into the following form, assuming vl evenly divides U:

(a) `red[0:vl-1:1] = |0|...|0|r|;`
     `for (i = 0; i < U; i += vl) {`
(b) `  red[0:vl-1:1] += a[i:i+vl-1:1];`
     `}`

(c) $r = \sum_{i=0}^{vl-1} red[i];$

Part (a) is implemented by generating a code sequence that constructs the appropriate reduction vector. Since the initial value of the accumulator is often a statically known constant, this part usually consists of simply loading a constant vector into a 128-bit register. Part (b) computes the partial results in this 128-bit register using the appropriate instruction to implement the reduction operator for the selected vector data type. Part (c) combines these partial results into the final scalar value with an instruction sequence that reduces the individual packed data elements into one value. This last step can still exploit some parallelism, since n partial results can be combined in $O(\log n)$ parallel steps by means of a reduction tree (Lewis 1994, Quinn 1987). Because this scheme as a whole relies on associative laws that are not necessarily true using finite floating-point arithmetic, vectorized floating-point reductions may produce a somewhat different answer than the original sequential code (large differences usually indicate a lack of numerical stability). Therefore, floating-point reductions are only vectorized in the fp:performance mode.

For example, if, in the sum reduction above U has the value 64, both the reduction variable r and array a have data type f64, the initial value of r is zero, and a is 16-byte aligned, the following vector code results:

```
    xorpd  xmm0, xmm0     ; red[0:1:1] = | 0.0 | 0.0 |
L:  addpd  xmm0, a[eax]   ; red[0:1:1] += a[i:i+1:1]
    add    eax,  16       ;
    cmp    eax,  512      ;
    jb     L              ; looping logic
                          ;
    haddpd xmm0, xmm0     ; | d1 |   d0 |
    movsd  r,    xmm0     ; | -- |d1+d0|
                          ; sum partial sums into r
```

For data type `f32`, part (c) of a sum reduction consists of applying `haddps` twice. Packed integer data types are summed by repetitively rearranging and adding the partial sums into one final scalar value (Bik et al. 2002; Bik, Girkar, and Haghighat 1999). Other kinds of reductions are vectorized similarly with obvious implementations of parts (a), (b), and (c). A bitwise-AND reduction like

```
u32 msk[256]; /* 16-byte aligned */
u32 x;
...
for (i = 0; i < 256; i++) {
   x &= msk[i];
}
```

translates into the following SIMD instructions, where a shuffle instruction must be used to set up the reduction vector because the initial value of the reduction variable x is not known at compile time.

```
      movd    xmm0, x            ; load from x
      pshufd  xmm0, xmm0, 0      ; red[0:3:1] = | x | x | x | x |
L:    pand    xmm0, msk[eax]     ; red[0:3:1] &= msk[i:i+3:1]
      add     eax,  16           ;
      cmp     eax,  1024         ;
      jb      L                  ; looping logic
                                 ;
      movdqa  xmm1, xmm0         ; | a3  | a2  |  a1  |  a0  |
      psrldq  xmm1, 8            ; | --  | --  |  a3  |  a2  |
      pand    xmm0, xmm1         ; | --  | --  |a3&a1|a2&a0|
      movdqa  xmm2, xmm0         ; | --  | --  |a3&a1|a2&a0|
      psrldq  xmm2, 4            ; | --  | --  |  -- |a3&a1|
      pand    xmm0, xmm2         ; store bitwise-AND of
      movd    x,    xmm0         ;   partial results into x
```

Even though the data type of the reduction variable should generally match the data type of the individual packed data elements in the vector data type, a few idiomatic mixed-type reductions can also be implemented efficiently, as discussed in Chapter 7. The quality of vector code for reductions can often be improved with traditional compiler optimizations such as coupled reduction recognition (Wolfe 1996), prelude and postlude code hoisting, and various forms of constant folding (Aho, Sethi, and Ullman 1986; Appel and Ginsburg 1998; Fischer and LeBlanc 1991; Muchnick 1997; Parsons 1992).

Private Variables

In the absence of conditional statements, only a few different situations can be distinguished for all remaining scalar memory references in a loop. A scalar that is only used—a read-only variable or literal constant, is vectorized with *scalar expansion* (Wolfe 1996, Zima and Chapman 1990), where the scalar is replicated into an expansion vector in the prelude to broadcast its value to all vector iterations. Because the iteration space is strip-mined by vl, a single 128-bit register suffices to implement this expansion vector.

```
                                   xexp[0:vl-1:1] = | x | ... | x |;
for (i = 0; i < U; i++) {          for (i = 0; i < U; i+=vl) {
   ... = x;                   →        ... = xexp[0:vl-1:1];
}                                  }
```

A scalar that is first defined at the left-hand side of an assignment and subsequently used or possibly even re-defined can be vectorized similarly despite the data dependence cycles that are caused by writing to and reading the same memory location. During execution of the vector loop, the scalar resides in an expansion vector, followed by a last value assignment in a postlude if the scalar is live (Aho, Sethi, Ullman 1986) upon exiting the loop. This last value assignment simply moves the highest data element in the expansion vector back into the scalar.

```
                                   for (i = 0; i < U; i+=vl) {
for (i = 0; i < U; i++) {             xexp[0:vl-1:1] = ...;
   x = ...;                   →          ... = xexp[0:vl-1:1];
   ... = x;                           }
}                                  x = xexp[vl-1];
```

A scalar that is used before it is defined in a loop causes carry-around behavior that generally cannot be effectively vectorized. The difference with the previous two situations is that the value of such a scalar is not private to each iteration and, hence, cannot easily be implemented with scalar expansion. A scalar that is assigned conditionally in a loop causes similar complications that generally can only be effectively vectorized under certain conditions. For more detailed information, see the section "Conditional Statements" later in this chapter.

Scalar expansion and last value assignment are implemented with the appropriate data rearranging and data movement instructions. The following instruction sequence, for instance, expands the lower word of the 32-bit register eax into the 128-bit register xmm0.

```
movd       xmm0, eax          ; |00|00|00|00|--|--|--| w|
punpcklwd  xmm0, xmm0         ; |--|--|--|--|--|--| w| w|
pshufd     xmm0, xmm0, 0      ; | w| w| w| w| w| w| w| w|
```

Likewise, the following instruction sequence implements the last value assignment by moving the highest word in register xmm0 back into eax.

```
psrldq xmm0, 14              ; |w7|w6|w5|w4|w3|w2|w1|w0|
movd   eax,  xmm0           ; |--|--|--|--|--|--|--|w7|
```

Similar data-rearranging instruction sequences can be given for all other vector data types. For literal constants, loading a compile-time expanded vector of constants from memory can be used as a more efficient alternative to run-time expansion. In addition, certain literal constants can be expanded into register xmm0 with just a few instructions, as illustrated below for packed integers, where T denotes one of b, w, d for packed bytes, words, and doublewords, respectively. See Intel (2003a) for more examples.

−1	0	1
pcmpeq xmm0,xmm0	pxor xmm0, xmm0	pxor xmm0, xmm0 pcmpeq xmm1, xmm1 psubT xmm0, xmm1

The following example illustrates some of these concepts:

```
/* arrays are 16-byte aligned */
s32 x[64], y[64], z[64], s;
...
for (i = 0; i < 64; i++) {
  s    = x[i];
  y[i] = s - 1;
  z[i] = s + 17;
}
```

The prelude expands the literal constants −1 and −17 into registers xmm3 and xmm4. The scalar variable s resides in expanded form in register xmm0 during execution of the vector loop and receives the value of the last iteration (s@63) from a last value assignment in the postlude.

```
   pcmpeq xmm3,  xmm3    ; expand 4 doublewords with -1
   movdqa xmm4,  _const  ; expand 4 doublewords with 17
L: movdqa xmm1,  xmm3    ; copy  4 doublewords
   movdqa xmm2,  xmm4    ; copy  4 doublewords
   movdqa xmm0,  x[eax]  ; load  4 doublewords from x
   paddd  xmm1,  xmm0    ; add   4 doublewords
```

```
paddd   xmm2,     xmm0    ; add    4 doublewords
movdqa  y[eax],   xmm1    ; store  4 doublewords into y
movdqa  z[eax],   xmm2    ; store  4 doublewords into z
add     eax,      16      ;
cmp     eax,      256     ;
jb      L                 ; looping logic
                          ;
psrldq  xmm0,     12      ; |s@63|s@62|s@61|s@60|
movd    s,        xmm0    ; | --  | --  | --  |s@63|
```

Although the data type of a scalar on the left-hand side of the expression must generally match the data type of the individual packed data elements in the selected vector data type, non-matching data types of read-only scalars can be dealt with using an appropriate type conversion and data rearrangement during scalar expansion. In fact, any loop invariant expression can be implemented with scalar expansion after code hoisting (Aho, Sethi, and Ullman 1986; Muchnick 1997) has been used to move the expression out of the loop. This optimization is illustrated as follows, where E denotes an arbitrary loop invariant expression:

```
                                  _t = (E);
for (i = 0; i < U; i++) {           for (i = 0; i < U; i++) {
   ... = ... (E) ... ;      →          ... = ... _t ... ;
}                                   }
```

The compiler-generated temporary variable _t is subsequently expanded during vectorization as explained previously. This method is particularly useful to enable the vectorization of loops where operations that cannot be vectorized appear in loop invariant subexpressions.

Alternating Private Variables

A special class of private variables is formed by variables that alternate between two values, as illustrated with the variable v below, where C denotes a loop invariant expression.

```
       for (i = 0; i < U; i++) {
S₁:       v = C - v;
S₂:       ... = v;
       }
```

Despite loop-carried data dependence, $S_1 \delta^o_{(<)} S_1$, $S_1 \delta^f_{(<)} S_1$, and $S_1 \delta^a_{(<)} S_1$ together with all data dependences that are caused by the subsequent use of v in S_2, the loop can still be vectorized by exploiting the mathematical equivalence C-(C-v) = v, as shown here:

S_2:
```
vexp[0:vl-1:1] = |v|C-v| ... |v|C-v|;
for (i = 0; i < U; i+=vl) {
    ... = vexp[i:i+vl-1:1];
}
```

Since the mathematical equivalence shown above may not be true in finite precision floating-point arithmetic, floating-point, alternating, private variables can only be vectorized in fp:performance mode.

The run-time expansion is implemented with a sequence of data rearranging and data movement instructions. Since a vector loop always executes an even number of iterations, no last value assignment is required for the alternating variable. Instead, the original value of this variable before the vector loop feeds directly into the next use after the vector loop.

Performance Example

These techniques for vectorizing scalar memory references can enhance performance substantially, as illustrated by compiling the computationally intensive FLOPS benchmark (Aburto 1992) with the Intel C/C++ compiler. This benchmark consists of eight different modules, each with a different mix of double-precision floating-point operations on a variety of induction, reduction, and private variables. Because a small data set is used, benchmark performance is independent of memory hierarchy performance. Figure 5.5 shows the performance in MFLOPS on a 3-gigahertz Pentium 4 processor for a sequential and vectorized version of the eight modules, sorted in decreasing order of operation mix complexity. The corresponding speedup is shown in the same figure using a secondary *y* axis. Five of the eight modules clearly benefit from intra-register vectorization. Only the performance of three modules that are dominated by high latency, double-precision floating-point divisions (flops7, flops2 and flops1) remains unaffected, even though the loops in these modules can be vectorized.

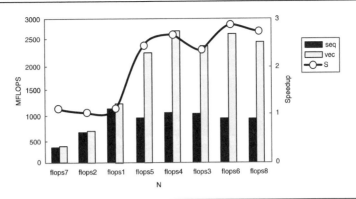

Figure 5.5   FLOPS Benchmark Performance—3-Gigahertz Pentium® 4
Processor

Operators

Operators are vectorized with SSE/SSE2/SSE3 instructions that simultaneously perform several of the corresponding operations on packed
data elements. Table 5.3 shows the instructions that, depending on the
selected vector data type, are used for the vectorization of arithmetic
operators.

Table 5.3   Vectorization of Arithmetic Operators

	packed bytes	**packed words**	**packed dwords**	**packed qwords**	**packed floats**	**packed doubles**
+ −	paddb psubb	paddw psubw	paddd psubd	paddq psubq	addps subps	addpd subpd
− (unary)	rewrite −x into 0−x					
* /		pmullw			mulps divps[3]	mulpd divpd
%					not applicable	

Unsupported cases, like multiplying packed doublewords, are left
open. Multiplications by a small constant can always be vectorized with
additive instructions (x*3 equals x+x+x). The pmullw instruction can be

---

[3] Single-precision floating-point division can be implemented alternatively by multiplying the
dividend with the results of applying rcpps to the divisor, possibly improved in accuracy with
Newton-Raphson iteration (Intel 2003a).

used to multiply packed words if only 16-bit precision is required for the final results, as in the following example:

```
s16 u[256], v[256], w[256];  /* 16-byte aligned */
...
for (i = 0; i < 256; i++) {
  u[i] = v[i] * w[i];
}
```

Even though the usual arithmetic conversions require 32-bit precision for multiplication, this fragment can exploit the following eight-way SIMD parallelism:

```
L: movdqa xmm0,    v[eax]   ; load  8 words from v
   pmullw xmm0,    w[eax]   ; mult  8 words from w
   movdqa u[eax],  xmm0     ; store 8 words into u
   add    eax,     16       ;
   cmp    eax,     512      ;
   jb     L                 ; looping logic
```

Table 5.4 shows the instructions that are used to vectorize bitwise operators for different vector data types. Only constructs where higher order bits of intermediate results do not essentially contribute to the final 16-bit results, such as a[i] >>= 2; for an array with data type s16, can be vectorized with arithmetic and logical shift-right operations on packed words. The shift operators compensate for some of the lack of support for integer arithmetic operators because x * 2^n is accomplished by logically shifting x to the left by n bits for signed and unsigned operands alike, while x / 2^n is obtained by logically shifting x to the right by n bits for unsigned operands. Note that signed operands require round-to-zero division. Consequently, the loop

```
u64 x[256];  /* 16-byte aligned */
...
for (i = 0; i < 256; i++) {
  x[i] /= 32;
}
```

can be vectorized with packed quadwords as vector data type:

```
L: movdqa xmm0,    x[eax]   ; load  2 quadwords from x
   psrlq  xmm0,    5        ; divide 2 quadwords by   32
   movdqa x[eax],  xmm0     ; store 2 quadwords into x
   add    eax,     16       ;
   cmp    eax,     2048     ;
   jb     L                 ; looping logic
```

Table 5.4   Vectorization of Bitwise Operators

	packed bytes	packed words	packed dwords	packed qwords
&	pand			
|	por			
^	pxor			
<< (logical) >> (arith.) >> (logical)		psllw psraw psrlw	pslld psrad psrld	psllq psrlq
~	rewrite ~x into x^(-1)			

Likewise, even though the modulus operator is not supported for any vector data type, expression $x \ \% \ 2^n$ can be rewritten into $x \ \& \ (2^n-1)$ for unsigned operands to enable vectorization by means of the pand instruction.

MIN, MAX, and ABS Operators

As explained in Chapter 3, idiom recognition converts programming constructs that compute a minimum, maximum, or absolute function into explicit operators. Table 5.5 shows the instructions that are used to vectorize these operators. All cases that are not directly supported by a multimedia instruction must be emulated.

Table 5.5   Vectorization of MIN/MAX/ABS Operators

	packed bytes (unsigned)	packed words (signed)	packed integers (other)	packed floats	packed doubles
MIN MAX	pminub pmaxub	pminsw pmaxsw	emulate emulate	minps maxps	minpd maxpd
ABS	emulate				

The fp:performance mode allows emulating the floating-point ABS(x), for example, in an efficient but not fully IEEE 754-compliant way by resetting the sign bit with an andps or andpd instruction. Furthermore, the following instruction sequences emulate MIN/MAX/ABS operators for packed doublewords (Bik, Girkar, and Haghighat 1999; Intel 1997 and 2003a), where the given implementation of the absolute function leaves the most negative integer value that can be represented unaffected.

MIN(xmm0,xmm1)	MAX(xmm0,xmm1)	ABS(xmm0)
movdqa xmm2, xmm0	movdqa xmm2, xmm0	pxor xmm1, xmm1
movdqa xmm3, xmm1	movdqa xmm3, xmm1	pcmpgtd xmm1, xmm0
pcmpgtd xmm0, xmm3	pcmpgtd xmm0, xmm3	pxor xmm0, xmm1
pxor xmm1, xmm2	pxor xmm1, xmm2	psubd xmm0, xmm1
pand xmm0, xmm1	pand xmm0, xmm1	
pxor xmm0, xmm2	pxor xmm0, xmm3	

A subtlety arises if packed bytes or words have been selected as vector data type because, like all other arithmetic operators, the MIN/MAX/ABS operators proceed in 32-bit precision for 8-bit and 16-bit operands. Since higher order bits can contribute to the final results, even if only a narrow precision is eventually required, care must be taken to preserve semantics. Fortunately, it is valid to use narrow precision instructions to implement comparisons between two narrow precision operands with a consistent zero or sign extension or between a narrow precision operand and an appropriate literal constant (Bik et al. 2002a).

Validity constraints are formalized using the following ϕ_t-condition on an expression e, where x_t denotes an arbitrary expression with data type t, V_t denotes the data type range of t, and c denotes a literal constant.

$$\phi_t(e) = \text{true iff. either} \begin{cases} e \text{ of the form } (\text{u32})x_t, & t \in \{\text{u8},\text{u16}\} \\ e \text{ of the form } (\text{s32})x_t, & t \in \{\text{u8},\text{u16},\text{s8},\text{s16}\} \\ e \text{ of the form } c, & c \in V_t \end{cases}$$

For example, both $\phi_{s8}((\text{s32})v)$, where v has type s8, and $\phi_{s8}(-3)$ are true under this definition, but $\phi_{s8}((\text{u32})v)$ and $\phi_{s8}(-129)$ are not. This ϕ_t-condition simplifies formulating validity tests for vectorizing MIN/MAX operators with narrow precision clipping instructions, as shown below. Note that similar validity tests apply to vectorizing MIN/MAX/ABS operators with narrow precision *emulation* instruction sequences.

Expression	Clipping	Validity Test
$\text{MIN}_{\text{s32/u32}}(\text{x, y})$	pminub	if $\phi_{u8}(x) \land \phi_{u8}(y)$
$\text{MAX}_{\text{s32/u32}}(\text{x, y})$	pmaxub	if $\phi_{u8}(x) \land \phi_{u8}(y)$
$\text{MIN}_{\text{s32}}(\text{x, y})$	pminsw	if $\phi_{s16}(x) \land \phi_{s16}(y)$
$\text{MAX}_{\text{s32}}(\text{x, y})$	pmaxsw	if $\phi_{s16}(x) \land \phi_{s16}(y)$

The restricted non-negative data type range of unsigned numbers allows both *signed* and *unsigned* MIN/MAX operators to be recognized as *unsigned* clipping idioms. For example, if array variable z has type $u8$, then both

$$MIN_{u32}((u32)\ z[i],\ 100u)$$

with $\phi_{u8}((u32)z[i]) \wedge \phi_{u8}(100u)$, as well as

$$MIN_{s32}((s32)\ z[i],\ 100)$$

with $\phi_{u8}((s32)z[i]) \wedge \phi_{u8}(100)$

can be mapped on the instruction pminub, even though the operators perform unsigned and signed arithmetic, respectively. This observation is useful in situations like the one following, where idiom recognition yields a signed MIN operator:

```
u8 u[256];   /* 16-byte aligned */
...
u8 x = 0xff;
for (i = 0; i < 256; i++) {
  if (u[i] < x) x = u[i];   →  x = (u8) MIN_s32( ((s32) x    ),
}                                                ((s32) u[i]) );
```

Since the usual arithmetic conversions require that the relational operator is applied to operands that have been promoted into type $s32$, the MIN operator has a signed 32-bit precision. However, an 8-bit *unsigned* precision suffices for this particular clipping idiom, and reduction in the i-loop can be vectorized with the instruction minub, because both operands satisfy the ϕ_{u8}-condition, as follows.

After the vector loop, the partial results are combined into one final scalar value to finalize the reduction.

```
   movdqa xmm0, _const   ; red[0:15:1] = | 0xff | ...| 0xff |
L: pminub xmm0, u[eax]    ; red[0:15:1] = MIN( red[0:15:1],
   add    eax,  16        ;                    u[i:i+15:1] )
   cmp    eax,  256       ;
   jb     L               ; looping logic
                          ;
   movdqa xmm4, xmm0      ; |m15| ...|m08|m07| ...|m00|
   psrldq xmm4, 8         ; |  - | ...|  - |m15| ...|m08|
   pminub xmm0, xmm4      ; reduce into 8 minima
   movdqa xmm3, xmm0      ; etc.
   psrldq xmm3, 4         ;
   pminub xmm0, xmm3      ; reduce into 4 minima
   movdqa xmm2, xmm0      ; etc.
```

```
psrldq xmm2, 2        ;
pminub xmm0, xmm2     ; reduce into 2 minima
movdqa xmm1, xmm0     ; etc.
psrldq xmm1, 1        ;
pminub xmm0, xmm1     ; reduce into final minumum
movd   x,    xmm0     ;  and store result into x
```

Chapter 7 discusses some advanced clipping and saturation idioms that may arise in MIN/MAX operators.

Type Conversions

As already seen in several examples, many expressions in C contain casts or implicit type conversions that arise from the usual arithmetic conversions. Effective intra-register vectorization of C programs must somehow be able to deal with these type conversions.

Integer Type Conversions

Integer type conversions between signed and unsigned operands with the same precision can simply be ignored, provided that all operators are implemented with appropriate vector instructions. For example, the following loop

```
s32 u[256];
s32 v[256];
u32 w[256]; /* all 16-byte aligned */
...
for (i = 0; i < 256; i++) {
  u[i] = (v[i] >> 2) + (w[i] >> 2);
  }
```

actually contains several implicit type conversions between the data types s32 and u32, as made explicit in the following program text:

$$u[i] = (s32) ((u32) (v[i] >>_{s32} 2) +_{u32} (w[i] >>_{u32} 2u));$$

Due to the usual arithmetic conversions, the two shift operators define an arithmetic and logical shift right, respectively, while the addition requires unsigned arithmetic. If packed doublewords are selected as vector data type, by itself a signless data type, the original type conversions affect instruction selection for the shift operators, but otherwise do not require any explicit implementation, as shown here:

```
L: movdqa xmm1,  v[eax] ; load  4 doublewords from v
   movdqa xmm0,  w[eax] ; load  4 doublewords from w
   psrad  xmm1,  2       ; shift 4 doublewords (arithmetic)
   psrld  xmm0,  2       ; shift 4 doublewords (logical)
```

```
paddd    xmm1,    xmm0    ; add    4 doublewords
movdqa   u[eax],  xmm1    ; store  4 doublewords into u
add      eax,     16      ;
cmp      eax,     1024    ;
jb       L                ; looping logic
```

Likewise, integer type conversions that keep the data *at least* as wide as the precision of the individual packed data elements in the vector data type may be ignored during intra-register vectorization provided that, as always, higher order bits of intermediate results cannot contribute to the precision of final results, and operators are implemented with the appropriate arithmetic. Despite two promotions—zero and sign extension—and two truncations in the following slightly contrived example, only eight bits of data are actually copied from elements of y into elements of x. Consequently, this loop can be vectorized with aligned data movement instructions movdqa that copy 16 bytes at a time.

```
u8 x[N], y[N]; /* 16-byte aligned */
...
for (i = 0; i < N; i++) {
  x[i] = ((u8) ((s32)((s8)((s32) y[i]))) );
}
```

Even a zero extension from an operand that has narrower precision than the precision of the individual packed data elements in the vector data type can be vectorized by replacing the type conversion by a bitwise operator, as illustrated by the following example:

```
s16 x[128]; /* 16-byte aligned */
...
for (i = 0; i < 128; i++) {
  x[i] = ((u8) x[i]);
}
```

Clearly, the appropriate vector data type for this loop consists of packed words. Truncating x[i] into the narrower data type u8 followed by a zero extension into a wider data type can be implemented as x[i]&0xff, as was exploited earlier for a narrower induction variable. Consequently, this loop can be converted into the following vector code:

```
   movdqa   xmm1,    _const  ; expand 8 words with 0xff
L: movdqa   xmm0,    x[eax]  ; load   8 words from x
   pand     xmm0,    xmm1    ; and    8 words with 0xff
   movdqa   x[eax],  xmm0    ; store  8 words into x
   add      eax,     16      ;
   cmp      eax,     256     ;
   jb       L                ; looping logic
```

Chapter 7 discusses more elaborate integer conversion idioms.

Floating-Point Type Conversions

Using either the fp:precision mode or the fp:performance mode determines how floating-point type conversions are vectorized. The fp:precision mode allows only vectorizing type conversions with multimedia instructions that preserve the exact precision. The fp:performance mode relaxes this restriction in favor of more vectorization opportunities by also allowing the vectorization of floating-point type conversions with multimedia instructions that merely preserve the precision that is actually required for the final results. Consider, for instance, the following loop:

```
f32 a[128];
f64 b[128]; /* both 16-byte aligned */
f64 c;
...
for (i = 0; i < 128; i++) {
  a[i] += b[i] * c;
}
```

All implicit type conversions in this fragment are made explicit in the following assignment statement:

$$a[i] = (f32) (((f64) a[i]) +_{f64} (b[i] *_{f64} c));$$

Since 64-bit precision is required for the arithmetic operators, the fp:precision mode allows only for the selection of packed, double-precision floating-point numbers as vector data type. The corresponding vector loop exploits two-way SIMD parallelism as follows. As already alluded to in the section "Unit-Stride Memory References" earlier in this chapter, the narrower 64-bit data movement instruction `movlps` must now be used for loading and storing the single-precision floating-point unit-stride memory references in order to match the vector length $vl = 2$ of the selected vector data type.

```
       movsd     xmm0,    c          ; load c
       unpcklpd  xmm0,    xmm0       ; expand    |  c  |  c  |
L:     movlps    xmm1,    a[eax]     ; load      |--|--|SP|SP|  from a
       cvtps2pd  xmm2,    xmm1       ; convert   |  DP  |  DP  |
       movapd    xmm1,    b[2*eax]   ; load   2 doubles from b
       mulpd     xmm1,    xmm0       ; mult. 2 doubles
       addpd     xmm1,    xmm2       ; add   2 doubles
       cvtpd2ps  xmm2,    xmm1       ; convert |--|--|SP|SP|
       movlps    a[eax],  xmm2       ; store 2 floats into a
       add       eax,     8          ; increment 2x4
       cmp       eax,     512        ;
       jb        L                   ; looping logic
```

The fp:performance mode, on the other hand, favors speed over accuracy by allowing four-way SIMD parallelism that is based on packed, single-precision floating-point numbers as vector data type. As shown below, the vector loop must now first convert variable c into a single-precision floating-point number to enable a scalar expansion that matches the vector length $vl = 4$ of the selected vector data type. Furthermore, two 128-bit data movement instructions and one unpack instruction are now used for loading the double-precision floating-point unit-stride memory reference in order to keep pace with this vector length.

```
      cvtsd2ss xmm0,    c            ; convert and expand
      shufps   xmm0,    xmm0, 0      ;   variable c into 4 floats
   L: cvtpd2ps xmm1,    b[2*eax]     ; convert 2 doubles into floats
      cvtpd2ps xmm2,    b[2*eax+16]  ; convert 2 doubles into floats
      movlhps  xmm1,    xmm2         ; combine into 4 floats
      mulps    xmm1,    xmm0         ; mult. 4 floats
      addps    xmm1,    a[eax]       ; add   4 floats
      movaps   a[eax],  xmm1         ; store 4 floats into a
      add      eax,     16           ;
      cmp      eax,     512          ;
      jb       L                     ; looping logic
```

Division operators are always excluded from such a precision lessening, because this kind of transformation could lose too much precision.

The following is another common example of vectorizing a floating-point type conversion, where single-precision floating-point numbers are accumulated into a double-precision accumulator:

```
f32 a[128]; /* 16-byte aligned */
...
f64 acc = 0;
for (i = 0; i < 128; i++) {
  acc += a[i];
}
```

Such a loop can exploit two-way SIMD parallelism as follows, where again the instruction movlps is used to match the vector length $vl = 2$ of the selected vector data type. Note that, although this translation preserves the 64-bit precision of the addition, this loop can be vectorized only in the fp:performance mode because the order in which partial results of the reduction are computed is changed.

```
      xorpd    xmm0, xmm0   ; red[0:1:1] =  | 0.0 | 0.0 |
   L: movlps   xmm1, a[eax] ; load         |--|--|SP|SP|
      cvtps2pd xmm2, xmm1   ; convert      | DP  | DP  |
```

```
addpd    xmm0, xmm2    ; red[0:1:1] +=  |  DP  |  DP  |
add      eax,  8       ; increment 2x4
cmp      eax,  512     ;
jb       L             ; looping logic
                       ;
haddpd   xmm0, xmm0    ; partial sums   |  d1  |  d0  |
movsd    acc,  xmm0    ; reduced into   |  --  |d1+d0 |
```

Mixed-Type Conversions

Type conversions between packed integer and floating-point data types with the same vector length are easily implemented with instructions cvtdq2ps and cvtps2dq. An example of such mixed-type loop vectorization is shown here:

```
f32 a[100], b[100]; /* 16-byte aligned */
s32 x[100];
...
for (i = 0; i < 100; i++) {
   a[i] = b[i] * x[i];
}
```

Integer elements of array x are converted into single-precision floating-point values with the four-way SIMD parallel instruction cvtdq2ps to enable vectorization of the loop with packed single-precision floating-point numbers, as can be seen in the following vector code:

```
L: cvtdq2ps xmm0,   x[eax] ; convert 4 doublewords from x
   mulps    xmm0,   b[eax] ; mult.   4 floats      from b
   movaps   a[eax], xmm0   ; store   4 floats      into a
   add      eax,    16     ;
   cmp      eax,    400    ;
   jb       L              ; looping logic
```

Although, in principle, any mixed-type conversion can be implemented with an appropriate sequence of data movement and data rearranging instructions, typically only type conversions that allow for a consistent vector length during the bulk of the operations can be translated into efficient vector code.

Mathematical Functions

Intel C++ and Fortran compilers are shipped with a short vector mathematical library developed at Intel Nizhny Novgorod Lab, Russia, to provide efficient software implementations for trigonometric, hyperbolic, exponential, logarithmic, and conversion functions on packed floating-point numbers. Table 5.6 lists all functions supported in the library, which uses the following general naming convention for the vector implementation of a mathematical function `Func()`:

`vmlsFunc4` (single-precision)   `vmldFunc2` (double-precision)

Table 5.6   Vectorization of Mathematical Functions

	packed floats	**packed doubles**

trigonometric	`vmlsSin4`
	`vmlsCos4`
	`vmlsTan4`
	`vmlsSinCos4`
		`vmldSin2`
		`vmldCos2`
		`vmldTan2`
		`vmldSinCos2`

inverse trigonometric	`vmlsAsin4`
	`vmlsAcos4`
	`vmlsAtan4`
	`vmlsAtan24`
		`vmldAsin2`
		`vmldAcos2`
		`vmldAtan2`
		`vmldAtan22`

hyperbolic	`vmlsSinh4`
	`vmlsCosh4`
	`vmlsTanh4`
		`vmldSinh2`
		`vmldCosh2`
		`vmldTanh2`

inverse hyperbolic	`vmlsAsinh4`
	`vmlsAcosh4`
	`vmlsAtanh4`
		`vmldAsinh2`
		`vmldAcosh2`
		`vmldAtanh2`

exponential	`vmlsExp4`
	`vmlsExp24`
	`vmlsPow4`
		`vmldExp2`
		`vmldExp22`
		`vmldPow2`

logarithmic	`vmlsLog104`
	`vmlsLog24`
	`vmlsLn4`
		`vmldLog102`
		`vmldLog22`
		`vmldLn2`

cubic root
square root (instruction)
reciprocal square root
	`vmlsCbrt4`
	`sqrtps`
	`vmlsInvSqrt4`[4]
		`vmldCbrt2`
		`sqrtpd`
		`vmldInvSqrt2`

conversion	`vmlsTrunc4` `vmlsRound4`	`vmldTrunc2` `vmldRound2`

The functions expect two double-precision or four single-precision packed floating-point numbers in register `xmm0` and return the results of applying the appropriate function to all data elements in the same register. Functions `vmlsPow4`, `vmldPow2`, `vmlsAtan24`, and `vmldAtan22` further expect a vector of second arguments in register `xmm1`. Functions

---

[4] Alternatively, this function can be directly implemented with instruction `rsqrtps`, possibly improved in accuracy with Newton-Raphson iteration (Intel 2003a).

`vmlsSinCos4` and `vmldSinCos2` simultaneously compute the sine and cosine of the arguments, returning the cosine results in a 128-bit memory region that is specified by an additional pointer argument. The conversion functions are useful to vectorize the Fortran intrinsics `AINT()` and `ANINT()`. The single-precision and double-precision square root functions are directly supported by an instruction.

A library that operates on packed data elements, rather than on full arrays of arbitrary length, enables the compiler to handle mathematical function calls simply as operators during intra-register vectorization. Vectorization of the following loop:

```
f64 a[256], b[256], c[256]; /* 16-byte aligned */
...
for (i = 0; i < 256; i++) {
  a[i] = pow(a[i], b[i]) + cos(c[i]);
}
```

can directly proceed for `vl = 2` using the function calls to `vmldPow2()` and `vmldCos2()` to vectorize the mathematical functions and the instruction `addpd` to vectorize the addition.

```
L: movapd xmm0, a[esi]    ; load     2 doubles from a
   movapd xmm1, b[esi]    ; load     2 doubles from b
   call   vmldPow2        ; pow      2 doubles
   movapd [esp], xmm0     ; save     2 doubles
   movapd xmm0,  c[esi]   ; load     2 doubles from c
   call   vmldCos2        ; cos      2 doubles
   movapd xmm1,   [esp]   ; restore  2 doubles
   addpd  xmm1,   xmm0    ; add      2 doubles
   movapd a[esi], xmm1    ; store    2 doubles into a
   add    esi,    16      ;
   cmp    esi,    2048    ;
   jb     L               ; looping logic
```

Mathematical functions of the standard C library (Plauger 1992) typically operate on double-precision operands, although many implementations also support single-precision versions that are obtained by appending `f` to the base function name; for example, `sin()` versus `sinf()`. As a result, the assignment statement in the following loop

```
f32 a[256], b[256]; /* 16-byte aligned */
...
for (i = 0; i < 256; i++) {
  a[i] = sin( b[i] ) + 1;
}
```

actually contains the following implicit type conversions:

```
a[i] = (f32) ( sin((f64) b[i]) +f64 1.0 );
```

Because the results are eventually converted back into data type `f32`, the fp:performance mode allows selecting packed, single-precision floating-point numbers as vector data type ($vl = 4$), effectively narrowing the precision of both the addition and sine functions to favor performance.

```
L: movaps xmm0,    b[esi]  ; load  4 floats from b
   call   vmlsSin4          ; sine  4 floats
   addps  xmm0,    _const   ; add   4 floats
   movaps a[esi], xmm0      ; store 4 floats into a
   add    esi,     16       ;
   cmp    esi,     1024     ;
   jb     L                 ; looping logic
```

Applications that make intensive use of mathematical functions can benefit greatly from this short vector mathematical library, which you can see by compiling the Sunset benchmark (Abrosimov, Zelenogorsky, and Kryukov 1999), which is available in both C and Fortran, with the Intel compiler. This rough-water surface simulation, based on the idea of Dmitry Abrosimov and further improved by Andrey Naraikin, provides real-time rendering of a sunset over the ocean. The main algorithm of the Sunset benchmark spends a substantial part of its computational time computing a sine function and dot product for every pixel in the picture. Table 5.7 reports the sequential and vectorized performance in frames-per-second for different picture sizes on a 3-gigahertz Pentium 4 processor. The results are identical for C and Fortran. The corresponding speedup S shows that taking advantage of the short vector mathematical library can achieve up to an eight-fold improvement for the performance of a mathematically intensive application as a whole.

Table 5.7 Sunset Performance—3-Gigahertz Pentium® 4 Processor

Picture Size	Seq	Vec	S
100 × 100	39.9 fps.	333.9 fps.	8.4
200 × 200	9.62 fps.	73.9 fps.	7.7
400 × 400	2.42 fps.	16.2 fps.	6.7
700 × 700	0.78 fps.	5.23 fps.	6.7

Conditional Statements

Loops with conditional statements can be vectorized with a technique that is called *bit masking* (Bistry et al. 1997). Vectorization of the statements in the following `if` statement that is under control of a condition `c(i)`

```
for (i = 0; i < U; i++) {
  if (c(i)) {
    lhs1[i] = rhs1[i];
  } else {
    lhs2[i] = rhs2[i];
  }
}
```

proceeds by generating code that constructs a bit-mask vector in which the packed data elements consist of an all-ones bit mask for each iteration in which `c(i)` is true and an all-zeros bit mask for each iteration in which `c(i)` is false. Subsequently, all statements in the `if` statement are vectorized according to the pattern that follows, where the final values consist of a masked combination of the left-hand side and right-hand side expressions:

```
for (i = 0; i < U; i+=vl) {
  g[0:vl-1:1] = bit_mask( c[i:i+vl-1:1] );
  lhs1[i:i+vl-1:1] = (lhs1[i:i+vl-1:1] & !g[0:vl-1:1])
                   | (rhs1[i:i+vl-1:1] &  g[0:vl-1:1]);
  lhs2[i:i+vl-1:1] = (lhs2[i:i+vl-1:1] &  g[0:vl-1:1])
                   | (rhs2[i:i+vl-1:1] & !g[0:vl-1:1]);
}
```

An `if` statement with only a true branch is handled similarly with a single masked statement. Analogously, if `lhs1` and `lhs2` denote the same array variable, bit masking can be easily condensed into one masked statement, as follows:

```
for (i = 0; i < U; i+=vl) {
  g[0:vl-1:1] = bit_mask( c[i:i+vl-1:1] );
  lhs1[i:i+vl-1:1] = (rhs1[i:i+vl-1:1] &  g[0:vl-1:1])
                   | (rhs2[i:i+vl-1:1] & !g[0:vl-1:1]);
}
```

Within masked expressions, common bitwise and arithmetic optimizations are used to simplify the resulting code. Such simplifications are particularly useful while vectorizing conditional reductions. Consider, for example, the following conditional sum reduction:

```
for (i = 0; i < U; i++) {
  if (c(i)) {
    x += rhs[i];
  }
}
```

Applying bit masking to the vector reduction scheme that was presented earlier in this chapter yields the following code:

```
red[0:vl-1:1] = |0|...|0|r|;
for (i = 0; i < U; i+=vl) {
  g[0:vl-1:1] = bit_mask( c[i:i+vl-1:1] );
  red[i:i+vl-1:1] =
    (red[i:i+vl-1:1]+rhs[i:i+vl-1:1] &  g[0:vl-1:1]) |
    (red[i:i+vl-1:1]                  & !g[0:vl-1:1]);
}
```
$$r = \sum_{i=0}^{vl-1} \text{red}[i];$$

Since zero is the identity element (Gilbert 1976) of addition, the vector reduction statement can be simplified into the following code:

```
  red[i:i+vl-1:1] += (rhs[i:i+vl-1:1] & g[0:vl-1:1]);
```

The next sections discuss several aspects of conditional statement vectorization in more detail.

Bit-Mask Vector Construction

The bit-mask vector is constructed using the vector instructions shown in Table 5.8 to implement the equality, relational, and logical operators that constitute the condition; packed quadwords are unsupported. For example, the bit-mask vector for the following condition:

```
s32 x[N], y[N];  /* 16-byte aligned */
...
for (i = 0; i < N; i++ {
  if (x[i] == y[i]) ...
}
```

is constructed as follows for packed doublewords:

```
movdqa    xmm0, x[eax]  ; load    4 doublewords from x
pcmpeqd   xmm0, y[eax]  ; compare 4 doublewords with y
```

Table 5.8   Vectorization of Equality, Relational, and Logical Operators

	packed bytes	packed words	packed dwords	packed floats	packed doubles
== !=	pcmpeqb pcmpneb	pcmpeqw pcmpnew	pcmpeqd pcmpned	cmpeqps cmpneqps	cmpeqpd cmpneqpd
<	emulate			cmpltps	cmpltpd
<=	with			cmpleps	cmplepd
>	pcmpgtb	pcmpgtw	pcmpgtd	emulate	
>=	(signed only)			(swap)	
&& ||	emulate with bitwise-AND/OR (short-circuit evaluation loss)				
!	emulate with bitwise-NOT				
& !	pandn			andnps	andnpd

A sample evaluation is illustrated in the following table.

x	11	15	22	88
y	11	15	22	17
xmm0	0xff..ff	0xff..ff	0xff..ff	0x00..00

Relational operators that are not directly supported can be emulated by swapping operands and performing the comparison with a different predicate ($a > b \equiv b < a$ and $a \geq b \equiv b \leq a$), possibly negated for integer operands ($a \leq b \equiv a$ NOT $> b$). The logical operators can be emulated as bitwise operators at the expense of losing short-circuit evaluation for the &&-operator and ||-operator, which still preserves semantics if all expressions are free of side effects. The frequently occurring combination of a bitwise AND/NOT has direct hardware support.

As seen earlier, a subtlety arises if packed bytes or words have been selected as vector data type, because the usual arithmetic conversions require 32-bit precision comparisons for narrow precision 8-bit and 16-bit operands. Since higher order bits can contribute to the final boolean result, care must be taken that vectorization preserves the semantics. Validity tests for vectorizing the signed >-operator, signed and unsigned ==-operator, or !=-operator with a narrow precision instruction are expressed as follows using the ϕ_t-condition that was defined earlier in this chapter:[5]

Expression	Comparison	Validity Test
(e1 $>_{\text{s32}}$ e2)	pcmpgtb	if ϕ_{s8}(e1) $\wedge$ ϕ_{s8}(e2)
	pcmpgtw	if ϕ_{s16}(e1) $\wedge$ ϕ_{s16}(e2)
(e1 $==_{\text{s32/u32}}$ e2)	pcmpeqb	if ϕ_{u8}(e1) $\wedge$ ϕ_{u8}(e2) or ϕ_{s8}(e1) $\wedge$ ϕ_{s8}(e2)
	pcmpeqw	if ϕ_{u16}(e1) $\wedge$ ϕ_{u16}(e2) or ϕ_{s16}(e1) $\wedge$ ϕ_{s16}(e2)
(e1 $!=_{\text{s32/u32}}$ e2)	pcmpneb	if ϕ_{u8}(e1) $\wedge$ ϕ_{u8}(e2) or ϕ_{s8}(e1) $\wedge$ ϕ_{s8}(e2)
	pcmpnew	if ϕ_{u16}(e1) $\wedge$ ϕ_{u16}(e2) or ϕ_{s16}(e1) $\wedge$ ϕ_{s16}(e2)

For example, because

$$\phi_{\text{s16}}(((\text{s32})\ \text{u[i]}))\ \wedge\ \phi_{\text{s16}}(10)$$

is true, vectorizing the comparison in the following loop with the narrow precision pcmpgtw instruction preserves the original semantics:

```
s16 u[800]; /* 16-byte aligned */
...
for (i = 0; i < 800; i++) {
  if (u[i] < 10) { /* i.e.: ((s32) u[i]) < 10 */
    u[i] = 0;
  } else {
    u[i] = 1;
  }
}
```

Compact vector code results because the masked expression involving the constant zero can be further optimized:

```
movdqa  xmm2,   _const1  ; expand  8 words with 10
movdqa  xmm3,   _const2  ; expand  8 words with 1
```

---

[5] For the equality and inequality operators, the ϕ_{s8}- and ϕ_{s16}-condition may be relaxed slightly to include casting the narrow precision operand into an unsigned operand as well. This situation occasionally arises after macro expansion.

```
L: movdqa   xmm1,    u[eax]    ; load     8 words from u
   movdqa   xmm0,    xmm2      ; copy     8 words
   pcmpgtw  xmm0,    xmm1      ; compare  8 words with 10
   pandn    xmm0,    xmm3      ; mask     8 !guards
   movdqa   u[eax],  xmm0      ; store    8 words into u
   add      eax,     16        ;
   cmp      eax,     1600      ;
   jb       L                  ; looping logic
```

Guarded Errors

Because bit masking eliminates conditional branches by executing both branches of an `if` statement, care must be taken that errors that were formerly guarded are not brought into the execution path. A simple example where conditionals guard against subscript out-of-bounds and null-pointer de-reference errors follows. Note that in practice, less straightforward correspondences between guards and potential errors will arise.

```
s32 x[N1], y[N2], *p = NULL;

if (flag) {
  p = malloc(sizeof(s32) * N);
}

for (i = 0; i < N; i++) {
  if (i < N1) x[i] = 0;
  if (i < N2) y[i] = 0;
  if (flag)   p[i] = 0;
}
```

Automatic vectorization may proceed only if the compiler can prove that bit masking does not introduce any errors into the execution path. A simple rule that already performs well in practice is based on the observation that if the same array expression appears in both branches of an `if` statement or in any other unconditional part of the loop body, including the condition of the `if` statement, then bit masking does not bring any error related to this memory reference into the execution path. Rules that are more complicated use more program context to disprove the introduction of such or other errors, or disprove the possibility of errors by means of run-time tests in the prelude (Bik, Girkar, and Haghighat 1999). The Intel C++ and Fortran compilers also use the rule that inserting *any* of the vectorization-enabling pragmas presented in Chapter 9 before a loop asserts that each `if` statement in the loop body may be vectorized without explicitly testing if bit masking could introduce any errors.

The short vector mathematical library discussed earlier in this chapter also provides masked versions of all functions, enabling the vectorization of loops that guard mathematical functions against invalid input values. The masked function names are obtained by concatenating the string `Mask` at the end of the original name (`vmldLn2Mask`) and expecting the bit mask in an additional 128-bit register (viz. `xmm1` or `xmm2`).

Conditional Scalar Assignments

In general, when a scalar is assigned conditionally in a loop, efficient vectorization may become difficult. Vectorization of such scalar memory references is usually only profitable if (a) the scalar implements a conditional reduction or (b) the scalar merely carries a temporary value in a conditional computation and is not live (Aho, Sethi, and Ullman 1986) upon exiting the loop. Situation (a) is simply handled by bit masking the computation of partial results in the loop body while situation (b) only requires bit masking the relevant store in the conditional computation. Both situations are illustrated with the following example:

```
          f64 a[128]; /* 16-byte aligned */
          f64 acc;
          ...
S₁:       acc = 0;
          for (i = 0; i < 128; i++) {
            if (a[i] < -1) {
S₂:              f64 t = a[i] + 1;
S₃:              acc += t * t - t;
            }
          }
```

Scalar `t` merely carries temporary values from statement S_2 into the conditional reduction in statement S_3. Consequently, only statement S_3 requires bit masking. Simplification of the masked expressions that result for this reduction eventually yields the vector code that follows:

```
      movapd   xmm0, _const1   ; expand      2 doubles with  1.0
      movapd   xmm1, _const2   ; expand      2 doubles with -1.0
      xorpd    xmm2, xmm2      ; reset accumulator
L:    movapd   xmm3, a[eax]    ; load        2 doubles from a
      movapd   xmm4, xmm3      ; copy        2 doubles
      addpd    xmm3, xmm0      ; increment   2 doubles by 1
      movapd   xmm5, xmm3      ; copy        2 doubles
      mulpd    xmm5, xmm5      ; multiply    2 doubles
      subpd    xmm5, xmm3      ; subtract    2 doubles
      cmpltpd  xmm4, xmm1      ; compare     2 doubles with -1.0
```

```
andpd    xmm5, xmm4        ; mask           2 guards
addpd    xmm2, xmm5        ; accumulate 2 partial sums
add      eax,  16          ;
cmp      eax,  1024        ;
jb       L                 ; looping logic
                           ;
haddpd   xmm2, xmm2        ; add partial sums
movsd    acc,  xmm2        ; store into acc
```

A different form of situation (b) is shown as follows. Here, a scalar that is defined in both branches S_4 and S_5 of an `if` statement carries a temporary value into an unconditionally executed statement S_6:

```
        f64 a[128], b[128]; /* 16-byte aligned */
        ...
        for (i = 0; i < 128; i++) {
          f64 t;
          if (a[i] < 0) {
S₄:         t = -1.0;
          } else {
S₅:         t = 1.0;
          }
S₆:       b[i] = t;
        }
```

Now, bit masking must be applied to the store of the scalar `t` to ensure that all statement instances of S_6 receive the appropriate values:

```
    movapd   xmm0,  _const1  ; expand  2 doubles with  1.0
    movapd   xmm1,  _const2  ; expand  2 doubles with -1.0
    xorpd    xmm2,  xmm2     ; setup zero
L:  movapd   xmm4,  a[eax]   ; load    2 doubles from a
    cmpltpd  xmm4,  xmm2     ; compare 2 doubles with zero
    movapd   xmm3,  xmm4     ; copy    2 doubles
    andpd    xmm4,  xmm1     ; mask    2  guards
    andnpd   xmm3,  xmm0     ; mask    2 !guards
    orpd     xmm4,  xmm3     ; combine 2 doubles
    movapd   b[eax], xmm4    ; store   2 doubles into b
    add      eax,   16       ;
    cmp      eax,   1024     ;
    jb       L               ; looping logic
```

Performance Example

Bit masking enables the parallel execution of conditional statements without branch instructions, which generally also positively influences branch prediction. A drawback of executing both branches of an `if` statement is that expensive operations that were formerly not executed are brought into the execution path, as illustrated in the following example with a conditionally executed, high-latency, floating-point division:

```
f32 a[N], b[N], c[N]; /* 16-byte aligned */

void divabc(s32 n) {
  s32 i;
  for (i = 0; i < n; i++) {
    if (a[i] > 0) {
      a[i] = b[i] / c[i];
    }
  }
}
```

Vectorizing this loop with bit masking yields the following code:

```
L: movaps   xmm0,   a[eax]   ; load     4 floats from a
   movaps   xmm2,   b[eax]   ; load     4 floats from b
   divps    xmm2,   c[eax]   ; divide   4 floats by   c
   xorps    xmm1,   xmm1     ; reset    4 floats
   cmpltps  xmm1,   xmm0     ; compare  4 floats with zero
   movaps   xmm3,   xmm1     ; copy     4 floats
   andnps   xmm3,   xmm0     ; mask     4 !guards
   andps    xmm2,   xmm1     ; mask     4  guards
   orps     xmm3,   xmm2     ; combine  4 floats
   movaps   a[eax], xmm3     ; store    4 floats into a
   add      eax,    16       ;
   cmp      eax,    ecx      ;
   jb       L                ; looping logic followed by
                             ; a sequential cleanup loop
```

Figure 5.6 shows the speed-up of vector code over sequential code on a 3-gigahertz Pentium 4 processor in case the number of positive elements in array a is 10 percent, 50 percent, and 90 percent and all divisions yield normalized values. Note that speedup is computed from execution times that were obtained by calling the function repeatedly and dividing the total run time accordingly. Because the sequential execution time increases with the probability of the branch being taken while the vector execution time remains virtually the same, the speedup increases with percentage of positive elements in array a.

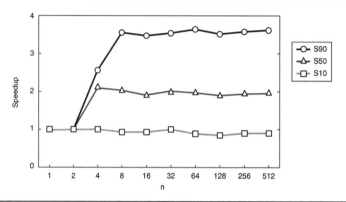

Figure 5.6   Bit-Masking Speedup—3-Gigahertz Pentium® 4 Processor

To avoid a slowdown that results from bringing an infrequently executed and expensive branch into the execution path, compilers use efficiency heuristics to decide whether vectorization of a loop by means of bit masking seems profitable. As explained in Chapter 9, the Intel C++ and Fortran compilers use either static analysis or profile-guided optimization to estimate important execution characteristics, such as the probability that a branch is taken. Based on these probabilities, the compiler subsequently estimates the sequential and vector run time of a loop to decide what version is generated. For the example shown above, vectorization for any branch-taken probability somewhat higher than 10 percent, seems already profitable.

Chapter 6

Alignment Optimizations

Due to the sensitivity of multimedia instructions to the memory alignment of operands, one important aspect of effective automatic intra-register vectorization is the ability of the compiler to enforce a favorable alignment on the memory references in vector loops. A memory location is called 2^n-byte aligned if its address a satisfies the condition

$$a \bmod 2^n = 0$$

or, stated differently, a $k \in \mathbb{N}$ exists such that $a = k \cdot 2^n$ (Knuth 1997). Instructions of the streaming-SIMD extensions are more efficient for memory operands that are aligned on a natural boundary: 64-bit memory operands that are 8-byte aligned and 128-bit memory operands that are 16-byte aligned. Such favorable alignments are enforced by selecting an appropriate alignment on data structures in a program, such as arrays, and by analyzing and optimizing programming constructs that access these data structures, such as loops and functions. This chapter presents static alignment optimizations that can be performed within or between functions and compiler hints or dynamic alignment optimizations that can be used in situations where the static optimizations have failed to enforce aligned memory references.

Intraprocedural Alignment Optimizations

This section discusses some compile-time alignment optimizations that require only local analysis of a single function.

Memory Allocation and Data Layout

In an imperative programming language like C, memory is typically managed using one of the following three memory allocation schemes (Aho, Sethi, and Ullman 1986, Chapter 7):

■ Static allocation, where memory is already reserved at compile time

■ Stack allocation, where memory is managed using a run-time stack

■ Heap allocation, where memory is dynamically allocated as needed

Static allocation is used for external (global) variables and for internal (local) variables that are declared static. Because statically allocated memory is already reserved at compile time, the compiler can enforce any favorable alignment on these variables. Generally, a data structure with a size of one, two or four, or eight bytes should be given a byte, double-word, or quadword alignment in memory, respectively. Larger data structures should be given a 16-byte, 32-byte, or even 64-byte alignment (Intel 2003a). If the compiler has access to *all* code that uses a compound data structure, such as during whole program compilation, advanced data layout transformations become applicable. For example, choosing a 16-byte alignment for the following data structure and padding the `struct` with four additional bytes enforces a 16-byte alignment on all sub-arrays at the expense of increasing memory requirements—`sizeof(struct a_s)` changes from 60 to 64 bytes.

```
struct a_s { s32 x[4], y[4], z[7]; } a[100];
```

Likewise, since C stores arrays in row-major order, the following dimension padding of a two-dimensional array that is 16-byte aligned enforces a 16-byte alignment on each row of the array as well:

```
u8 u[31][31];   → dimension padding →   u8 u[31][32];
```

Stack allocation is used for internal variables that are automatic—variables that come into existence on entry of a function and disappear again on exit of the function. Memory that is required by each instance of a function is organized in an *activation record*, which is pushed onto a run-time stack on entry of the function and popped again on exit of the function (Aho, Sethi, and Ullman 1986; Appel and Ginsburg 1998; Fischer and LeBlanc 1991; van de Goo, 1989; Parsons 1992). Although the compiler has no direct control of the exact memory locations used for the different activation records during program execution, a statically known alignment can still be enforced on all local variables with run-time padding instructions in the prelude and postlude of the function and an appropriate data layout for the activation record (Intel 2003a).

Finally, heap allocation is used for variables that are explicitly allocated and de-allocated by the programmer, using standard C library functions like `malloc()` and `free()` or operators like `new` and `delete` in C++ (Stroustrup 1991). Without control over the implementation that is used for the library, the compiler cannot enforce a particular alignment on heap-allocated memory. If allowed, however, a modified version that always returns properly aligned data can be used instead.

Intraprocedural Alignment Analysis

Information on the selected alignment of variables together with only intraprocedural analysis of the program context often suffices to determine the alignment of memory references at compile time. Based on the property

$$a \bmod 2^n = o \iff (a + i \cdot 2^n) \bmod 2^n = o$$

the compiler is able to determine that an offset o with respect to a base 2^n in memory is unaffected by adding or subtracting any multiple of that base.

Consider, for instance, the following program fragment:

```
        f32 a[60][60]; /* 32-byte aligned */
        ...
        for (i = 0; i < 60; i++) {
          for (j = 0; j < 60; j++) {
  Sᵢ:         a[i][j] = 0;
          }
        }
```

Since row-major order stores `a[i][j]` at memory address

$$a = \text{Addr(a)} + 240 \cdot i + 4 \cdot j$$

the compiler can conclude that in *any* iteration of the i-loop, the memory references of S_1 in the j-loop *start* at an address a that is 16-byte aligned—Addr(a) mod 16 = 0, 240 mod 16 = 0 and j = 0 on entry of the innermost loop, but not guaranteed 32-byte aligned since 240 mod 32 ≠ 0. Because vector instructions continue to access memory in chunks of 16 bytes, the implication is that the j-loop can be vectorized with aligned data movement instructions.

The use of pointer variables and pointer arithmetic can substantially complicate proper alignment analysis, because the initial value of a pointer variable has to be chased back to an address or set of addresses with a statically known alignment. In the following fragment,

```
           s32 *p = q+1; /* same as &q[1] */
           for (i = 0; i < N; i++) {
S₂:            x += *p++;
           }
```

the compiler is able to conclude that each memory reference through the pointer variable p in statement S_2 resides at memory address

$$a = \text{Addr(q)} + 4 + 4 \cdot i$$

in each iteration of the i-loop. Consequently, if q denotes an array variable with 16-byte alignment, memory references *start* at an address a that has an offset $o = 4$ with respect to the base 16—Addr(q) + 4 mod 16 = 4 and i = 0 on entry of the loop. Similarly, if in the following example:

```
        if (...) {
S₁:     p = &q[0];
        }
        else {
S₂:     p = malloc( N * sizeof(s32) );
        }
        for (i = 0; i < N; i++) {
S₃:     x += *p++;
        }
```

array variable q is now 32-byte aligned and the compiler may use a version of `malloc()` that returns 16-byte aligned data, then the alignments defined in S_1 and S_2 imply that the memory references through pointer variable p start at an address that is at least 16-byte aligned. Note that this meeting of two alignments during analysis is further formalized in the section "Interprocedural Alignment Optimizations" later in this chapter.

Intraprocedural alignment analysis can be supplemented with program transformations. Advanced pointer-to-array access conversion (van Engelen and Gallivan 2001) can make code with obscure pointer-based memory references more amenable to alignment analysis. Loop peeling can resolve an initial memory misalignment of $a \bmod 2^n = o$ for a memory reference with element size s by peeling off $(2^n - o) / s$ iterations from the loop if $(2^n - o) \bmod s = 0$ and the loop has sufficient iterations. Loop distribution, where applicable, can isolate memory references with different initial memory misalignments before such loop peeling is applied. In the following code, for example, combining loop distribution with peeling enforces an initial 16-byte alignment in both resulting loops, which can subsequently be vectorized with aligned data movement instructions:

```
u16 x[99]; /* both 16-byte */              for (i = 0; i < 92; i++) {
u16 y[99]; /*      aligned */                x[i] = 0;
...                                        }
for (i = 0; i < 92; i++) {      →         y[7] = 0xffff;
  x[i] = 0;                                for (i = 1; i < 92; i++) {
  y[i+7] = 0xffff;                           y[i+7] = 0xffff;
}                                          }
```

Cache Line Split Optimizations

Loop peeling and distribution cannot resolve different initial misalignments in a single statement, although compiler hints can suggest an alternative memory alignment to resolve even some of these complications, as further discussed in Chapter 9. In such cases, a suitable peeling factor is based on the majority of memory references, after which some access patterns necessarily remain unaligned.

Enforcing an aligned access pattern on each of the four memory references in the following fragment, for example, requires a peeling factor of 0, 3, 2, and 1, respectively:

```
f32 a[40], b[41], c[42], d[43]; /* all 32-byte aligned */
...
for (i = 0; i < 40; i++) {
  a[i] = b[i+1] * c[i+2] * d[i+3];
}
```

Breaking the tie in favor of the store operation yields three unaligned load instructions and one aligned store instruction in the vector loop.

```
L: movups xmm2,   b[eax+4]   ; load   4 floats from b
   movups xmm0,   c[eax+8]   ; load   4 floats from c
   movups xmm1,   d[eax+12]  ; load   4 floats from d
   mulps  xmm2,   xmm0       ; mult.  4 floats
   mulps  xmm2,   xmm1       ; mult.  4 floats
   movaps a[eax], xmm2       ; store  4 floats into a
   add    eax,    16         ;
   cmp    eax,    160        ;
   jb     L                  ; looping logic
```

The access patterns of these four data movement instructions with respect to the 32-byte cache line that is supported by the Pentium III processor are illustrated in Figure 6.1.

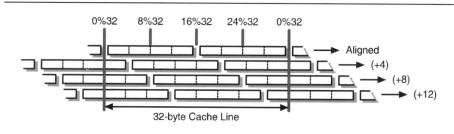

Figure 6.1   Cache Line Splits—32-Byte Cache Line

Aligned data movement instructions always access data that is contained within one cache line. On the other hand, the unaligned data movement instructions alternate between accessing data that is contained within one cache line and data that is split over two cache lines. For the 64-byte cache line supported by the Pentium 4 processor, every fourth unaligned data movement instruction crosses a cache line. Because a *cache line split* incurs a large performance penalty (Intel 2003a), an unaligned data movement instruction that crosses a cache line is implemented more efficiently with a special instruction sequence that avoids such splits altogether at the expense of some data rearranging. A 128-bit load instruction movups xmm0, mem that crosses a cache line by either $c = 4$, $c = 8$, or $c = 12$ bytes, for example, is implemented more efficiently with one of the following instruction sequences that combine the results of several narrower load instructions so that each remains within a single cache line. Note that the unsafe load at (!) may access 4 bytes past the end of a data structure.

$c = 4$	$c = 8$	$c = 12$
| ```
movlps  xmm1,mem
movss   xmm0,mem+8
movhps  xmm0,mem+12(!)
shufps  xmm1,xmm0,0x84
``` | ```
movlps  xmm0,mem
movhps  xmm0,mem+8
``` | ```
movss   xmm1,mem
movhps  xmm1,mem+4
movlps  xmm0,mem+8
shufps  xmm1,xmm0,0x48
``` |

For the previous example, the implication is that in order to alleviate the performance penalties of cache line splits on a Pentium III processor, the compiler first must duplicate the loop body of the vector loop in order to separate unaligned data movement instructions that remain within a cache line from unaligned data movement instructions that cross a cache line. After duplicating the loop body, each cache line split is avoided by replacing the corresponding unaligned data movement instruction with the appropriate instruction sequence, as follows:

```
L: movups xmm2,    b[eax+4]  ; ++ original loop body
   movups xmm0,    c[eax+8]  ; ++
   movups xmm1,    d[eax+12] ; ++
   mulps  xmm2,    xmm0      ; ++
   mulps  xmm2,    xmm1      ; ++
   movaps a[eax],  xmm2      ; ++
                             ;
   movss  xmm3,    b[eax+28] ; -- copy of loop body
   movlps xmm7,    b[eax+20] ; --
   movhps xmm3,    b[eax+32] ; --
   shufps xmm7,    xmm3, 132 ; -- split for array b (c = 4)
   movlps xmm4,    c[eax+24] ; --
   movhps xmm4,    c[eax+32] ; -- split for array c (c = 8)
   movss  xmm6,    d[eax+28] ; --
   movhps xmm6,    d[eax+32] ; --
   movlps xmm5,    d[eax+36] ; --
   shufps xmm6,    xmm5, 72  ; -- split for array d (c = 12)
   mulps  xmm7,    xmm4      ; --
   mulps  xmm7,    xmm6      ; --
   movaps a[eax+16], xmm7    ; --
                             ;
   add    eax,     32        ;
   cmp    eax,     160       ;
   jb     L                  ; looping logic (iterates 5 times)
```
```

In general, if a vector loop has at least one irresolvable data movement instruction with a statically known initial misalignment with respect to a cache line size C, then $\frac{C}{16}$-fold *loop unrolling* is applied to the vector loop to unify the amount of data handled in each iteration, now $\frac{C}{16} \times 16 = C$, with the cache line size (Muchnick 1997, Padua and Wolfe 1986, Wolfe 1996, Zima and Chapman 1990). After this loop unrolling, the compiler knows exactly which of the two ($C = 32$) or four ($C = 64$) copies of the unaligned data movement instruction crosses a cache line, so that this instruction can be replaced with an appropriate instruction sequence. Although full cache line split support would require $15 \times 3 \times 2 = 90$ instruction sequences—for every cross factor $0 < c \leq 15$ and any of the three instructions movdqu, movups, or movupd as load or store instruction—only a few of these sequences commonly occur in practice.

Failure to use cache line split instruction sequences can have a dramatic impact on performance, as illustrated by the following loop that operates on integer arrays x and y:

```
s32 x[256], y[257]; /* both 64-byte aligned */
...
for (i = 0; i < n; i++) {
  x[i] = (x[i] + y[i+1]) >> 1;
}
```

Naïve vectorization of this loop yields the following implementation, which uses aligned data movement instructions to access array x and unaligned data movement instructions to access array y:

```
L: movdqu xmm0,   y[eax+4] ; load  4 doublewords from y
   paddd  xmm0,   x[eax]   ; add   4 doublewords from x
   psrad  xmm0,   1        ; shift 4 doublewords
   movdqa x[eax], xmm0      ; store 4 doublewords into x
   add    eax,    16       ;
   cmp    eax,    ecx      ;
   jb     L                ; looping logic, followed by
   ...                     ; a sequential cleanup loop
```

The statically known initial misalignment $a \bmod 64 = 4$ for the access pattern of y, however, enables the compiler to optimize the vector loop for the 64-byte cache line that is supported by the Pentium 4 processor, as shown in the following.

```
L: movdqu xmm0,   y[eax+4] ; load  4 doublewords from y
   paddd  xmm0,   x[eax]   ; add   4 doublewords from x
   psrad  xmm0,   1        ; shift 4 doublewords
   movdqa x[eax], xmm0      ; store 4 doublewords into x
                           ;
```

```
movdqu xmm1,       y[eax+20] ; load  4 doublewords from y
paddd  xmm1,       x[eax+16] ; add   4 doublewords from x
psrad  xmm1,       1         ; shift 4 doublewords
movdqa x[eax+16], xmm1       ; store 4 doublewords into x
                             ;
movdqu xmm2,       y[eax+36] ; load  4 doublewords from y
paddd  xmm2,       x[eax+32] ; add   4 doublewords from x
psrad  xmm2,       1         ; shift 4 doublewords
movdqa x[eax+32], xmm2       ; store 4 doublewords into x
                             ;
movd       xmm6,   y[eax+52] ; total scalar split
movd       xmm3,   y[eax+60] ;    for array y
movd       xmm5,   y[eax+56] ;
movd       xmm4,   y[eax+64] ;
punpckldq xmm6,    xmm3      ;
punpckldq xmm5,    xmm4      ;
punpckldq xmm6,    xmm5      ;
paddd      xmm6,   x[eax+48] ; add   4 doublewords from x
psrad      xmm6,   1         ; shift 4 doublewords
movdqa     x[eax+48], xmm6   ; store 4 doublewords into x
add        eax,    64        ;
cmp        eax,    ecx       ;
jb         L                 ; looping logic, followed by
...                          ; a sequential cleanup loop
```

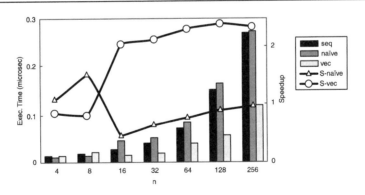

Figure 6.2   Cache Line Split Performance—3-Gigahertz Pentium® 4 Processor)

Figure 6.2 shows the execution time on a 3-gigahertz Pentium 4 processor of a sequential version—seq, the unoptimized vector implementation—naïve, and the optimized vector implementation—vec, for increasing values of n. Execution times were obtained by running the loop repeatedly and dividing the total run time accordingly. The corresponding speedup is shown in the same figure using a secondary *y* axis. The naïve implementation exhibits speedup up to the point where cache line splits occur ($4 \leq n < 16$). The optimized vector implementation exhibits speedup as soon as sufficient iterations exist ($16 \leq n$). Without further trip count information, the optimized vector implementation seems the best choice for the Pentium 4 processor.

On the Pentium 4 processor with HT Technology, the SSE3 instruction lddqu provides an alternative load instruction that alleviates some of the performance penalties of cache line splits. The implication is that the loop shown above can also be implemented without loop unrolling, as follows:

```
L:  lddqu   xmm0,   y[eax+4] ; load  4 doublewords from y
    paddd   xmm0,   x[eax]   ; add   4 doublewords from x
    psrad   xmm0,   1        ; shift 4 doublewords
    movdqa  x[eax], xmm0     ; store 4 doublewords into x
    add     eax,    16       ;
    cmp     eax,    ecx      ;
    jb      L                ; looping logic, followed
    ...                      ; by sequential cleanup
```

Figure 6.3 shows the execution time on a 2.8-gigahertz Pentium 4 processor with HT Technology of a sequential version—seq, the vector implementation shown above—lddqu and the implementation that has been optimized to avoid cache line splits—vec, for increasing values of n. Again, execution times were obtained by running the loop repeatedly and dividing the total run time accordingly. The corresponding speedup is shown along a secondary y axis. Although ultimately the highest speedup is still obtained with a cache line split instruction sequence, the lddqu instruction provides a viable, more compact alternative.

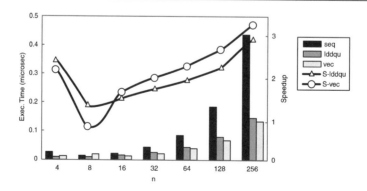

Figure 6.3   Cache Line Split Performance—2.8-Gigahertz Pentium® 4 with HT Technology

Interprocedural Alignment Optimizations

Analysis of a single function is often hampered by a lack of knowledge about the alignment of data structures that are associated with formal pointer arguments. For example, even though intraprocedural analysis of the function

```
void f(s32 *p, s32 n) {
  while (--n >= 0) {
    *p++ = 0; /* aligned access? */
  }
}
```

can detect a well-behaved loop that accesses p[0] through p[n-1], without further information on the memory addresses used as actual arguments for formal pointer argument p, the compiler must conservatively assume an unaligned access pattern. Quite often, however, different data structures that are associated with a formal pointer argument have some common alignment properties that can be exploited in the function. This section presents a method for gathering interprocedural alignment information and exploiting the common properties. Although this method was developed independently at the Intel Compiler Lab, similar approaches to alignment analysis were proposed by others (Larsen, Witchel, and Amarasinghe (2002); Pryanishnikov, Krall, and Horspool (2003).

Interprocedural Alignment Analysis

Interprocedural alignment analysis consists of finding maximal values 2^n in a mapping align such that

$$\text{align}(f,p) = \langle 2^n, o \rangle$$

indicates that all actual arguments associated with formal *pointer* argument p of function f() evaluates to a memory address a that satisfies $a \bmod 2^n = o$.

By defining an alignment lattice and jump functions, this problem can be solved using a modified version of the interprocedural constant propagation algorithm described in Callahan et al. (1986). Call by reference arguments supported in languages such as C++ and Fortran are handled similarly.

Alignment Lattice

The alignment lattice $(V, \wedge)$ consists of the set

$$V = \{\top\} \cup \{ \langle 2^n, o \rangle \mid 0 \le o < 2^n \text{ with } n, o \in \mathbb{N} \}$$

and a meet operator $\wedge$ that is defined as $v \wedge \top = v$ for each $v \in V$ and otherwise as

$$\langle 2^n, o \rangle \wedge \langle 2^{n'}, o' \rangle = \langle 2^{n''}, o'' \rangle$$

for the following n'' and o'':

$$\begin{cases} n'' = \max\{ 0 \le m \le \min(n, n') \mid o \bmod 2^m = o' \bmod 2^m \} \\ o'' = o \bmod 2^{n''} \end{cases}$$

For example, $\langle 4, 0 \rangle \wedge \langle 4, 2 \rangle$ is equal to $\langle 2, 0 \rangle$ under this definition, since the latter forms the greatest lower bound of the former two alignments. This way, the meet operator defines the infinite lattice (Gilbert 1976) illustrated as follows, where $\langle 1, 0 \rangle$ serves as $\bot$, since $v \wedge \bot = \bot$ holds for every $v \in V$.

$$\top$$
$$\vdots$$

$$\langle 32, 0 \rangle \; \ldots \qquad\qquad\qquad\qquad\qquad \ldots \; \langle 32, 31 \rangle$$
$$\langle 16, 0 \rangle \langle 16, 8 \rangle \langle 16, 4 \rangle \langle 16, 12 \rangle \ldots \qquad \ldots \langle 16, 3 \rangle \langle 16, 11 \rangle \langle 16, 7 \rangle \langle 16, 5 \rangle$$
$$\langle 8, 0 \rangle \quad \langle 8, 4 \rangle \; \langle 8, 2 \rangle \langle 8, 6 \rangle \langle 8, 1 \rangle \langle 8, 5 \rangle \quad \langle 8, 3 \rangle \quad \langle 8, 7 \rangle$$
$$\langle 4, 0 \rangle \qquad \langle 4, 2 \rangle \qquad \langle 4, 1 \rangle \qquad \langle 4, 3 \rangle$$
$$\langle 2, 0 \rangle \qquad\qquad\qquad \langle 2, 1 \rangle$$
$$\langle 1, 0 \rangle$$
$$\bot$$

The values in this lattice represent alignment information that has not yet been determined ($\top$), a known alignment at a particular offset from a certain base ($\langle 2^n, o \rangle$), and the least informative alignment information at any byte in memory ($\langle 1, 0 \rangle$ or $\bot$).

Alignment Jump Functions

The accuracy of interprocedural analysis depends on the sophistication of so-called jump functions, which define correspondences between formal and actual arguments at call sites. For the interprocedural alignment analysis problem under consideration, the following alignment jump functions provide sufficient sophistication to handle many cases that occur in practice.

Given any type T and calling structure

```
       f(..., T *x_i, ...) {
          ...                              g(..., T *y_j, ...) {
s:        g(..., a_j, ...);                   ...
          ...                              }
       }
```

the jump function $J_s(y_j)$ for the formal pointer argument y_j of function g() at call site s in the body of function f() is defined as follows:

1. If actual argument a_j evaluates to a memory address with a statically known alignment $\langle 2^n, o \rangle$, then $J_s(y_j) = \langle 2^n, o \rangle$.

2. If the equivalence $a_j \equiv x_i + c$ holds for some constant c and the implicit definition of the formal argument in the function header f() is the only reaching definition of x_i at call site s, then:

$$J_s(y_j) = \begin{cases} \top & \text{if } \texttt{align}(\texttt{f},\texttt{x}_i) = \top \\ \langle 2^n, (o+c) \bmod 2^n \rangle & \text{if } \texttt{align}(\texttt{f},\texttt{x}_i) = \langle 2^n, o \rangle \\ \bot & \text{if } \texttt{align}(\texttt{f},\texttt{x}_i) = \bot \end{cases}$$

3. In all other cases, $J_s(y_j) = \bot$.

Case (2) handles common pass through arguments with $c = 0$. This case can also be generalized by discarding arbitrary expressions of the form $2^m \cdot e$ in the sum, provided that $\min(2^n, 2^m)$ is used as the base in the result.

Interprocedural Alignment Propagation Algorithm

Interprocedural alignment analysis now proceeds similar to the interprocedural constant propagation algorithm presented in Callahan et al. (1986). First, mapping `align` is initialized to $\top$ and each function in the program is added to a working set as follows:

```
work := {}; /* empty set */
for each function f
  for each formal pointer argument xᵢ of function f
    align(f,xᵢ) := ⊤;
  endfor
  work := work ∪ { f };
endfor
```

Subsequently, a function is picked and removed from the working set, followed by an update of the mapping `align` by evaluating alignment jump functions for all call sites in the function. If a change occurs, the called function is added to the working set. This process is repeated until no changes occur and the working set becomes empty.

```
while (work != {})
  pick a function f from work;
  work := work - { f };
  for each call site s in body of f that calls function g
    for each formal pointer argument yⱼ given a value at s
      oldval := align(g,yⱼ);
      align(g,yⱼ) := oldval ∧ Jₛ(yⱼ);
      if (align(g,yⱼ) != oldval) work := work ∪ {g};
    endfor
  endfor
endwhile
```

The algorithm as given assumes that the complete call graph is available to the compiler to enable iterating over all functions and call sites in a program (Ryder 1979, Zima and Chapman 1990). An incomplete call graph can still be dealt with, however, by initializing mapping `align` to $\perp$ for all formal pointer arguments of functions for which not all callers are available. Because the maximum alignment chosen by the compiler defines a finite subset of the alignment lattice in which the alignment of each formal argument can only be reduced a bounded number of times, the algorithm is guaranteed to terminate.

Interprocedural Alignment Propagation Example

Interprocedural alignment propagation is illustrated by the following program, where the selected alignments serve the purpose of illustration only. Because the complete call graph is available to the compiler, mapping align is initialized to ⊤ and all functions are added to the working set.

```
        u8 a[16]; /* 16-byte aligned */
        u8 b[32]; /* 32-byte aligned */

        main() {
s₁:       f(a,b,b+4);   /* same as f(&a[0],&b[0],&b[4]); */
        }
        void f(u8 *x, u8 *y, u8 *z) {
s₂:       g(x,y,z);

s₃:       g(y,x,z+8);
        }
        void g(u8 *u, u8 *v, u8 *w) {
          if (...) {
s₄:           f(u,v,w);
          }
          ...
        }
```

Function main() is visited next. Because the actual arguments at call site s_1 evaluate to memory addresses with a statically known alignment, evaluating the following jump functions of case (1) gives rise to updating the mapping align for the formal arguments of f() as in the following:

$$J_{s_1}(x) = \langle 16,0 \rangle \quad \text{hence} \quad \text{align}(f,x) = \top \wedge \langle 16,0 \rangle = \langle 16,0 \rangle$$

$$J_{s_1}(y) = \langle 32,0 \rangle \quad \text{hence} \quad \text{align}(f,y) = \top \wedge \langle 32,0 \rangle = \langle 32,0 \rangle$$

$$J_{s_1}(z) = \langle 32,4 \rangle \quad \text{hence} \quad \text{align}(f,z) = \top \wedge \langle 32,4 \rangle = \langle 32,4 \rangle$$

Visiting function f() gives rise to the updates

$$J_{s_2}(u) = \langle 16,0 \rangle \quad \text{hence} \quad \text{align}(g,u) = \top \wedge \langle 16,0 \rangle = \langle 16,0 \rangle$$

$$J_{s_2}(v) = \langle 32,0 \rangle \quad \text{hence} \quad \text{align}(g,v) = \top \wedge \langle 32,0 \rangle = \langle 32,0 \rangle$$

$$J_{s_2}(w) = \langle 32,4 \rangle \quad \text{hence} \quad \text{align}(g,w) = \top \wedge \langle 32,4 \rangle = \langle 32,4 \rangle$$

and subsequently

$$J_{s_3}(u) = \langle 32,0 \rangle \quad \text{hence} \quad \text{align}(g,u) = \langle 16,0 \rangle \wedge \langle 32,0 \rangle = \langle 16,0 \rangle$$

$$J_{s_3}(v) = \langle 16,0 \rangle \quad \text{hence} \quad \text{align}(g,v) = \langle 32,0 \rangle \wedge \langle 16,0 \rangle = \langle 16,0 \rangle$$

$$J_{s_3}(w) = \langle 32,12 \rangle \quad \text{hence} \quad \text{align}(g,w) = \langle 32,4 \rangle \wedge \langle 32,12 \rangle = \langle 8,4 \rangle$$

by evaluating the alignment jump functions of case (2) at call sites s_2 and s_3. After this, function g() is taken from the working set, which gives rise to updating the mapping align as follows:

$$J_{s_4}(x) = \langle 16,0 \rangle \quad \text{hence} \quad \text{align(f,x)} = \langle 16,0 \rangle \wedge \langle 16,0 \rangle = \langle 16,0 \rangle$$

$$J_{s_4}(y) = \langle 16,0 \rangle \quad \text{hence} \quad \text{align(f,y)} = \langle 32,0 \rangle \wedge \langle 16,0 \rangle = \langle 16,0 \rangle$$

$$J_{s_4}(z) = \langle 8,4 \rangle \quad \text{hence} \quad \text{align(f,z)} = \langle 32,4 \rangle \wedge \langle 8,4 \rangle = \langle 8,4 \rangle$$

Because this operation changes the mapping align for two formal arguments of f(), this function is added back to the working set. Re-evaluating the jump functions at call sites s_2 and s_3 does not give rise to any more changes, however, and the algorithm terminates.

Exploiting Interprocedural Alignment Information

Information obtained by interprocedural alignment analysis is subsequently used during local optimization of a single function, discussed at the beginning of this chapter. For example, if

$$\text{align(f,p)} = \langle 16,15 \rangle$$

holds in the function

```
void f(u8 *p) {
  s32 i;
  for (i = 0; i < 49; i++) {
    p[i] = 0;
  }
}
```

then the compiler can conclude that peeling off one iteration from the i-loop ensures that the memory references through formal pointer argument p start at a memory address that is 16-byte aligned. As a result, this loop can be vectorized using aligned data movement instructions, as follows:

```
      pxor   xmm0,    xmm0    ; setup vector zero
      mov    [edx],   0       ; store 1   byte   into p
      mov    eax,     1       ;
L:    movdqa [edx+eax], xmm0  ; store 16 bytes into p
      add    eax,     16      ;
      cmp    eax,     49      ;
      jb     L                ; looping logic
```

Several other interprocedural optimizations can make intra-register vectorization more effective. Interprocedural constant propagation can improve local analysis of array subscripts and trip counts of well-behaved loops (Callahan et al. 1986). Procedure cloning can be used to generate a few copies of a function such that each copy is tailored to specific alignment properties at multiple sets of call sites (Allen and Kennedy 2002; Cooper, Hall, and Kennedy 1992; Cooper, Kennedy, and Torczon 1986).

Improving Alignment Optimizations

Static alignment optimizations alone cannot always detect or enforce aligned memory references. This section discusses compiler hints and dynamic alignment optimizations that can be used in these situations.

Compiler Hints for Alignment

The programmer can use compiler hints to convey alignment properties to the compiler that may otherwise remain undetected. For example, the programmer can use the following alignment hint to tell the compiler that all memory regions associated with formal pointer argument p are 16-byte aligned:

```
void fill(s16 *p) {
  __assume_aligned(p, 16);
  ...
}
```

The use of such compiler hints ensure that, independent of the results of compiler alignment analysis, all optimizations of function `fill()` take advantage of this incoming alignment. A complete list of alignment hints supported by Intel C++ and Fortran compilers is given in Chapter 9.

Multi-Version Code

Generating multi-version code that tests the initial alignment of each memory reference at run time can be an effective way to optimize a loop with statically unknown alignments (Bik et al. 2002b and 2001; Krall and Lelait 2000; Pryanishnikov, Krall, and Horspool 2003). For instance, suppose that no static alignment information is available for the formal pointer arguments `dx` and `dy` in the following C implementation of the

Level 1 BLAS kernel DDOT (Lawson et al. 1979a and 1979b) that computes the dot product of two vectors:

```
f64 ddot(f64 *dx, f64 *dy, s32 n) {
  s32 i;
  f64 d = 0;
  for (i = 0; i < n; i++) { d += dx[i] * dy[i]; }
  return d;
}
```

Testing the initial alignment of each memory reference at run time against the two most likely offsets a mod 16 = 0 and a mod 16 = 8, since 8-byte alignment forms the natural boundary of data type f64, yields the following five-way multi-version code:

```
u32 offx = dx & 0x0f; /* dx's offset wrt. base 16 */
u32 offy = dy & 0x0f; /* dy's offset wrt. base 16 */

if (offx == 0 && offy == 0) {
  for (i = 0; i < n; i++) { d += dx[i] * dy[i]; }
}
else if (offx == 0 && offy == 8) {
  for (i = 0; i < n; i++) { d += dx[i] * dy[i]; }
}
else if (offx == 8 && offy == 0) {
  for (i = 0; i < n; i++) { d += dx[i] * dy[i]; }
}
else if (offx == 8 && offy == 8) {
  for (i = 0; i < n; i++) { d += dx[i] * dy[i]; }
}
else {
  for (i = 0; i < n; i++) { d += dx[i] * dy[i]; }
}
```

Each branch of this multi-version code can subsequently be optimized according to the initial alignment of both memory references. The loop in the first branch is simply vectorized with aligned data movement instructions. Likewise, the loop in the branch with identical nonzero offsets can be vectorized with aligned data movement instructions after peeling off one iteration from the loop. The loops in the two branches with a zero and nonzero offset, on the other hand, can only be vectorized with one aligned and one unaligned data movement instruction. Finally, because the last branch handles all cases where memory references are not even properly 8-byte aligned, the loop in this branch is typically best implemented sequentially.

If a similar approach is used for the following C implementation of the Level 1 BLAS kernel SDOT (Lawson et al. 1979a and 1979b),

```
f32 sdot(f32 *sx, f32 *sy, s32 n) {
  s32 i;
  f32 s = 0;
  for (i = 0; i < n; i++) { s += sx[i] * sy[i]; }
  return s;
}
```

then testing the initial alignment of each memory reference at run time against the four most likely offsets a mod $16 = 0$, a mod $16 = 4$, a mod $16 = 8$, and a mod $16 = 12$, since 4-byte alignment forms the natural boundary of data type f32, gives rise to the 17-way multi-version code sketched here:

```
u32 offx = sx & 0x0f; /* sx's offset wrt. base 16 */
u32 offy = sy & 0x0f; /* sy's offset wrt. base 16 */

if (offx == 0 && offy == 0) {
  for (i = 0; i < n; i++) { s += sx[i] * sy[i]; }
}
else if (offx == 0 && offy == 4) {
  for (i = 0; i < n; i++) { s += sx[i] * sy[i]; }
}
else if (offx == 0 && offy == 8) {
  for (i = 0; i < n; i++) { s += sx[i] * sy[i]; }
}
else if (offx == 0 && offy == 12) {
  for (i = 0; i < n; i++) { s += sx[i] * sy[i]; }
}
  ⋮
else if (offx == 12 && offy == 8) {
  for (i = 0; i < n; i++) { s += sx[i] * sy[i]; }
}
else if (offx == 12 && offy == 12) {
  for (i = 0; i < n; i++) { s += sx[i] * sy[i]; }
}
else {
  for (i = 0; i < n; i++) { s += sx[i] * sy[i]; }
}
```

In general, multi-version code that tests m different offsets with respect to a certain base for n different memory references gives rise to m^n separate branches, plus one else-branch that is required if not all possible offsets are covered. Enabling cache-line split optimizations for the most likely offsets with respect to a cache line size 64, for instance, increases the number of branches from 5 ($2^2 + 1$) to 65 ($8^2 + 1$) for DDOT and from 17 ($4^2 + 1$) to 257 ($16^2 + 1$) for SDOT. Multi-version code that deals with more misalignments, up to $m = 64$ to test $a \bmod 64 = 0$, $a \bmod 64 = 1$ up to $a \bmod 64 = 63$, or more memory references—which increases n—gives rise to even more branches. Although the resulting multi-version code can often be improved by merging branches that are implemented similarly, the potential code size explosion is clearly too prohibitive to make this approach a generally applicable dynamic alignment optimization. Therefore, the next section explores an alternative way to deal with the trade-off between limited code size and testing overhead versus improved performance for each combination of alignments.

Dynamic Loop Peeling

If the initial alignment of a single memory reference in a loop is not known at compile time, the compiler can generate a prelude that first executes a few iterations sequentially until the access pattern becomes 16-byte aligned (Bik et al. 2002b and 2001; Larsen, Witchel, and Amarasinghe 2002). Applying this *dynamic loop peeling* to the following loop with a statically unknown value of p

```
u8 *p;
...
for (i = 0; i < U; i++) {
  p[i] = 0;
}
```

yields the following code with a sequential peeling loop in the prelude and a second loop that can be vectorized using aligned data movement instructions:

```
u32 peel = p & 0x0f;
if (peel != 0) {
  peel = 16 - peel;
  for (i = 0; i < MIN(peel,U); i++) {
    p[i] = 0; /* peeling loop */
  }
}
for (i = peel; i < U; i++) {
  p[i] = 0;   /* aligned loop */
}
```

Note that dynamic loop peeling for one memory reference also enforces a known alignment on other memory references that have statically known relative offsets to this former memory reference. For instance, even though no memory reference in the following loop has an initial alignment that is known at compile time, all relative offsets between the memory references are known statically:

```
for (i = 0; i < U; i++) {
  x += p[i] + p[i+8] + p[i+16];
}
```

Consequently, applying dynamic loop peeling to memory reference p[i] also enforces an aligned access pattern for memory reference p[i+16] and gives memory reference p[i+8] a known initial misalignment of eight bytes, enabling the compiler to avoid the penalty of cache line splits, as in the following:

```
u32 peel = p & 0x0f;
if (peel != 0) {
  peel = 16 - peel;
  for (i = 0; i < MIN(peel,U); i++) {
    x += p[i] + p[i+8] + p[i+16];
  }
}
/*
 * Now the following alignment properties hold */
 *   aligned         : p[i] and p[i+16]
 *   misaligned (+8): p[i+8]
 */
for (i = peel; i < U; i++) {
  x += p[i] + p[i+8] + p[i+16];
}
```

Similar statically known relative offsets arise between memory references that involve different variables in the same COMMON block in Fortran (Kaufman and Friedman 1990), since such blocks generally impose a fixed data layout on all declared components. In the following Fortran example, for instance, the memory references A(I) and B(I) access two array elements in the same COMMON block PDATA that are always 160 bytes apart, assuming a 4-byte implementation of the data type REAL:

```
        COMMON /PDATA/ A(40), B(40)
        REAL A, B
        ...
        DO 10 I = K, 40
          A(I) = B(I) * 2.0
10      CONTINUE
```

As a result, any optimization that enforces a 16-byte alignment on memory reference A(I) in this loop automatically enforces a 16-byte alignment on memory reference B(I).

If a loop contains several memory references with statically unknown and unrelated alignments, the compiler first applies dynamic loop peeling to the most important memory reference. The compiler can subsequently optimize the loop with a known initial alignment for this and related memory reference and either [a] assume that all other memory references are unaligned or [b] resort to multi-version code generation to test the resulting alignment of one or more other important memory references. Alignment strategy [a] provides a reasonable trade-off in favor of code size, whereas alignment strategy [b] increases performance opportunities at the expense of an increase in code size. This increase still can be controlled by restricting both the number of other memory references involved in the multi-code and the number of different offsets that are tested—simply testing for aligned or unaligned only rather than testing the resulting alignment against several offsets. As an example, both strategies generate the following prelude for the kernel SDOT that was considered in the previous section, where sy[i] is arbitrarily selected as most important memory reference:

```
peel = sy & 0x0f;
if (peel != 0) {
  peel = (sy & 0x03) ? n : (16 - peel) / 4;
  for (i = 0; i < MIN(peel,n); i++) {
    d += sx[i] * sy[i];
  }
}
...
```

The prelude first dynamically peels the loop according to the initial misalignment of memory reference sy[i]. If sy is not properly 4-byte aligned, the access pattern can never be made to align, and the peeling loop executes *all* iterations sequentially. Under alignment strategy [a], the following loop directly follows this prelude:

```
...
for (i = peel; i < n; i++) { /* only sy aligned */
  d += sx[i] * sy[i];
}
```

Under alignment strategy [b], the following slightly more elaborate code follows the prelude, which enables the compiler to specifically optimize the situation in which both access patterns become aligned after dynamic loop peeling:

```
...
if (((sx + peel) & 0x0f) == 0) {
  /* both sy and sx aligned */
  for (i = p; i < n; i++) { d += sx[i] * sy[i]; }
}
else {
  /* only sy aligned */
  for (i = p; i < n; i++) { d += sx[i] * sy[i]; }
}
```

This example clearly shows that dynamic loop peeling avoids the code explosion that is inherent to general multi-version code generation, while still providing enough flexibility to optimize loops for commonly occurring alignment situations.

Performance Examples

When compiled for the Pentium 4 processor, the Intel C/C++ Compiler vectorizes the earlier considered kernel DDOT with alignment strategy [b] and accelerates the reduction by incorporating an additional 128-bit accumulator after unrolling the vector loop to enable more computational overlap between independent addition-multiplication pairs. Figure 6.4 shows speedups of this compiler-generated vector loop (*S*-vec) and an assembly version (*S*-asm) that has been hand-optimized for the Pentium 4 processor (courtesy Henry Ou) over a sequential version for increasing values of the trip count n and for different alignment properties of the formal pointer arguments dx and dy. The information in Figure 6.4 is based on execution times that were obtained by running the kernel repeatedly and dividing the total run time accordingly. The suffix *x/y* denotes that dx mod 16 = *x* and dy mod 16 = *y*.

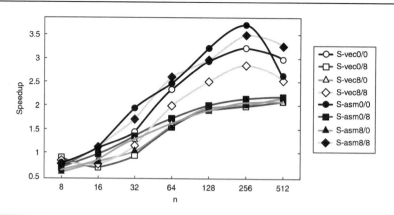

Figure 6.4 DDOT Speedup—1.5-Gigahertz Pentium® 4 Processor

The performance trends reveal that automatically generating code provides a viable alternative to hand optimization. Both implementations make the common case fast but are also able to adapt to other likely alignment properties. Above n = 512, the 8-kilobyte size of the L1 cache starts to dominate performance.

A flavor of how dynamic loop peeling can help a larger application is given by compiling the Linpack benchmark (Dongarra et al. 1994), available in both C and Fortran, with the Intel C++ and Fortran compilers. This benchmark reports the performance of solving a system of linear equations with a separate factorization and solve phase, where most of the execution time results from repetitively applying vector updates to different parts of columns in the coefficient matrix during the factorization phase. The vector updates are implemented with the Level 1 BLAS kernel SAXPY and DAXPY (Lawson et al. 1979a and 1979b) in, respectively, the single-precision and double-precision floating-point version of the Linpack benchmark, obtained by defining either macro name SP or DP. A simplified C implementation of the latter kernel follows:

```
void daxpy(f64 *dx, f64 *dy, f64 s, s32 n) {
  s32 i;
  for (i = 0; i < n; i++) {
    dy[i] += s * dx[i];
  }
}
```

The Intel C/C++ Compiler vectorizes this kernel with dynamic data dependence analysis to resolve possible data dependences between memory references through the formal pointer arguments dx and dy and with alignment strategy [b] of dynamic loop peeling to enforce aligned access patterns through these pointer variables. Table 6.1 summarizes some alignment properties of the memory regions associated with formal pointer arguments dx and dy while solving a system defined by a 100×100 coefficient matrix that, for comparison purposes, is stored in two benchmark-defined two-dimensional arrays with leading dimensions lda = 200 and lda = 201. The compiler selects a 32-byte alignment for both arrays. The table lists the number of times address a, passed as actual argument for either dx or dy, satisfies

$$a \bmod 16 = o$$

for offsets $o = 0$, $o = 4$, $o = 8$, and $o = 12$. The last two columns show how many times dx and dy have an *identical* misalignment—so that dynamic loop peeling can make both access patterns aligned—or a *different* misalignment, which implies that one access pattern must remain unaligned. These properties already reveal that the best performance can be expected for lda = 200.

Table 6.1   Linpack Alignment Properties

100×100		$o = 0$	$o = 4$	$o = 8$	$o = 12$	identical	different
lda = 201	dx	25	2575	25	2524	1250	3899
	dy	1374	1250	1275	1250		
lda = 200	dx	1324	1300	1275	1250	5149	0
	dy	1324	1300	1275	1250		

Table 6.2 shows the single-precision and double-precision floating-point performance reported by a sequential and vectorized version of the Linpack benchmark on a 3-gigahertz Pentium 4 processor. The ability to vectorize loops despite incomplete data dependence and alignment information has a clear positive impact on performance. The single-precision speedups in the range 11.7–17.2 are quite excessive due to a large number of denormal assists (Intel 2003a) in the FPU-based sequential version. Note that speedups compared to scalar SSE code fall in the more realistic range of 1.2–1.8. The double-precision speedups in the range 1.2–1.3, on the other hand, are representative of speedups observed for numerical applications as a whole.

Table 6.2   Linpack Performance—3-Gigahertz Pentium® 4 Processor

MFLOPS 100 × 100	single-prec		double-prec	
	Seq	Vec	Seq	Vec
lda = 201	125	1469	1193	1502
lda = 200	125	2150	1186	1544

Although multimedia extensions were originally designed to boost the performance of multimedia or internet applications, this benchmark shows that the extensions are also useful for exploiting data parallelism in more traditional scientific and engineering applications. Another interesting point is that the numbers reported by the C and Fortran implementation of the Linpack benchmark, when compiled with the Intel C++ and Fortran compilers, are quite similar, even though Fortran's aliasing restrictions on formal arguments enable the compiler to vectorize the kernel DAXPY without dynamic dependence analysis. Hence, dynamic dependence analysis provides a valuable method to tackle one of the problems that has traditionally been held responsible for potential performance differences between the two programming languages. For both languages, dynamic loop peeling provides an essential method to deal with the sensitivity of multimedia instructions to varying memory alignment.

Chapter 7

Supplemental Optimizations

This chapter discusses a number of supplemental optimizations that can be used to improve the effectiveness of automatic intra-register vectorization. First, recognizing and exploiting idioms that are directly supported in the multimedia instruction set generally increases performance and reduces code size. Second, the SSE3 instruction set supports a few instructions that particularly benefit applications that use single-precision and double-precision complex data types. Third, because computational improvements have little impact on code that is constrained by memory performance, vectorization sometimes becomes effective only when supplemented with high-level and low-level optimizations for the memory hierarchy.

Idiom Recognition

Recognizing programming constructs that can be mapped onto compact idiomatic instructions has a positive impact on performance and code size, as further discussed in this section for conversion, arithmetic, reduction, and saturation idioms, as well as search loops.

Conversion Idioms

Unpack instructions enable the vectorization of mixed-type loops in which narrow precision integer operands must be promoted into wider precision operands that match the individual data elements of the selected vector data type. Zero extension is implemented by moving a cleared register into the higher part, while sign extension requires replicating the sign bit. If packed words are selected as vector data type (vl = 8), for example, then an 8-bit unit-stride memory reference can still be vectorized with either zero or sign extension as follows, where data movement instruction movq loads eight bytes into the lower part of the 128-bit register xmm0:

u8→u16/s16 (zero extension)	s8→u16/s16 (sign extension)
`movq        xmm0, m64`	`movq          xmm0, m64`
`pxor        xmm1, xmm1`	`punpcklbw     xmm0, xmm0`
`punpcklbw xmm0, xmm1`	`psraw         xmm0, 8`

In combination with the conversion instructions, these two instruction sequences and others like them enable vectorization of a variety of mixed-type loops. Consider, for example, the following fragment, in which the usual arithmetic conversions require that operands are promoted into data type s32 before the sum is truncated back into data type s16:

```
u8  x[N];
s16 y[N]; /* both 16-byte aligned */
...
for (i = 0; i < N; i++) {
  y[i] += x[i];/* (s16) (((s32) y[i]) + ((s32) x[i])) */
}
```

Because a 16-bit precision suffices for this loop and simultaneous zero extension of eight bytes into eight words can be implemented with the instruction sequence shown above, the loop can be vectorized with packed words as vector data type as follows:

```
      pxor      xmm1,      xmm1      ; setup zero
L:    movq      xmm0,      x[eax]    ; load        8 bytes from x
      punpcklbw xmm0,      xmm1      ; zero ext. 8 bytes
      paddw     xmm0,      y[2*eax]  ; add         8 words from y
      movdqa    y[2*eax], xmm0       ; store       8 words into y
      add       eax,       8         ;
      cmp       eax,       ecx       ;
      jb        L                    ; looping logic
```

To vectorize the following loop, in which a byte value is converted into a single-precision floating-point number, a slightly modified instruction sequence is required:

```
f32 a[N];
s8  z[N]; /* both 16-byte aligned */
...
for (i = 0; i < N; i++) {
  a[i] = z[i];
}
```

This loop can exploit four-way SIMD parallelism by implementing the type conversion of data type s8 into f32 with the following multimedia instructions. First the data movement instruction movd is used to load four bytes into the lower part of xmm0. The data movement instruction is then followed by a sign extension into four doublewords and a final conversion into single-precision floating-point numbers by means of the conversion instruction cvtdq2ps.

```
L: movd       xmm0,      z[eax]   ; load 4 bytes from z
   punpcklbw  xmm0,      xmm0     ; sign extend
   punpcklwd  xmm0,      xmm0     ;    4 bytes into
   psrad      xmm0,      24       ;    4 doublewords
   cvtdq2ps   xmm1,      xmm0     ; convert into 4 floats
   movaps     a[4*eax],  xmm1     ; store 4 floats into a
   add        eax,       4        ;
   cmp        eax,       ecx      ;
   jb         L                   ; looping logic
```

Arithmetic Idioms

Chapter 5 shows how to vectorize the multiplication of two word operands with the instruction pmullw if only a 16-bit result is required. Likewise, if the high word of the 32-bit result is then shifted into the low word $((x[i]*y[i])>>16)$, the expression as a whole can be vectorized for packed words using the arithmetic instruction pmulhuw or pmulhw, depending on whether both word operands are involved in either a zero extension or sign extension, respectively, before multiplication. This idiom can be generalized slightly by observing that any shift factor $s \geq 16$ can be implemented by subsequently shifting the 16-bit results of the idiom by $s - 16$, as illustrated by the following code:

```
s16 x[N], y[N], z[N]; /* 16-byte aligned */
...
for (i = 0; i < N; i++) {
  x[i] = (y[i] * z[i]) >> 18;
}
```

Multiplying and shifting the operands after sign extension is an idiom that shifts the high word of the product two bits to the right, enabling generation of the following compact eight-way SIMD parallel code:

```
L: movdqa xmm0,    y[eax]   ; load  8 words from y
   pmulhw xmm0,    z[eax]   ; mult. 8 words from z
   psraw  xmm0,    2        ; shift 8 words to right
   movdqa x[eax],  xmm0     ; store 8 words into x
   add    eax,     16       ;
   cmp    eax,     ecx      ;
   jb     L                 ; looping logic
```

Even a mixed-type loop that stores the 32-bit result of multiplying two word operands can be vectorized by combining the results of the lower and higher multiplication instructions. The low word is always computed with the instruction pmullw, while either pmulhuw or pmulhw is used for the high word, depending on whether both word operands are involved in either a zero extension or sign extension, respectively, before multiplication. Both words are then combined by means of a data movement instruction. In the following example, the product of two word operands after sign extension is stored into a doubleword array:

```
s16 u[N];
s32 v[N]; /* both 16-byte aligned */
...
for (i = 0; i < N; i++) {
  v[i] = u[i] * u[i];
}
```

Recognizing the arithmetic idiom in this mixed-type loop gives rise to the following eight-way SIMD parallel code. Note that two data movement instructions are required to store the results back into array v to keep up with the vector length (vl = 8).

```
L: movdqa    xmm0,       u[eax]      ; load 8 words from u
   movdqa    xmm1,       xmm0        ; copy 8 words
   pmulhw    xmm0,       xmm0        ; multiply high
   pmullw    xmm1,       xmm1        ; multiply low
   movdqa    xmm2,       xmm1        ; combine
   punpckhwd xmm1,       xmm0        ;   products
   punpcklwd xmm2,       xmm0        ;     into 2x4 doublewords
   movdqa    v[2*eax],   xmm2        ; store low  4 doublewords
   movdqa    v[2*eax+16], xmm1       ;   and high 4 doublewords
   add       eax,        16          ;   into v
   cmp       eax,        ecx         ;
   jb        L                       ; looping logic
```

An averaging computation such as $(x[i]+y[i]+1)>>1$ is vectorized with packed bytes or packed words as vector data type using the arithmetic instruction `pavgb` or `pavgw`, respectively. An example follows:

```
u8 x[N], y[N];   /* 16-byte aligned */
...
for (i = 0; i < N; i++) {
  x[i] = (x[i] + y[i] + 1) >> 1;
}
```

The idiom in this loop can be directly mapped onto a single instruction:

```
L: movdqa xmm0,    x[eax]  ; load     16 bytes from x
   pavgb  xmm0,    y[eax]  ; average 16 bytes from y
   movdqa x[eax], xmm0     ; store    16 bytes into x
   add    eax,     16      ;
   cmp    eax,     ecx     ;
   jb     L                ; looping logic
```

The average idiom can be generalized by observing that expression $(a[i]+c)>>1$ for a constant $c \geq 1$ within the data type range can be vectorized similarly by rewriting this expression into $(a[i]+(c-1)+1)>>1$ first.

Reduction Idioms

As discussed in Chapter 5, the data type of the reduction variable must generally match the data type of the individual elements in the vector data type. Two idiomatic exceptions are formed by accumulating the product of two signed word operands into a signed doubleword and accumulating the absolute differences of unsigned byte operands into a word or doubleword, which can easily be implemented using the arithmetic instructions `pmaddwd` and `psadbw`, respectively. In particular, recognition of the latter idiom can yield quite compact vector code, as illustrated by the following loop:

```
u8 x[N], y[N]; /* 16-byte aligned */
...
s32 red = 0;
for (i = 0; i < N; i++) {
  s32 temp = x[i] - y[i];
  if (temp < 0) temp = -temp;
  red += temp;
}
```

In this fragment, the operator

```
ABSs32(temp)
```

is recognized first, followed by forward substitution of `temp` into

$$ABS_{s32}(((s32)x[i])-((s32)y[i]))$$

These transformations subsequently expose the accumulation of absolute differences, which is compactly vectorized as follows:

```
      pxor   xmm0, xmm0      ; setup zero
L:    movdqa xmm1, x[eax]    ; accumulate sum of 16
      psadbw xmm1, y[eax]    ;    absolute differences as
      paddd  xmm0, xmm1      ;    words w0/w4 into
      add    eax,  16        ;    doublewords d0/d2 (!)
      cmp    eax,  ecx       ;
      jb     L               ; looping logic
                             ;
      movdqa xmm1, xmm0      ; copy  |--|d2|--|d0|
      psrldq xmm1, 8         ; shift |--|--|--|d2|
      paddd  xmm0, xmm1      ; add
      movd   ecx,  xmm0      ;
      mov    red,  ecx       ;
```

Because each pair of words computed by `psadbw` accumulates into doubleword zero and two in `xmm0`, a single addition suffices to compute the final sum. This example also illustrates how a stepwise approach to idiom recognition enables the compiler to bridge the semantic gap between high-level programming constructs on one hand and low-level idiomatic instructions on the other hand. Such a stepwise approach also forms the basis for detecting saturation idioms, as discussed in the next section.

Saturation Idioms

Due to the lack of support for saturation arithmetic in the C programming language, saturation operations must be coded in a relatively obscure way, where conditional constructs explicitly saturate the values obtained with conventional wrap-around arithmetic. Operator overloading of C++ (Stroustrup 1991) can hide some of these implementation details from the programmer, but ultimately all details are visible to the compiler. As a result, a semantic gap arises between the elaborate high-level programming constructs that are used for saturation arithmetic and the compact low-level saturation instructions that can be used to implement these constructs in an efficient manner. For example, Chapter 1 demonstrates the performance advantages of mapping the sequential code that follows at the left-hand side into the saturation instructions shown at the right-hand side.

```
u16 x[N], y[N], z[N];
...
for (i = 0; i < N; i++) {
  s32 t = x[i] + y[i];
  z[i] = (t <= 65535)
       ? t : 65535;
}
```

```
L: movdqa  xmm0,   x[eax]
   paddusw xmm0,   y[eax]
   movdqa  z[eax], xmm0
   add     eax,    16
   cmp     eax,    ecx
   jb      L
```

how?

→

This section discusses how the compiler can achieve such a translation without directly resorting to high-level pattern matching. A stepwise methodology that bridges the semantic gap with a number of fine-grained rewriting rules (Bik et al. 2002a) is presented. These rules, combined with traditional compiler optimizations, first rewrite saturation constructs into a uniform intermediate representation. Subsequently, constructs that implement saturation arithmetic are easily recognized and exploited in MIN/MAX operators that result in this intermediate representation. Validity tests for the rewriting rules are formulated using the ϕ_t-condition on an expression e, introduced in Chapter 5. For convenience, the definition of this condition is repeated in the following, where x_t denotes an arbitrary expression with data type t, V_t denotes the data type range of t, and c denotes a literal constant:

$$\phi_t(e) = \text{true iff. either} \begin{cases} e \text{ of the form } (u32)x_t, & t \in \{u8,u16\} \\ e \text{ of the form } (s32)x_t, & t \in \{u8,u16,s8,s16\} \\ e \text{ of the form } c, & c \in V_t \end{cases}$$

Rewriting Rules

The original program is converted into a uniform intermediate representation by recognizing MIN/MAX operators as explained in Chapter 3 and moving additive operators into MIN/MAX operators if this rewriting is useful (it may expose a saturation operation) and valid (it preserves semantics). Rewriting rules that move an addition or subtraction into signed MIN/MAX operators are shown as follows, where x denotes an arbitrary expression, and c and d denote literal constants:

$$d +_{s32} \text{MIN}_{s32}(x, c) \quad \rightarrow \quad \text{MIN}_{s32}(d +_{s32} x, d+c)$$
$$d +_{s32} \text{MAX}_{s32}(x, c) \quad \rightarrow \quad \text{MAX}_{s32}(d +_{s32} x, d+c)$$
$$d -_{s32} \text{MIN}_{s32}(x, c) \quad \rightarrow \quad \text{MAX}_{s32}(d -_{s32} x, d-c)$$
$$d -_{s32} \text{MAX}_{s32}(x, c) \quad \rightarrow \quad \text{MIN}_{s32}(d -_{s32} x, d-c)$$

These rewriting rules are useful if the resulting literal constant $d \pm c$ is equal to 127, 255, 32,767 or 65,535 for a resulting MIN operator, or −32,768, −128 or 0 for a resulting MAX operator. A conservative but practical validity test is to combine the usefulness test with the tests

$$\phi_{u8}(x) \vee \phi_{u16}(x) \vee \phi_{s8}(x) \vee \phi_{s16}(x)$$

and $-65,535 \le d \le 65,535$. These validity tests prevent, for example, rewriting an expression

```
1 +s32 MINs32(x, 0x7fffffff)
```

that always yields 1+x into the following expression that always evaluates to the second argument:

```
MINs32(x +s32 1, 0x80000000)
```

Rewriting rules for moving an addition or subtraction into unsigned MIN/MAX operators are quite similar, although a signed MIN/MAX operator must be used in the replacing expressions if operands can become negative. The following rewriting rules are applied if the new constant is equal to 255 or 65,535 for a resulting MIN operator, or 0 for a resulting MAX operator and, additionally, $0 \le d \le 65,535$ and $\phi_{u8}(x) \vee \phi_{u16}(x)$:

```
d +u32 MINu32(x, c)      →          MINu32(d +u32 x       , d+c)
MAXu32(x, c) -u32 d      →          (u32) MAXs32((s32) x -s32 d, c-d)
d -u32 MINu32(x, c)      →          (u32) MAXs32(d -s32 (s32) x, d-c)
d -u32 MAXu32(x, c)      →          (u32) MINs32(d -s32 (s32) x, d-c)
```

These rewriting rules, together with commutative equivalents, are applied repeatedly to the intermediate representation in combination with the rewriting rules for MIN/MAX idiom recognition and traditional compiler optimizations like constant/copy propagation, forward substitution, constant folding, and expression simplification until no further replacements occur (Aho, Sethi, and Ullman 1986; Appel and Ginsburg 1998; Fischer and LeBlanc 1991; Muchnick 1997; Parsons 1992). The actual saturation idiom recognition then occurs, as explained next.

Unsigned Saturation Arithmetic in Single Clipping

Unsigned saturation addition and subtraction idioms typically arise in single clippings. The expressions shown in the following table, together with commutative equivalents, can be effectively implemented with the given unsigned saturation instructions if the validity tests on the operands are satisfied:

Expression	Saturation	Validity Test
$\text{MIN}_{u32}(x +_{u32} y, \quad 255u)$	paddusb	if $\phi_{u8}(x) \wedge \phi_{u8}(y)$
$\text{MIN}_{s32}(x +_{s32} y, \quad 255\ )$	paddusb	if $\phi_{u8}(x) \wedge \phi_{u8}(y)$
$\text{MAX}_{s32}(x -_{s32} y, \quad 0\ )$	psubusb	if $\phi_{u8}(x) \wedge \phi_{u8}(y)$
$\text{MIN}_{u32}(x +_{u32} y, 65535u)$	paddusw	if $\phi_{u16}(x) \wedge \phi_{u16}(y)$
$\text{MIN}_{s32}(x +_{s32} y, 65535\ )$	paddusw	if $\phi_{u16}(x) \wedge \phi_{u16}(y)$
$\text{MAX}_{s32}(x -_{s32} y, \quad 0\ )$	psubusw	if $\phi_{u16}(x) \wedge \phi_{u16}(y)$

Both signed and unsigned MIN operators can map onto unsigned saturation additions. Making the sign of negative constants explicit (expressing $x + c$ with $c < 0$ as $x - |c|$) increases the probability of finding unsigned saturation subtractions in signed MAX operators. The validity tests ensure that the 32-bit operations implied by the programming language standard may actually be implemented with narrow precision saturation instructions.

Signed Saturation Arithmetic in Double Clipping

Signed saturation addition and subtraction idioms typically arise in double clippings because the result of adding or subtracting two *signed* operands may exceed either the minimum or maximum value of the data type range. The expressions shown in the following table, together with commutative and associative equivalents can effectively be implemented with the given signed saturation instructions if the validity tests on the operands are satisfied.

Expression	Saturation	Validity Test
$\text{MAX}_{s32}(\\ \quad \text{MIN}_{s32}(\text{x} +_{s32} \text{y}, \quad 127),\\ \quad -128)$	paddsb	if $\phi_{s8}(\text{x}) \wedge \phi_{s8}(\text{y})$
$\text{MAX}_{s32}(\\ \quad \text{MIN}_{s32}(\text{x} -_{s32} \text{y}, \quad 127),\\ \quad -128)$	psubsb	if $\phi_{s8}(\text{x}) \wedge \phi_{s8}(\text{y})$
$\text{MAX}_{s32}(\\ \quad \text{MIN}_{s32}(\text{x} +_{s32} \text{y}, 32767),\\ -32768)$	paddsw	if $\phi_{s16}(\text{x}) \wedge \phi_{s16}(\text{y})$
$\text{MAX}_{s32}(\\ \quad \text{MIN}_{s32}(\text{x} -_{s32} \text{y}, 32767),\\ -32768)$	psubsw	if $\phi_{s16}(\text{x}) \wedge \phi_{s16}(\text{y})$

Signed Saturation Arithmetic in Single Clipping

Under certain conditions, as illustrated in Figure 7.1, signed saturation addition and subtraction idioms also arise in single clippings. The expressions and their commutative equivalents, validity tests, and corresponding instructions for packed bytes are shown in the following table:

Expression	Saturation	Validity Test
$\text{MIN}_{s32}(\text{c} +_{s32} \text{x}, \quad 127)$	paddsb	if $\phi_{s8}(\text{x}) \wedge 0 < c \leq 127$
$\text{MAX}_{s32}(\text{c} +_{s32} \text{x}, \quad -128)$	paddsb	if $\phi_{s8}(\text{x}) \wedge -128 \leq c < 0$
$\text{MIN}_{s32}(\text{c} -_{s32} \text{x}, \quad 127)$	psubsb	if $\phi_{s8}(\text{x}) \wedge 0 < c \leq 127$
$\text{MAX}_{s32}(\text{c} -_{s32} \text{x}, \quad -128)$	psubsb	if $\phi_{s8}(\text{x}) \wedge -128 \leq c < 0$

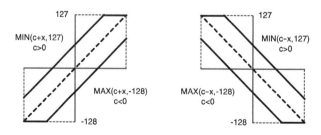

Figure 7.1 Signed Saturation in Single Clipping

Similar expressions and validity tests are used to recognize the idiomatic instructions that operate on packed words, as shown in the following table:

Expression	Saturation	Validity Test
$MIN_{s32}(c +_{s32} x, \quad 32767)$	paddsw	if $\phi_{s16}(x) \ \wedge \ 0 < c \le 32767$
$MAX_{s32}(c +_{s32} x, -32768)$	paddsw	if $\phi_{s16}(x) \ \wedge \ -32768 \le c < 0$
$MIN_{s32}(c -_{s32} x, \quad 32767)$	psubsw	if $\phi_{s16}(x) \ \wedge \ 0 < c \le 32767$
$MAX_{s32}(c -_{s32} x, -32768)$	psubsw	if $\phi_{s16}(x) \ \wedge \ -32768 \le c < 0$

Signed and Unsigned Saturation Conversion in Double Clipping

The pack instructions enable the vectorization of mixed-type loops in which an operand is converted into a narrower data type by means of saturation. The resulting mismatch in vector length is most easily resolved by restricting the operand x in the expressions shown in the following table—together with commutative and associative equivalents—to a direct cast of a unit-stride memory reference with data type s16 or s32 into data type s32 in a loop that is vectorized with packed bytes or packed words as vector data type, respectively.

Expression	Saturation	Validity Test
$MAX_{s32}(MIN_{s32}(x, \quad 127), \quad -128)$	packsswb	if $\phi_{s16}(x)$
$MAX_{s32}(MIN_{s32}(x, \quad 255), \quad 0)$	packuswb	if $\phi_{s16}(x)$
$MAX_{s32}(MIN_{s32}(x, 32767), -32768)$	packssdw	

This restriction on x simplifies code generation, since the memory reference can be loaded by directly feeding two 128-bit packed doublewords or words through the pack instruction into the remaining computation on packed words or bytes, as shown in the example in the following section.

Saturation Examples

The stepwise methodology presented in the previous sections has made recognizing the saturation idiom in the example given in Chapter 1 rather straightforward. First, the MIN operator is recognized in the conditional construct, as follows:

```
u16 x[N], y[N], z[N];
...
for (i = 0; i < N; i++) {
  s32 t = x[i] + y[i];
  z[i] = (t <= 65535) ? t : 65535;  →   z[i] = MIN_{s32}(t, 65535);
}
```

Subsequently, forward substitution is applied to the expression assigned to variable t, where all implicit type conversions have been made explicit in the program text, as shown in the following:

```
for (i = 0; i < N; i++) {
  z[i] = (s16) MIN_{s32}(((s32) x[i]) + ((s32) y[i]), 65535);
}
```

Now, the right-hand side expression is easily recognized as an idiom that can be implemented with the unsigned saturation instruction paddusw, since the following validity test is satisfied:

$$\phi_{u16}(\ ((s32)\ x[i])\ ) \wedge \phi_{u16}(\ ((s32)\ y[i])\ )$$

The detection of a saturation conversion is illustrated by the following example, which converts signed words from array y into unsigned bytes in array x while saturating all values into the data type range:

```
u8  x[N];
s16 y[N]; /* both 16-byte aligned */
...
for (i = 0; i < N; i++) {
  s32 t = y[i];
  if (t < 0)   t = 0;
  if (t > 255) t = 255;
  x[i] = t;
}
```

The compiler first rewrites the complete loop body into the single assignment statement as follows:

```
x[i] = (u8) MIN_{s32}( MAX_{s32}((s32) y[i], 0), 255 );
```

The following vector loop is then generated. In this vector loop, the unit-stride memory reference of the narrower data type is implemented by feeding two 128-bit operands with signed packed words into the pack instruction that generates unsigned packed bytes.

```
L: movdqa   xmm0,    y[2*eax]       ; saturate 16 words from y
   packuswb xmm0,    y[2*eax+16]    ; into      16 bytes
   movdqa   x[eax],  xmm0           ; store     16 bytes into x
   add      eax,     16             ;
   cmp      eax,     edx            ;
   jb       L                       ; looping logic
```

Instruction selection can be made more advanced. Note that the value of any expression recognized as either a narrow precision clipping idiom, discussed in Chapter 5, or saturation idiom remains within the range of the corresponding data type. Extending the definition of the ϕ_t-condition accordingly enables the detection of nested idioms, as illustrated by the following example:

```
u8 u[N], v[N];
...
for (i = 0; i < N; i++) {
  s32 x = (u[i] < 200) ? u[i]+55 : 255;
  if (x > v[i]) v[i] = x;
}
```

First, the MIN and MAX operator are recognized as follows, where all type conversions have been made explicit in the program text.

```
for (i = 0; i < N; i++) {
  s32 x = 55 + MIN_s32(((s32) u[i]), 200);
  v[i] = (u8) MAX_s32(x, ((s32)v[i]));
}
```

Next, the literal constant is moved into the MIN operator. Combined with forward substitution, this operation eventually yields the following rewritten fragment:

```
for (i = 0; i < N; i++) {
  v[i] = (u8) MAX_s32(
              MIN_s32(((s32) u[i]) + 55, 255),
              ((s32)v[i])
           );
}
```

Next, the MIN operator is recognized as an unsigned saturation addition that can be implemented with the instruction `paddusb` because the following validity test is satisfied:

$$\phi_{u8}(((s32)\ u[i])) \wedge \phi_{u8}(55)$$

The extended definition of the ϕ_{u8}-condition observed above satisfies the validity test for recognizing a clipping idiom in the MAX operator, as follows:

$$\phi_{u8}(MINs32(((s32)\ u[i]),\ 200)) \wedge \phi_{u8}(((s32)\ u[i]))$$

Eventually, intra-register vectorization yields the following vector code in which the nested idiom has been fully exploited:

```
      movdqa   xmm1,    _const1   ; expand |55| ... |55|
L:    movdqa   xmm0,    u[eax]    ; load  16 bytes from u
      paddusb  xmm0,    xmm1      ; add   16 bytes and saturate
      pmaxub   xmm0,    v[eax]    ; max   16 bytes from v
      movdqa   v[eax],  xmm0      ; store 16 bytes into v
      add      eax,     16        ;
      cmp      eax,     ecx       ;
      jb       L                  ; looping logic
```

To show how the stepwise methodology performs on a real-world application, intra-register vectorization has been applied to the benchmark GSM appearing in both the MediaBench suite (Lee, Potkonjak, and Mangione-Smith 1997) and the MiBench embedded benchmark suite (Guthaus et al. 2001). This full-rate speech transcoding application defines saturation arithmetic with the following macros:

```
#define MAX_WORD (32767)
#define MIN_WORD ((-32767)-1)

#define GSM_ADD(a, b)((ltmp=(int)(a)+(int)(b)) >= MAX_WORD \
        ? MAX_WORD : ltmp <= MIN_WORD ? MIN_WORD : ltmp)

#define GSM_SUB(a, b)((ltmp=(int)(a)-(int)(b)) >= MAX_WORD \
        ? MAX_WORD : ltmp <= MIN_WORD ? MIN_WORD : ltmp)
```

A typical use like the one that follows is easily recognized by the stepwise methodology as a loop that can be implemented with the instructions `paddsw` and `psubsw` for the two macro occurrences:

```
s16 x[N], y[N], dp[N], dq[N]; /* 16-byte aligned */
...
for (i = 0; i < N; i++) {
  s32 ltmp; /* required by macro */
```

```
      dp[i] = GSM_ADD(x[i], y[i]);
      dq[i] = GSM_SUB(x[i], y[i]);
}
```

Even though macro expansion initially results in a rather obscure intermediate representation of this code, repeatedly applying rewriting rules to this fragment eventually yields the following form for this loop, in which the saturation idioms are easily recognized:

```
for (i = 0; i < N; i++) {
   dp[i] = MIN(MAX(x[i] + y[i], -32768), 32767);
   dq[i] = MIN(MAX(x[i] - y[i], -32768), 32767);
}
```

The vector code that is generated for this loop is as follows:

```
L: movdqa xmm2,   x[eax]   ; load     8 words from x
   movdqa xmm1,   y[eax]   ; load     8 words from y
   movdqa xmm0,   xmm2     ; copy     8 words
   paddsw xmm0,   xmm1     ; add      8 words and saturate
   psubsw xmm2,   xmm1     ; subtract 8 words and saturate
   movdqa dp[eax], xmm0    ; store    8 words into dp
   movdqa dq[eax], xmm2    ; store    8 words into dq
   add    eax,    16       ;
   cmp    eax,    ecx      ;
   jb     L                ; looping logic
```

This section concludes with some performance results for the following important loop in the data decompression application 164.gzip in the industry-standardized benchmark suite Standard Performance Evaluation Corporation 2000[1] (SPEC CPU2000):

```
u16 head[N]; /* 16-byte aligned */
...
for (i = 0; i < N; i++) {
  u32 m = head[i];
  head[i] = (m >= 32768) ? m-32768 : 0;
}
```

First, the loop body is rewritten into the following assignment statement, which exposes an unsigned maximum function:

```
head[i] = (u16) ( MAX_u32(((u32) head[i]), 32768u) - 32768 );
```

Then, the subtraction is moved into the unsigned MAX operator, which requires a signed MAX operator in the replacing expression:

```
head[i] = (u16) MAX_s32(((s32) head[i]) - 32768, 0);
```

---

[1] SPEC® is a registered trademark of the Standard Performance Evaluation Corporation. For more information, go to www.spec.org.

Finally, intra-register vectorization of this loop proceeds by recognizing the unsigned saturation idiom in the signed maximum function, which results in the following eight-way SIMD parallel code:

```
    movdqa  xmm0,      _const     ; expand   8 words with 32768
L:  movdqa  xmm1,      head[eax]  ; load     8 words from head
    psubusw xmm1,      xmm0       ; subtract 8 words and saturate
    movdqa  head[eax], xmm1       ; store    8 words into head
    add     eax,       16         ;
    cmp     eax,       ecx        ;
    jb      L                     ; looping logic
```

Figure 7.2 plots the execution times of a sequential and vectorized version on a 3-gigahertz Pentium 4 processor for increasing values of N, obtained by running the loop repeatedly and dividing the total run time accordingly. The corresponding speedup is shown in the same figure using a secondary y axis. The speedup steadily increases up to eight for N = 4K, after which the size of the L1 cache becomes a restricting factor. The impact of the performance improvements on the application as a whole, where N = 32K, is shown in Chapter 9.

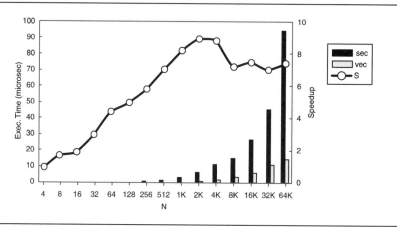

Figure 7.2   Saturation Performance—3-Gigahertz Pentium® 4 Processor

Search Loops

Loops that are not well-behaved may still be amenable to optimization with multimedia extensions (Zhou and Ross 2002). In particular, loops that iterate until a certain condition on the input data is met can often exploit SIMD parallelism during the search. Consider, for example, the following function:

```
f32 a[N]; /* 16-byte aligned */

s32 search(f32 x) {
  s32 i = 0;
  for (i = 0; i < N; i++) {
    if (a[i] == x) {
      return i;
    }
  }
  return -1; /* not found */
}
```

The search loop in this function can be vectorized as follows. First, four elements of array a are simultaneously compared against scalar expanded values of x with comparison instruction cmpeqps. Next, the resulting 128-bit mask is converted into a 4-bit mask in a general-purpose register with data movement instruction movmskps, which enables executing a single conditional branch based on the outcome of four comparisons. While all tests fail, i is incremented by four and the next four elements of array a are considered. As soon as one of the tests succeeds, however, the loop is exited. At that stage, the final value of the loop index that must be fed into the return statement can be constructed as $i + i - 1$, where i denotes the least significant nonzero bit in the 4-bit mask—the first of the last four iterations for which the comparison succeeded. This correspondence is illustrated in the following table:

mask	i	mask	i	mask	i	mask	i
0000	-	0100	3	1000	4	1100	3
0001	1	0101	1	1001	1	1101	1
0010	2	0110	2	1010	2	1110	2
0011	1	0111	1	1011	1	1111	1

Rather than scanning for this first nonzero bit at run time, $i - 1$ can be quickly computed as fbit[mask] using the following 16-entry lookup table:

```
static const s32 fbit[] = { 0,0,1,0,
                            2,0,1,0,
                            3,0,1,0,
                            2,0,1,0 };
```

The following is an implementation of this scheme:

```
     xor        eax,  eax          ; i = 0;
     movss      xmm1, [ebp+8]      ;
     shufps     xmm1, xmm1, 0      ; expand scalar x
L:   movaps     xmm0, a[4*eax]     ; load      4 floats from a
     cmpeqps    xmm0, xmm1         ; compare   4 floats with x
     movmskps   ebx,  xmm1         ; construct 4-bit mask
     test       ebx,  ebx          ; if any set
     jne        E                  ;   goto exit
     add        eax,  4            ;
     cmp        eax,  ecx          ;
     jb         L                  ; looping logic
     ...                           ;
     mov        eax,  -1           ; not found
     jmp        R                  ;
E:   add        eax,  fbit[4*ebx]  ; found
R:   ...                           ;
     ret                           ; return sequence
```

Figure 7.3 compares execution times on a 3-gigahertz Pentium 4 processor, obtained by calling the function repeatedly and dividing the total run time accordingly, of a sequential version of function search() and the vectorized version shown above for fixed N = 32 and varying positions of the first element equal to x, where position 32 indicates that no element equals x. The corresponding speedup, shown in the same figure using a secondary y axis, reveals the potential benefits of vectorizing search loops. For this particular case, reducing the number of conditional branches that are executed with four-way SIMD parallelism already becomes profitable when the search loops iterate only twice. Similar forms of search loops can be vectorized in the same manner using one of the instructions movmsk[ps,pd] or pmovmskb to move a 128-bit mask into a general-purpose register. For the latter instruction, run-time scanning for the least significant nonzero bit in the 16-bit mask may be preferable over using a 64K-entry lookup table fbit[]. Note that, although sequential cleanup loops generally avoid out-of-bounds comparisons when the vector length does not evenly divide a trip count that does not exceed input data length, some care must be taken to avoid reading past the end of data structures for search loops that instead rely on sentinel values to flag the end of input data.

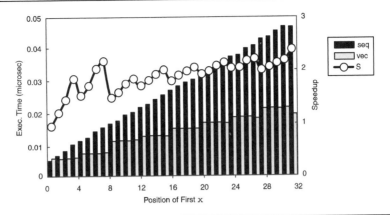

Figure 7.3   Search-Loop Performance—3-Gigahertz Pentium® 4 Processor

Complex Data

To simplify programming with complex numbers, the C99 standard (ISO 1999) extended the basic data types of the C programming language with two built-in complex data types, for which c32 and c64 were introduced as shorthand in Chapter 3. This section shows that some SSE3 instructions are particularly useful to optimize numerical programs that operate on the complex data types.

Complex Numbers

A *complex number* $c \in \mathbb{C}$ has the form

$$c = x + y \cdot i$$

where $x, y \in \mathbb{R}$ denote the *real part* and the *imaginary part*, respectively. Common operations on complex numbers are addition, subtraction, multiplication, division, and the complex conjugate. Two complex numbers $c, c' \in \mathbb{C}$ are added or subtracted as follows:

$$c + c' = (x + y \cdot i) + (x' + y' \cdot i) = (x + x') + (y + y') \cdot i$$
$$c - c' = (x + y \cdot i) - (x' + y' \cdot i) = (x - x') + (y - y') \cdot i$$

The product of two complex numbers $c, c' \in \mathbb{C}$ is computed using the following formula for multiplication:

$$c \cdot c' = (x + y \cdot i) \cdot (x' + y' \cdot i) = (x \cdot x' - y \cdot y') + (x \cdot y' + y \cdot x') \cdot i$$

Division of two complex numbers $c, c' \in \mathbb{C}$ is more elaborate:

$$c / c' = (x + y \cdot i) / (x' + y' \cdot i) = \left(\frac{x \cdot x' + y \cdot y'}{x'^2 + y'^2} \right) + \left(\frac{y \cdot x' - x \cdot y'}{x'^2 + y'^2} \right) \cdot i$$

Finally, the complex conjugate of $c \in \mathbb{C}$, denoted as $\bar{c}$, is obtained by negating the imaginary part, as follows:

$$\bar{c} = \overline{(x + y \cdot i)} = x - y \cdot i$$

The operations are expressed in C99 by applying any of the operators +, -, *, / to operands with data types c32 and c64. The complex conjugate of an expression with data type c32 or c64 is computed with function conjf() or conj(), respectively. The usual arithmetic conversions are extended to include type conversions that first promote an integer or floating-point operand into the complex data type of the other operand.

Single-Precision Complex Data Types

Recall from Chapter 3 that a single-precision complex array

```
c32 c[N];
```

has the data layout in memory illustrated in Figure 7.4, where $c_r[i]$ and $c_i[i]$ denote the real part and imaginary part of the complex element c[i], respectively, and a denotes the first memory address that is used for the array.

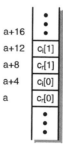

Figure 7.4   Data Layout of a Single-Precision Complex Array

As a result, loading a double quadword from memory address *a* into the 128-bit register xmm0 with the data movement instruction movups or movaps effectively loads two complex numbers into the register, as illustrated here:

xmm0: | $c_i[1]$ | $c_r[1]$ | $c_i[0]$ | $c_r[0]$ |

Having four single-precision floating-point numbers that belong to two complex numbers in a single operand enables the exploitation of SIMD parallelism in complex operations.

Vectorizing a complex addition or subtraction is straightforward, as illustrated by the following loop:

```
c32 c[N], d[N]; /* 16-byte aligned */
...
for (i = 0; i < N; i++) {
  c[i] += d[i]
}
```

Since a complex sum is defined as the pair-wise sums of the real and the imaginary parts, this loop is vectorized as follows where, even though the vector instructions exploit four-way SIMD parallelism, the vector length is actually vl = 2, since each vector iteration handles only two complex numbers simultaneously:

```
L: movaps xmm0,    c[eax]  ; load  2 complex from c
   addps  xmm0,    d[eax]  ; add   2 complex from d
   movaps c[eax], xmm0     ; store 2 complex into c
   add    eax,     16      ;
   cmp    eax,     ecx     ;
   jb     L                ; looping logic
```

Vectorizing a complex multiplication or division is more elaborate due to interaction between the real and imaginary parts of the operands. A multiplication like

```
for (i = 0; i < N; i++) {
  c[i] *= d[i]
}
```

is compactly implemented with the following instructions:

```
L: movaps    xmm0,    c[eax]       ; |c1_i|c1_r|c0_i|c0_r|
   movsldup  xmm2,    d[eax]       ; |d1_r|d1_r|d0_r|d0_r|
   mulps     xmm2,    xmm0         ; 1st cross products
   movshdup  xmm1,    d[eax]       ; |d1_i|d1_i|d0_i|d0_i|
   shufps    xmm0,    xmm0, 177    ; |c1_r|c1_i|c0_r|c0_i|
   mulps     xmm1,    xmm0         ; 2nd cross products
```

```
addsubps   xmm2,    xmm1        ; add/subtract cross products
movaps     c[eax],  xmm2        ; store 2 complex into c
add        eax,     16          ;
cmp        eax,     ecx         ;
jb         L                    ; looping logic
```

Similarly, the following complex division

```
for (i = 0; i < N; i++) {
  c[i] /= d[i]
}
```

can be translated into the following vector code:

```
L: movaps    xmm0,    c[eax]       ; |c1_i|c1_r|c0_i|c0_r|
   movaps    xmm2,    d[eax]       ; |d1_i|d1_r|d0_i|d0_r|
   mulps     xmm2,    xmm2         ; 1st cross products
   movsldup  xmm3,    d[eax]       ; |d1_r|d1_r|d0_r|d0_r|
   haddps    xmm2,    xmm2         ; sum cross products
   unpcklps  xmm2,    xmm2         ;          and expand
   movshdup  xmm1,    d[eax]       ; |d1_i|d1_i|d0_i|d0_i|
   mulps     xmm1,    xmm0         ; 2nd cross products
   shufps    xmm0,    xmm0, 177    ; |c1_r|c1_i|c0_r|c0_i|
   mulps     xmm3,    xmm0         ;
   addsubps  xmm3,    xmm1         ; add/subtract cross products
   shufps    xmm3,    xmm3, 177    ;          and rearrange
   divps     xmm3,    xmm2         ; divide results
   movaps    c[eax],  xmm3         ; store 2 complex into c
   add       eax,     16           ;
   cmp       eax,     ecx          ;
   jb        L                     ; looping logic
```

The complex conjugate function `conjf()` is vectorized efficiently by simply swapping the sign bit of the two imaginary parts with an `xorps` instruction. Promotion of any operand with the data type `f32` into data type `c32` is vectorized by means of unpack instructions. The fp:precision mode also provides more accurate implementations of all single-precision complex operators that trade some performance for higher precision during intermediate computations.

As usual, all loop invariant computations are moved to the vector prelude, as illustrated with the following C implementation of the Level 1 BLAS single-precision complex kernel CAXPY (Lawson et al. 1979a and 1979b).

```
c32 cx[N], cy[N], ca; /* arrays are 16-byte aligned */
...
for (i = 0; i < N; i++) {
  cy[i] += ca * cx[i]
}
```

The two terms in the cross products arising from the single-precision complex scalar ca can already have been set up in the prelude, as follows:

```
       movss     xmm0,     ca          ; | -- | -- | -- |ca_r|
       movss     xmm1,     ca+4        ; | -- | -- | -- |ca_i|
       unpcklps  xmm0,     xmm1        ; | -- | -- |ca_i|ca_r|
       shufps    xmm0,     xmm0, 68    ; |ca_i|ca_r|ca_i|ca_r|
       movaps    xmm1,     xmm0        ;
       shufps    xmm1,     xmm1, 177   ; |ca_r|ca_i|ca_r|ca_i|
  L:   movsldup  xmm2,     cx[eax]     ; |cx1r|cx1r|cx0r|cx0r|
       mulps     xmm2,     xmm0        ; 1st cross products
       movshdup  xmm3,     cx[eax]     ; |cx1i|cx1i|cx0i|cx0i|
       mulps     xmm3,     xmm1        ; 2nd cross products
       addsubps  xmm2,     xmm3        ; add/subtract cross products
       addps     xmm2,     cy[eax]     ; add   2 complex from cy
       movaps    cy[eax],  xmm2        ; store 2 complex into cy
       add       eax,      16          ;
       cmp       eax,      ecx         ;
       jb        L                     ; looping logic
```

Figure 7.5 plots the execution times of a sequential, FPU-based version of CAXPY and the vectorized version shown above on a 2.8-gigahertz Pentium 4 processor with HT Technology for increasing values of N, obtained by running the kernel repeatedly and dividing the total run time accordingly. The corresponding speedup is shown in the same figure using a secondary y axis. The figure clearly reveals that SSE3 instructions allow for effective intra-register vectorization that already exhibits speedup for $N \geq 2$.

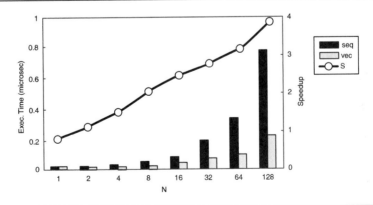

Figure 7.5   CAXPY Performance2.8-Gigahertz Pentium® 4 with HT Technology

Double-Precision Complex Data Types

A double-precision complex array stored at memory address a

```
c64 c[N];
```

has the data layout in memory illustrated in Figure 7.6.

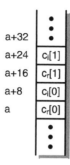

Figure 7.6   Data Layout of a Double-Precision Complex Array

Hence, loading a double quadword from memory address a into the 128-bit register xmm0 with the data movement instruction movupd or movapd loads only one complex number into the register, as illustrated:

xmm0 : | $c_i[0]$ | $c_r[0]$ |

Similar to the situation in the previous section, having two double-precision floating-point numbers that belong to one complex number in a single operand enables exploiting SIMD parallelism in complex operations. The following example

```
c64 c[N], d[N], e[N]; /* 16-byte aligned */
...
for (i = 0; i < N; i++) {
  c[i] += d[i] * e[i];
}
```

can be implemented as follows:

```
L: movddup   xmm2,   e[eax]   ; | e_r | e_r |
   movddup   xmm1,   e[eax+8] ; | e_i | e_i |
   movapd    xmm0,   d[eax]   ; | d_i | d_r |
   mulpd     xmm2,   xmm0     ; 1st cross products
   shufpd    xmm0,   xmm0, 1  ; | d_r | d_i |
   mulpd     xmm1,   xmm0     ; 1nd cross products
```

```
addsubpd xmm2,    xmm1      ; add/subtract cross products
addpd    xmm2,    c[eax]    ; add    one complex from c
movapd   c[eax],  xmm2      ; store one complex into c
add      eax,     16        ;
cmp      eax,     ecx       ;
jb       L                  ; looping logic (iterates N times)
```

Similar instruction sequences can be given for the other complex operations. Note that even though the resulting code exploits two-way SIMD parallelism, the loop is not actually vectorized since only one complex data element is processed at a time ($vl = 1$). As such, implementing double-precision complex operations by means of multimedia instructions is actually more a form of advanced instruction selection (Smith, Bik, and Tian 2004).

Memory Hierarchy Optimizations

Computational optimizations have little impact on code fragments that spend most of the execution time waiting for operands to arrive from memory. Therefore, effective intra-register vectorization must usually be supplemented with optimizations that improve memory hierarchy utilization. Such memory optimizations can be subdivided into high-level optimizations, typically based on loop restructuring, and low-level optimizations that use machine-dependent methods to enhance memory performance.

High-Level Optimizations

Because memory hierarchies exploit the principle of locality of reference, compiler optimizations for improving memory hierarchy utilization focus mainly on enhancing the locality characteristics of a program. Although a detailed description of compiler optimizations for the memory hierarchy would be beyond the scope of this book, this section briefly reviews some loop optimizations that are particularly useful in the context of intra-register vectorization. For more information, see Allen and Kennedy (2002, Chapter 9); Appel and Ginsburg (1998, Chapter 21); Gallivan, Jalby, and Gannon (1988); Muchnick (1997, Chapter 20); and Wolfe (1996, Chapter 10).

One of the most important high-level transformations is *loop interchanging* (Allen and Kennedy 2002, Padua and Wolfe 1986, Wolfe 1996, Zima and Chapman 1990), which swaps two adjacent control statements in a nested loop. This transformation is valid if *none* of the data dependences has a data dependence direction vector of the form

$$(=,...,=,\underset{\smile}{<,>},...)$$

in the marked position of the two loops, since that would violate an essential execution order constraint on the statement instances. Loop interchanging serves many purposes such as changing loop-carried behavior of data dependences, moving loops with high trip counts to a higher or lower nesting depth, changing spatial and temporal locality characteristics, and increasing the number of unit-stride memory references.

An example of the latter modification is shown below, where loop interchanging changes a non-unit-stride memory reference caused by row-major order storage of the two-dimensional array a into a unit-stride memory reference.

```
for (j = 0; j < N; j++) {          for (i = 0; i < M; i++) {
  for (i = 0; i < M; i++) {          for (j = 0; j < N; j++) {
    a[i][j] = 0;          →            a[i][j] = 0;
  }                                  }
}                                  }
```

The resulting nested loop exhibits better spatial locality, which enables better cache utilization, while the unit-stride memory reference is more amenable to effective vectorization than the non-unit-stride memory reference in the original nested loop. Not surprisingly, therefore, most vectorizing compilers include at least loop interchanging in their assortment of loop transformations. The observation that any combination of loop interchanging or loop permutation, skewing, and reversal (Allen and Kennedy 2002, Banerjee 1993, Wolfe 1986 and 1996), including the wave-front method (Lamport 1974) as special case, can actually be represented by a single *unimodular transformation* (Ancourt and Irigoin 1991, Banerjee 1990 and 1993, Dowling 1990, Wolf and Lam 1991a and 1991b, Wolfe 1996) prompted a step forward from the ad-hoc loop restructuring methods used in early compilers. This observation, later also generalized into non-singular transformations, eliminates the need to consider the order, validity, and usefulness of each elementary transformation in isolation (Ayguadé and Torres 1993, Barnett and Lengauer 1992, Li and Pingali 1992a and 1992b, Xue 1994). Instead, the compiler simply constructs a single transformation that simultaneously optimizes locality, vector, parallel, and/or other characteristics of a nested loop.

Another important high-level transformation that was already introduced to isolate data dependence cycles during vectorization is loop distribution, or *loop fission*. This transformation can also be used to reduce the amount of data that is referenced in each resulting loop, which may reduce competition for cache space and other hardware resources. The opposite transformation, *loop fusion*, combines two lexically adjacent loops with a similar control structure into one loop (Allen and Kennedy 2002, Loveman 1977, Padua and Wolfe 1986, Wolfe 1996). Fusing loops that reference the same data enhances temporal locality. Moreover, *loop blocking*, also called *loop tiling*, combines strip mining with loop interchanging to obtain a restructured nested loop in which inner loops operate on small tiles of data that exhibit enhanced temporal and spatial locality in the outer loops (Allen and Kennedy 2002, Wolfe 1996).

Vector Register Reuse

The ratio of arithmetic operations over memory operations in a vector loop can sometimes be improved by exposing more opportunities for reusing vector registers (Dongarra and Eisenstat 1984), as illustrated by the following nested loop:

```
for (i = 0; i < M; i++) {
  for (j = 0; j < N; j++) {
    b[j] += a[i][j];
  }
}
```

Since only unit-stride memory references appear in the innermost loop, the j-loop is easily vectorized as follows:

```
for (i = 0; i < M; i++) {
  for (j = 0; j < N; j += vl) {
    b[j:j+vl-1:1] += a[i][j:j+vl-1:1];
  }
}
```

Applying loop interchanging after this form of strip mining enables the reuse of a vector register for all iterations of the i-loop, as sketched in the following, with the direct use of the 128-bit register xmm0. The resulting code performs only one vector load operation per vector addition, compared to three vector load-and-store operations per vector addition in the code shown above.

```
for (j = 0; j < N; j += vl) {
  xmm0 = b[j:j+vl-1:1];
  for (i = 0; i < M; i++) {
    xmm0 += a[i][j:j+vl-1:1];
  }
  b[j:j+vl-1:1] = xmm0;
}
```

Figure 7.7 compares the speedup on a 3-gigahertz Pentium 4 processor of this optimized version over a sequential version with the speedup of the original vectorized version for single-precision floating-point arrays with a fixed value N = 4,096 and varying values for M. The comparison was based on execution times that were obtained by running the nested loop repeatedly and dividing the total run time accordingly. For M = 1, the two versions are identical, while for M = 32, the 256-kilobyte L2 cache size becomes the dominating factor. For intermediate values of M, however, optimizing the loop nest for vector register reuse is clearly advantageous.

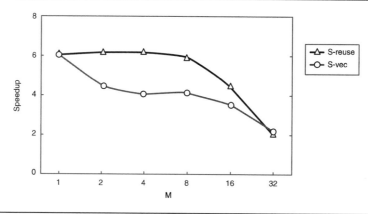

Figure 7.7   Register Reuse Speedup3-Gigahertz Pentium® 4 Processor

Applying such a transformation directly to a nested loop in which the outer loop can be vectorized, without going through all intermediate transformations, is sometimes referred to as *outer loop vectorization* (Wolfe 1996, Chapter 12).

Reusing a vector register that implements a reduction has the advantage that the prelude and postlude of the reduction is executed fewer times, as illustrated with the following nested loop that sums all dot products into a single accumulator `red`:

```
f64 a[M][N], b[N]; /* 16-byte aligned */
...
f64 red = 0;
for (i = 0; i < M; i++) {
  for (j = 0; j < N; j++) {
    red += a[i][j] * b[j];
  }
}
```

Vectorizing the j-loop in isolation results in code that executes the prelude and postlude of the reduction M times. Reusing the vector register that implements the reduction yields code in which the prelude and postlude are executed only once, as shown in the following, for constant trip counts M = N = 50:

```
        xor     ecx, ecx        ; i = 0
        xorpd   xmm0, xmm0      ; setup zero
L2:     ...                     ; set ebx to next row of a
        xor     eax, eax        ; j = 0
L1:     movapd  xmm1, a[ebx+eax*8]  ; load      2 doubles from a
        mulpd   xmm1, b[eax*8]  ; multiply 2 doubles from b
        addpd   xmm0, xmm1      ; accumulate
        add     eax, 2          ;
        cmp     eax, 50         ;
        jb      L1              ; looping logic (j-loop)
        ...                     ;
        add     ecx, 1          ;
        cmp     ecx, 50         ;
        jb      L2              ; looping logic (i-loop)
                                ;
        haddpd  xmm0, xmm0      ; store final sum
        movsd   red, xmm0       ;  into red
```

Opportunities for improving memory hierarchy utilization in a loop generally increase with nesting depth. Not surprisingly, therefore, the progression of the standardization of the important Basic Linear Algebra Subroutines (BLAS) from Level 1 BLAS vector-vector operations, to Level 2 BLAS matrix-vector operations and Level 3 BLAS matrix-matrix operations was mainly driven by exposing more opportunities to exploit memory hierarchies—vector register and cache reuse (Dongarra et al. 1988a, 1998b, 1990a, 1990b, 1991 and Lawson et al. 1979a and 1979b).

Low-Level Optimizations

The cacheability control instructions minimize cache pollution for streaming data—non-temporal data that is referenced once and not re-used in the immediate future. The compiler can take advantage of these instructions by replacing an aligned instruction that stores a large volume of non-temporal data by one of the instructions `movntps`, `movntpd`, or `movntdq`. Potential performance improvements that result from using these streaming stores are illustrated by the following four kernels from the Stream benchmark (McCalpin 1991):

```
f64 a[HUGE], b[HUGE], c[HUGE]; /* all 16-byte aligned */
...
/* copy */
for (j = 0; j < HUGE; j++) {
  c[j] = a[j];
}
...
/* scale */
for (j = 0; j < HUGE; j++) {
  b[j] = scalar * c[j];
}
...
/* add */
for (j = 0; j < HUGE; j++) {
  c[j] = a[j] + b[j];
}
...
/* triad */
for (j = 0; j < HUGE; j++) {
  a[j] = b[j] + scalar * c[j];
}
```

The high trip count—the value HUGE = 10,000,000 was used in the benchmark—effectively makes all arrays streaming data. As a result, the Intel C/C++ Compiler uses streaming stores for all vector store operations, as illustrated here, for the first kernel:

```
L: movapd  xmm0,    a[eax]   ; load  2 doubles from a
   movntpd c[eax], xmm0      ; store 2 doubles into c (streaming)
   add     eax,     16       ;
   cmp     eax,     ecx      ;
   jb      L                 ; looping logic
```

Figure 7.8 compares the performance in megabytes per second on a 3-gigahertz Pentium 4 processor of a sequential, vector, and streaming vector version of this benchmark. The results clearly reveal that intra-register vectorization becomes effective only after the non-temporal data movement instruction is exploited. For loops with a statically unknown trip count, static analysis or profile-guided optimization can be used to estimate the trip count, which is subsequently used to identify potential streaming data in a program.

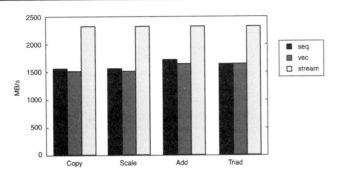

Figure 7.8   Stream Performance—3-Gigahertz Pentium® 4 Processor

Prefetch instructions can hide the latency of cache misses by preloading data ahead of time without actually stalling the processor. The insertion of explicit prefetch instructions is called *software prefetching* (Callahan, Kennedy, and Porterfield 1991; Allen and Kennedy 2002, Chapter 9). Because each prefetch instruction loads one cache line, redundant or conditionally executed prefetching can be avoided by unrolling a vector loop $C/16$-fold for a cache line size C before inserting prefetch instructions. Consider, for example, the following loop:

```
f32 a[N], b[N], c[N]; /* all 16-byte aligned */
...
for (i = 0; i < N; i++) {
  a[i] = b[i] + c[i];
}
```

When this code is compiled specifically for the Pentium III processor, which supports a cache line size $C = 32$, two-fold unrolling of the vector loop unifies the amount of data that is accessed by each vector iteration with the cache line size. In the vector code shown below, each prefetch instruction loads a cache line with elements of array a or b that are accessed by future iterations of the unrolled vector loop.

As illustrated in Figure 7.9, prefetch distance 64 loads a cache line that is used two unrolled-vector iterations later.

```
L: movaps       xmm0,        b[eax]      ; load  4 floats from b
   movaps       xmm1,        b[eax+16]   ; load  4 floats from b
   addps        xmm0,        c[eax]      ; add   4 floats from c
   addps        xmm1,        c[eax+16]   ; add   4 floats from c
   prefetchnta b[eax+64]                 ; prefetch cache line for b
   prefetchnta c[eax+64]                 ; prefetch cache line for c
   movaps       a[eax],      xmm0        ; store 4 floats into a
   movaps       a[eax+16],   xmm1        ; store 4 floats into a
   add          eax,         32          ;
   cmp          eax,         ecx         ;
   jb           L                        ; looping logic
```

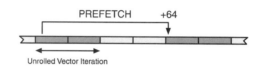

Figure 7.9   Prefetch Distance—32-Byte Cache Line

Selecting an appropriate prefetch distance (64 in the example) and locality hint (one of t0, t1, t2, or nta) can have a substantial impact on the effectiveness of prefetching. A prefetch distance that is either too large or too small or a hint that specifies a cache level that is either too near or too far unnecessarily increases memory traffic either with cache lines that are evicted before actually used or instruction bandwidth with prefetch instructions that are of little use to subsequently stalled load instructions. Advanced hardware prefetching in the Intel NetBurst® microarchitecture, discussed in Chapter 2, has, however, significantly diminished the importance of software prefetching for the current generation of IA-32 processors.

Chapter 8

Vectorization Beyond Loops

The focus in previous chapters has been on exploiting multimedia extensions in innermost loops, since this is typically where most execution time is spent (Booth 1997). As observed by Larsen and Amarasinghe (2000), however, the short vector length supported by most multimedia instruction sets also allows for exploiting more fine-grained SIMD parallelism. Consider, for example, the following straightline code that operates on three 16-byte aligned single-precision floating-point arrays:

S_1: a[0] = b[0] * c[0];
S_2: a[3] = b[3] * c[3];
S_3: a[2] = b[2] * c[2];
S_4: a[1] = b[1] * c[1];

The statement reordering S_1; S_4; S_3; S_2 is valid; that is, it preserves semantics and reveals that the four statements apply the same operation to operands that are adjacent in memory. Consequently, this straightline code can be implemented with just a few SSE instructions, as follows:

```
movaps xmm0, b     ; load     4 elements from b
mulps  xmm0, c     ; multiply 4 elements with c
movaps a,    xmm0  ; store    4 elements into a
```

Larsen and Amarasinghe proposed an approach where SIMD parallelism is extracted directly from isomorphic statements in straightline code, which are statements that contain the same operations in the same order, possibly combined with the generation of data rearranging instructions for operands that are not adjacent in memory. In this approach, loop vectorization is considered a special case of extracting SIMD parallelism from the body of a loop that has been unrolled by an appropriate unrolling factor.

This chapter presents a simpler approach in which statements that apply identical operations to operands that are or can be easily made adjacent in memory are first converted into explicit loops. Loops that materialize in this manner are subsequently dealt with by the loop vectorization methods presented in earlier chapters. Low trip count loops that remain sequential are eventually unrolled back into straightline code to avoid unnecessary loop overhead. Although potentially less general than the approach of Larsen and Amarasinghe, SIMD parallelism that is found in this manner can usually be implemented without any data-rearranging instructions. The relatively high costs of such instructions in current hardware forces one to choose a scheme that misses some opportunities that ultimately cannot be exploited in an effective way as viable alternative to more powerful approaches. Furthermore, because the loop materialization phase can be implemented and tested independently of the loop vectorization and unrolling phase, the loop-oriented scheme allows for a clean separation of concerns. The latter phase can now be used to deal with loops that appear in the original program as well as loops that materialize from straightline code. Finally, the simplicity of the scheme allows for an efficient implementation that is still quite capable of exploiting fine-grained SIMD parallelism in real-world applications, as demonstrated throughout this chapter.

Loop Materialization

This section presents a framework for *loop materialization*—the conversion of statements in straightline code into explicit loops.

Rollable Statements and Expressions

A chain of consecutive assignment statements

S_1: $\text{lhs}_1 = \text{rhs}_1;$
        $\vdots$
S_n: $\text{lhs}_n = \text{rhs}_n;$

with $n > 1$ is called rollable, denoted by $\Delta_n(S_1,...,S_n)$, if and only if the chains of left-hand side expressions and right-hand side expressions are simultaneously rollable, as follows:

$$\Delta_n(S_1,...,S_n) \Leftrightarrow \Delta_n(\text{lhs}_1,...,\text{lhs}_n) \wedge \Delta_n(\text{rhs}_1,...,\text{rhs}_n)$$

For expressions, recursive rules define the rollable property for a chain of binary or unary arithmetic operators in terms of the operands.

■ For any binary arithmetic operator $\oplus$:

$$\Delta_n(x_1 \oplus y_1,...,x_n \oplus y_n) \Leftrightarrow \Delta_n(x_1,...,x_n) \wedge \Delta_n(y_1,...,y_n)$$

■ For any unary arithmetic operator $\ominus$:

$$\Delta_n(\ominus x_1,...,\ominus x_n) \Leftrightarrow \Delta_n(x_1,...,x_n)$$

The recursive definition of the rollable property terminates in an expression chain that satisfies either a Δ_n^E- or Δ_n^A-property, as follows:

■ For any other chain of expressions $e_1,...,e_k$:

$$\Delta_n(e_1,...,e_n) \Leftrightarrow \Delta_n^E(e_1,...,e_n) \vee \Delta_n^A(e_1,...,e_n)$$

The Δ_n^E-property holds for any chain of *equivalent* constants or memory references, such as $\Delta_2^E(3.14, 3.14)$, $\Delta_2^E(\text{xval}, \text{xval})$, and $\Delta_2^E(\text{a[0]}, \text{a[0]})$. The Δ_n^A-property holds for any chain of *adjacent* memory references—a chain of same-type expressions that satisfy the following equivalences for a certain run-time memory address a, where s denotes the data type size of the expressions.

$$e_1 \equiv \text{Mem}[a : a+s-1]$$
$$\vdots$$
$$e_n \equiv \text{Mem}[a+(n-1)\cdot s : a+n\cdot s-1]$$

The effectiveness of loop materialization strongly depends on the ability of the compiler to evaluate or enforce the Δ_n^A-property. For example, a simple implementation can determine that $\Delta_3^A(\text{a[k]}, \text{a[k+1]}, \text{a[k+2]})$ holds for three adjacent array elements. A more advanced implementation can also see that, for example, $\Delta_3^A(\text{p->x}, \text{p->y}, \text{p->z})$ holds for a *locally invariant* pointer variable p to a structure with three same-type members x, y, and z that are adjacent in the data layout of the structure.

In all cases, however, the address calculations must be locally invariant within the chain. The previous property does not hold, for example, for the chain of right-hand expressions in the following, slightly contrived program fragment, because the value of the pointer variable p varies in the chain:

```
struct cyclic { struct cyclic *x, *y, *z; } *p;
         ...
S₁:      p = p->x;
S₂:      p = p->y;
S₃:      p = p->z;
```

Loop Materialization and Collapsing

If $\Delta_n(S_1,\ldots,S_n)$ with $n > 1$ holds for a chain of consecutive statements, this chain can materialize into a semantically equivalent loop

```
S₁:  lhs₁ = rhs₁;               for (_t = 0; _t < n; _t++) {
      ⋮                   →         τ(S₁,_t);
S_n:  lhs_n = rhs_n;            }
```

where $\tau(S_1,\_t)$ denotes the translation of statement S_1 that replaces each subexpression that was involved in the Δ_n^A-property with a load or store of the corresponding memory location $\text{Mem}[a + \_t \cdot s]$. Note that expressing this translation at source code level can become quite elaborate. If the chain of statements constitutes the loop body of an enveloping well-behaved loop with index i for which the statement instances satisfy the stronger property $\Delta_{n+1}(S_1(i),\ldots,S_n(i),S_1(i+1))$ for any iteration i = i, then loop materialization can be immediately followed by *loop collapsing* (Wolfe 1996, Chapter 9; Padua and Wolfe 1986).

```
      for (i = 0; i < U; i++) {
S₁:      lhs₁ = rhs₁;                     for (i = 0; i < U*n; i++) {
          ⋮                                   τ(S₁,i);
S_n:      lhs_n = rhs_n;          →         }
      }                                    i = U; /* last value (U>0) */
```

This conversion is a generalized form of *loop rerolling* (Zima and Chapman 1990), a transformation that is widely used to convert manually unrolled loops in legacy Fortran code back into a form that is more amenable to analysis and optimization. Sophisticated evaluation of the

Δ_n^A-property makes the combination of loop materialization and collapsing more general than loop rerolling, as illustrated by the following example:

```
        struct { f32 x, y; } a[100];
        ...
        for (i = 0; i < 100; i++) {
S₁:         a[i].x = 0;
S₂:         a[i].y = 0;
        }
```

Since $\Delta_3^A(\texttt{a[i].x}, \texttt{a[i].y}, \texttt{a[i+1].x})$ holds for an adjacent data layout of the array-of-structures (AoS) arrangement, the loop that materializes from the two assignment statements can be collapsed into the enveloping i-loop, as expressed at source code level with a union that linearizes the data structure as whole, as follows:

```
        union { /* a[i].x ≡ lin[2*i], a[i].y ≡ lin[2*i+1] */
            struct { f32 x, y; } a[100];
            f32 lin[200];
        } u;
        ...
        for (i = 0; i < 200; i++) {
S₁:         u.lin[i] = 0;
        }
```

This single unit-stride memory reference is more amenable to effective vectorization by a traditional loop-oriented method than the two non-unit-stride memory references in the original loop.

Inexpensive Loop Materialization

An inexpensive loop materialization method can be implemented as follows. First, the source program is subdivided into maximum chains of consecutive assignment statements. Given such a maximum chain of n statements, the rollable property is evaluated recursively for the chain of left-hand side expressions and the chain of right-hand side expressions. During this recursive evaluation, if the rollable property fails due to some mismatches, the top-level chain is broken into sub-chains at all places that cause mismatches.[1]

---

[1] Ties arising in a chain of expressions like a[0],a[0],a[1] which can be broken according to either $\Delta_2^E(\texttt{a[0]}, \texttt{a[0]})$ or $\Delta_2^A(\texttt{a[0]}, \texttt{a[1]})$, are relatively rare and, for the sake of simplicity, are resolved in favor of the first mismatch.

At this point, instead of re-evaluating the rollable property for the resulting sub-chains at the top levels that already have been visited, where any sub-chain simply inherits the rollable property from its original chain, the recursion continues to evaluate rollable properties for all sub-chains at the expression depth where the recursion detects the most recent mismatches. The recursion eventually terminates when the maximum expression depth has been reached or no further fragmentation can occur. Because each sub-expression is visited only once during this recursive evaluation, the computational requirements of this implementation of loop materialization are proportional to the size of the source program.

Consider, for example, the following chain of assignment statements:

```
S₁:   x = x + a[0];
S₂:   x = x + a[1];
S₃:   x = x + a[2] * y;
S₄:   x = x + a[3] * y;
S₅:   x = x + a[4] * (y+1);
```

Evaluation of $\Delta_5(S_1,S_2,S_3,S_4,S_5)$ starts with assessing the rollable property for the chain of left-hand side expressions. Since Δ_5^E (x, x, x, x, x) holds, the rollable property is then evaluated for the chain of right-hand side expressions. The recursion proceeds into the chain of +-operators and the corresponding chain of left-hand side operands without mismatches. For the chain of right-hand side operands, however, the first mismatch occurs. This mismatch, caused by the *-operator in the last three statements at the current recursion depth, breaks the top chain into $S_1;S_2$ and $S_3;S_4;S_5$. The recursion has reached the maximum expression depth for the first sub-chain, so property $\Delta_2(S_1,S_2)$ can be immediately recorded. For the second sub-chain, however, the recursion proceeds into the chain of right-hand side operands of the *-operator, which causes the top chain to be further broken into $S_3;S_4$ and S_5. Because the maximum expression depth has been reached for the former sub-chain, whereas no further fragmentation is possible for the latter, property $\Delta_2(S_3,S_4)$ is recorded. The recorded rollable properties give rise to the following loop materialization:

```
       for (i = 0; i < 2; i++) {
S₁:       x = x + a[i];
       }
       for (i = 0; i < 2; i++) {
S₃:       x = x + a[2+i] * y;
       }
S₅:   x = x + a[4] * (y+1);
```

Improved Loop Materialization

The rollable property can sometimes be enforced on a chain of assignment statements by program transformations, data layout transformations, or a combination of the two. A simple example of the former appears in the introduction to this chapter. A more elaborate example follows:

```
        s32 z[4];

        void f(void) {
          s32 i, j, k, l;
          ...
S₁:       z[0] = i + 8;
S₂:       z[2] = j + 4;
S₃:       z[1] = k + 9;
S₄:       z[3] = l + 2;
        }
```

Statement reordering $S_1; S_3; S_2; S_4$ is valid and enforces the Δ_4^A-property on the chain of left-hand side expressions. For the left-hand side operands of the +-operator, the Δ_4^A-property can be enforced after this statement reordering by choosing an adjacent data layout for i, k, j, and l, which is possible since the C standard (Kernighan and Ritchie 1988) does not strictly define a stack layout for local variables. The Δ_4^A-property can be enforced on the right-hand side operands by choosing an adjacent data layout for these constants in a read-only array. Combined, these transformations enforce the property $\Delta_4(S_1; S_3; S_2; S_4)$ that enables loop materialization at source-code level, as follows:

```
void f(void) {
  union { /* i≡loc[0], k≡loc[1], j≡loc[2], l≡loc[3] */
    struct { s32 i, k, j, l; } s;
    s32 loc[4];
  } u;
  static const s32 _c[] = { 8, 9, 4, 2 };
  ...
  for (i = 0; i < 4; i++) {
S₁:  z[i] = u.loc[i] + _c[i];
  }
}
```

An aggressively optimizing compiler could try many different valid statement permutations and data layouts in an attempt to extract the most SIMD parallelism from all straightline code regions in a program. In practice, however, slightly modifying the inexpensive method presented in the previous section can enhance the effectiveness of loop materialization while preserving the low computational requirements of the method. If mismatches are found while recursively evaluating the rollable property for a chain of statements, first an attempt is made to repair the mismatches locally with a valid statement reordering or data layout modification, provided that neither of these transformations conflicts with previously established rollable properties. Subsequently, the chain is broken according to all mismatches that could not be easily repaired, and the recursion continues.

Sophisticated Δ_n^A-property evaluation and collapsing loops that materialize from straightline code into enveloping loops form two other important aspects of effective loop materialization. To illustrate both aspects, consider the following program fragment:

```
typedef struct { f32 x, y;      } pair;
typedef struct { pair e[2][2]; } matrix;

void add(matrix *a, f32 s) {
  s32 i, j;
  for (i = 0; i < 2; i++) {
    for (j = 0; j < 2; j++) {
```
S_1:
S_2:
```
      a->e[i][j].x += s;
      a->e[i][j].y += s;
    }
  }
}
```

The loop that materializes from $S_1;S_2$ can be collapsed into *both* enveloping loops, as becomes apparent by completely unrolling the double loop.

```
S₁:  a->e[0][0].x += s;
S₂:  a->e[0][0].y += s;
S₃:  a->e[0][1].x += s;
S₄:  a->e[0][1].y += s;
S₅:  a->e[1][0].x += s;
S₆:  a->e[1][0].y += s;
S₇:  a->e[1][1].x += s;
S₈:  a->e[1][1].y += s;
```

S_1: `a->e[0][0].x += s;`
S_2: `a->e[0][0].y += s;`
S_3: `a->e[0][1].x += s;`
S_4: `a->e[0][1].y += s;`
S_5: `a->e[1][0].x += s;`
S_6: `a->e[1][0].y += s;`
S_7: `a->e[1][1].x += s;`
S_8: `a->e[1][1].y += s;`

If evaluation of the Δ_n^A-property includes various forms of adjacent elements within a structure and around array dimensions, the compiler can use property

$$\Delta_8^4(\,a\text{->}e[0][0].x, a\text{->}e[0][0].y, a\text{->}e[0][1].x, a\text{->}e[0][1].y,$$
$$a\text{->}e[1][0].x, a\text{->}e[1][0].y, a\text{->}e[1][1].x, a\text{->}e[1][1].y\,)$$

to conclude $\Delta_8(S_1;S_2;S_3;S_4;S_5;S_6;S_7;S_8)$. Consequently, a loop with eight iterations materializes from this straightline code at source-code level with a cast of the formal pointer argument, as follows:

```
f32 *linear = (f32) a;
for (i = 0; i < 8; i++) {
  linear[i] += s;
}
```

Independent of whether the loop that materializes from the original fragment is directly collapsed into the enveloping double loop or explicit unrolling into straightline code must first be performed, both versions must ultimately materialize into the single loop shown above, because either format could be used by the programmer.

Performance Considerations

After the loop materialization phase, the compiler applies conventional loop vectorization and unrolling methods to all loops in the resulting program. Low trip-count loops are implemented either with a few efficient SIMD instructions or otherwise fully unrolled into straightline code to avoid unnecessary loop overhead. High trip-count loops usually allow more flexibility in using the more advanced intra-register vectorization methods described in previous chapters or in otherwise selecting an unrolling factor appropriate for the target architecture. Even though the second phase handles loops appearing in the original program as well as loops that materialize from straightline code, this section focuses on some performance considerations that are more prevalent in the latter kind of loops.

Low Trip-Count Loops

Because loops that materialize from straightline code typically have a low trip count, three issues must be carefully dealt with while vectorizing such loops. First, low trip-count loops do not allow for advanced alignment strategies that dynamically peel iterations until access patterns become aligned. Due to the high costs of unaligned data movement instructions, low trip-count loops that are dominated by unaligned memory references should be converted back into straightline code. For example, vectorization of the loop that materializes from the first two statements $S_1;S_2$ in the following fragment is probably more worthwhile than vectorization of the loop that materializes from the last two statements $S_3;S_4$:

```
f64 a[3];      /* 16-byte aligned */
```

S_1:   `a[0] = 0.0;`   →   `xorpd  xmm0, xmm0`
S_2:   `a[1] = 0.0;`   `movapd a,     xmm0`

        . . .

S_3:   `a[1] = 0.0;`   →   `xorpd  xmm0, xmm0`
S_4:   `a[2] = 0.0;`   `movupd a+8,   xmm0`

Second, intra-register vectorization of a low trip-count loop that reads or writes data that was written recently or will be read shortly read by sequential code may suffer large performance penalties caused by a lack of store-to-load forwarding on the Intel NetBurst® microarchitecture, as described in Chapter 2.

For example, although the loop that materializes from the middle four statements $S_2;S_3;S_4;S_5$ in the following fragment can be implemented without data rearranging instructions, the resulting instructions marked with (!) suffer from a lack of store-to-load forwarding:

```
s32 x[4], y[4], z[4];   /* 16-byte  aligned */
    . . .
```

S_1: `y[0] = ...`   `mov    y,     eax`
S_2: `x[0] = y[0] + z[0];`   `movdqa xmm0, y     (!)`
S_3: `x[1] = y[1] + z[1];`   →   `paddd  xmm0, z`
S_4: `x[2] = y[2] + z[2];`   `movdqa x,     xmm0`
S_5: `x[3] = y[3] + z[3];`   `mov    eax,  x+4  (!)`
S_6: `...  = x[1];`

Although data rearranging instructions can avoid some store-to-load forwarding problems by explicitly forwarding the required part of a 128-bit register into a subsequent load, the compiler usually decides to unroll back into sequential straightline code a low trip-count loop with a potential lack of store-to-load forwarding.

Third, low trip-count loops are sometimes just a few iterations short of the vector lengths that are directly supported by multimedia instructions, as illustrated with the following fragment:

```
s16 u[7], v[7];
...
```
S_1: `u[0] += v[0];`
S_2: `u[1] += v[1];`
S_3: `u[2] += v[2];`
S_4: `u[3] += v[3];`
S_5: `u[4] += v[4];`
S_6: `u[5] += v[5];`
S_7: `u[6] += v[6];`

Vectorizing this loop with packed words as vector data type requires at least eight iterations. By padding the two arrays and statement sequence with one additional dummy data element (s16 u[8], v[8];) and dummy operation (u[7] += v[7];) the fragment is easily implemented with eight-way SIMD parallelism, as illustrated here:

```
movdqa xmm0, u     ; load  8 words from u
paddw  xmm0, v     ; add   8 words to   v
movdqa u,    xmm0  ; store 8 words into u
```

In general, padding data structures and statement sequences with a few redundant data elements and operations may expose more exploitable parallelism at the expense of slightly increasing the storage and computational requirements of the original program. Similar operation padding can be applied within a statement, as illustrated here:

```
s32 x[4], y[4];
...
```
S_1: `x[0] = y[0];`
S_2: `x[1] = y[1] + 1;`
S_3: `x[2] = y[2] + 3;`
S_4: `x[3] = y[3] + 5;`

By padding a dummy addition into S_1 (x[0] = y[0] + 0;), a loop that can be vectorized materializes from this straightline code:

```
static const s32 _c[] = { 0, 1, 3, 5 };
for (i = 0; i < 4; i++) {                      movdqa xmm0, _c
  x[i] = y[i] + _c[i];              →          paddd  xmm0, y
}                                               movdqa x,    xmm0
```

High Trip-Count Loops

Occasionally, a loop with a reasonably high trip count materializes directly from straightline code, as illustrated with the following code in function dist1() of the MPEG encoder in the MediaBench suite (Lee, Potkonjak, and Mangione-Smith 1997):

```
        static s32 dist1( ... ) {
            u8 *p1, *p2;
            s32 s, v;
            . . .
S₁:         if ((v = p1[0]   - p2[0])   < 0) v = -v; s+=v;
S₂:         if ((v = p1[1]   - p2[1])   < 0) v = -v; s+=v;
S₃:         if ((v = p1[2]   - p2[2])   < 0) v = -v; s+=v;
S₄:         if ((v = p1[3]   - p2[3])   < 0) v = -v; s+=v;
S₅:         if ((v = p1[4]   - p2[4])   < 0) v = -v; s+=v;
S₆:         if ((v = p1[5]   - p2[5])   < 0) v = -v; s+=v;
S₇:         if ((v = p1[6]   - p2[6])   < 0) v = -v; s+=v;
S₈:         if ((v = p1[7]   - p2[7])   < 0) v = -v; s+=v;
S₉:         if ((v = p1[8]   - p2[8])   < 0) v = -v; s+=v;
S₁₀:        if ((v = p1[9]   - p2[9])   < 0) v = -v; s+=v;
S₁₁:        if ((v = p1[10]  - p2[10])  < 0) v = -v; s+=v;
S₁₂:        if ((v = p1[11]  - p2[11])  < 0) v = -v; s+=v;
S₁₃:        if ((v = p1[12]  - p2[12])  < 0) v = -v; s+=v;
S₁₄:        if ((v = p1[13]  - p2[13])  < 0) v = -v; s+=v;
S₁₅:        if ((v = p1[14]  - p2[14])  < 0) v = -v; s+=v;
S₁₆:        if ((v = p1[15]  - p2[15])  < 0) v = -v; s+=v;
            . . .
        }
```

Idiom recognition makes the hidden ABS operator explicit in each statement sequence (S_1: s += ABS(p1[0]-p2[0])), and 16 rollable statements appear. The resulting straightline code subsequently materializes into a loop that translates into only a few vector instructions:

```
movdqu xmm2, [edx]   ; load 16 bytes from p1
movdqu xmm0, [eax]   ; load 16 bytes from p2
psadbw xmm2, xmm0    ; add  16 absolute differences
                     ;
movdqa xmm1, xmm2    ; compute final sum
psrldq xmm1, 8       ;  from two doublewords
paddd  xmm2, xmm1    ;
movd   edi, xmm2     ;
```

Even though the trip count provides sufficient iterations for a single vector operation on packed bytes, the trip count does not allow for more advanced intra-register vectorization methods, like dynamic loop peeling for alignment. More typically, such methods become feasible for loops that arise from combining loop materialization with loop collapsing. Take, for example, the following function m4() that multiplies a series of elements in an array with four different factors:

```
void m4(f32 *dst, f32 *src, s32 n) {
  s32 i;
  for (i = 0; i < n; i++) {
    *(dst)   = 0.5f * *(src);
    *(dst+1) = 0.2f * *(src+1);
    *(dst+2) = 0.1f * *(src+2);
    *(dst+3) = 0.4f * *(src+3);
    dst += 4; src += 4;
  }
}
```

S_1:
S_2:
S_3:
S_4:

The loop that materializes from $S_1;S_2;S_3;S_4$ can be collapsed into the enveloping i-loop after eliminating the induction variables and converting the array used to enforce adjacent storage of the constants into a rotating read-only memory reference, expressed at source-code level as follows:

```
static const f32 _c[] = { 0.5f,0.2f,0.1f,0.4f };
for (i = 0; i < 4*n; i++) {
  dst[i] = _c[i % 4] * src[i];
}
```

S_1:

The run-time data dependence testing overhead of disproving overlap between the formal pointer arguments can now be amortized over many iterations. In addition, higher trip counts also enable dynamic loop peeling for alignment. Dynamic loop peeling slightly complicates code generation for the read-only memory reference, since the rotation vector must be initialized to the following value, where p denotes the run-time peeling factor, as follows:

$$rot[0:3:1] = |\_c[(p+3)\%4]|\_c[(p+2)\%4]|\_c[(p+1)\%4]|\_c[(p+0)\%4]|$$

This initialization is conveniently implemented by repeating the first three constants in the read-only array once

```
static const f32 _cx[] = {0.5f,0.2f,0.1f,0.4f,0.5f,0.2f,0.1f};
```

and using an unaligned 128-bit data movement instruction from element p%4 as follows, assuming that the peeling factor resides in esi:

```
and    esi, 3          ; compute  p%4
movups xmm0, _c[esi*4] ; load _cx[p%4]
```

Due to the small size of the loop body after loop materialization, the compiler uses alignment strategy [b], introduced in Chapter 6, where the dynamic peeling loop forces an aligned access pattern through the formal pointer variable dst. Based on the outcome of a run-time test on the resulting alignment for src, either the following vector code or otherwise similar code in which an unaligned load is used for src is executed:

```
L: movaps xmm1,      [esi+eax]  ; load  4 floats from src
   mulps  xmm1,      xmm0       ; mult. 4 floats
   movaps [edi+eax], xmm1       ; store 4 floats into dst
   add    eax,       16         ;
   cmp    eax,       ecx        ;
   jb     L                     ; looping logic
```

Figure 8.1 compares the execution times of a sequential implementation of function m4() with a naïve implementation, in which vectorization of only the materialized loop is forced and the collapsed vector implementation is shown above on a 3-gigahertz Pentium 4 processor for increasing values of n and 16-byte aligned arrays. Execution times were obtained by running the function repeatedly and dividing the total run time accordingly. The corresponding speedup is shown along a secondary y axis.

The repeated overhead of dynamic data dependence analysis together with the inability to generate aligned data movement instructions is responsible for the poor performance of the naïve implementation. Combining loop materialization with loop collapsing, however, results in a vector loop that must execute the run-time data dependence test only once per function call and with sufficient iterations to justify peeling for alignment. In this case, loop collapsing made the difference between a loop that is better left sequential and a vector loop with satisfactory performance, as shown in Figure 8.1.

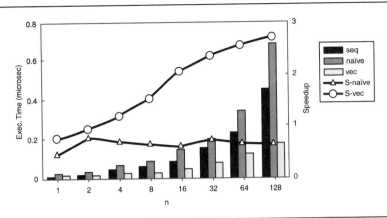

Figure 8.1   Materialized Loop Performance—3-Gigahertz Pentium® 4
Processor

As stated earlier, the combination of loop collapsing and loop materialization is sometimes simply a form of loop rerolling, as demonstrated with the unrolled version of the Linpack benchmark (Dongarra et al. 1994) studied at the end of Chapter 6 (obtained by defining macro name UNROLL). In this alternative implementation, all important loops have been manually unrolled to improve performance on traditional scalar architectures, as for the function daxpy(), as follows:

```
          void daxpy( ... ) {
              . . .
S₁:       m = n % 4;
          if (m != 0) {
L₁:          for (i = 0; i < m; i++)
S₂:              dy[i] = dy[i] + da*dx[i];
             if (n < 4) return;
          }
L₂:       for (i = m; i < n; i += 4) {
S₃:          dy[i]   = dy[i]   + da*dx[i];
S₄:          dy[i+1] = dy[i+1] + da*dx[i+1];
S₅:          dy[i+2] = dy[i+2] + da*dx[i+2];
S₆:          dy[i+3] = dy[i+3] + da*dx[i+3];
          }
          . . .
          }
```

The Intel® C/C++ Compiler leaves the programmer-defined cleanup loop L_1 sequential, because the assignment to variable m in S_1 limits the trip count to three iterations at most. The straightline code $S_3;S_4;S_5;S_6$ materializes into a loop that is subsequently collapsed into loop L_2 and vectorized. This combination effectively rolls the loop back into a form that enables the compiler to generate code that executes most of the iterations with vector instructions. An aggressive optimizing compiler could even go one step further and first use elaborate pattern matching to combine L_1 and L_2 back into one loop that executes all iterations.

Table 8.1 shows the single-precision and double-precision performance of the unrolled Linpack benchmark that is reported for the two benchmark-defined leading dimensions lda = 200 and lda = 201 on a 3-gigahertz Pentium 4 processor by a sequential version, a vectorized version with loop materialization disabled—labeled Vec- in the table, and the vectorized version described above. The performance results show that loop materialization enables the compiler to recover some of the vector optimizations that were lost by manual loop unrolling.

Table 8.1 Unrolled Linpack Performance—3-Gigahertz Pentium® 4 Processor

MFLOPS 100 × 100	single-prec			double-prec		
	Seq	Vec-	Vec	Seq	Vec-	Vec
lda = 201	125	1226	1253	1215	1205	1260
lda = 200	125	1205	1891	1167	1193	1353

A quick comparison with Table 6.2 also shows that the overhead of executing the programmer-defined cleanup loop unnecessarily limits performance. A general programming guideline, therefore, is to avoid manual loop unrolling altogether. Most modern compilers can automatically unroll loops that have not been optimized otherwise.

Chapter 9

Vectorization with the Intel Compilers

Previous chapters have given a detailed account of methods used by Intel® C++ and Fortran compilers to convert sequential code into a form that exploits multimedia extensions. In principle, programmers who use intrinsics or inline assembly to take advantage of a particular multimedia instruction set can take the same approach. With precise knowledge of the application domain and more control over the generated code, this explicit approach has the potential for the highest performance. Since the size of most applications renders hand optimizing all parts impossible, a more practical way to improve performance is to let a vectorizing compiler automatically take advantage of multimedia extensions, then to run performance analysis to determine where additional optimization is required. This chapter shows how to use Intel compilers to exploit multimedia extensions effectively with a minimum of engineering effort.

Vectorization Overview

Intel C++ and Fortran compilers offer programmers a rich set of machine-independent and machine-specific optimizations to maximize software performance. This section summarizes compiler switches and hints that are useful in the context of intra-register vectorization for the Intel MMX technology and streaming-SIMD extensions.[1]

Compiler Switches

The C/C++ compiler is invoked on the command line as

```
=> icl [switches] source.c
```

and the Fortran compiler as

```
=> ifort [switches] source.f
```

where `[switches]` denotes a list of optional compiler switches. Table 9.1 lists compiler switches that are specific to intra-register vectorization.

Table 9.1 Compiler Switches for Intra-Register Vectorization

Windows Switch	Semantics
-QxK or -QaxK -QxN or -QaxN -QxB or -QaxB -QxP or -QaxP	generate code for Pentium III processor generate code for Pentium 4 processor generate code for Pentium M processor generate code for Pentium 4 processor with HT
-Qvec_report	control level of vectorization diagnostics:
0 1 2 3	disable vectorization diagnostics report successfully vectorized code as 1 + report failure diagnostics for loops as 2 + report all prohibiting data dependences

The switch `-Qx{KNBP}` enables code generation in general and, hence, intra-register vectorization in particular, for the instruction sets supported by the Pentium III, Pentium 4, Pentium M, and Pentium 4 processor with HT Technology, respectively. The switch `-Qax{KNBP}` enables *automatic processor dispatch*. Under this option, the compiler generates a generic version that runs on any IA-32 processor but, if

---

[1] The summary uses syntax specific to the Microsoft Windows-based C/C++ compiler. Equivalent functionality with a slightly different syntax exists for the Fortran compiler and all Linux-based compilers. Refer to the documentation (Intel 1998–2004) for a complete description.

deemed profitable, the compiler also generates a version that has been optimized for the specified processor. At run time, the program automatically selects the appropriate optimized version based on the actual processor that is used to run the program.

The switch -Qvec_report0 disables all vectorization diagnostics, which is useful if a silent compilation is desired. The -Qvec_report1 switch provides feedback for all code fragments that have been successfully vectorized. Each diagnostic reports the source file with the line and column number of the first statement in the vectorized code fragment. For example, suppose the contents of a source file main.c are as follows, where line numbers have been made explicit with comments:

```
/* 01 */ #define N 32
/* 02 */ float a[N], b[N], c[N], d[N];
/* 03 */
/* 04 */ doit() {
/* 05 */   int i;
/* 06 */   for (i = 0; i < N/2; i++) a[i] = i;
/* 07 */   for (i = 1; i < N; i++) {
/* 08 */     b[i] = b[i-1] + 2; /* data dependence cycle */
/* 09 */     c[i] = 1;
/* 10 */   }
/* 11 */   d[0] = 10;
/* 12 */   d[1] = 10;
/* 13 */   d[2] = 10;
/* 14 */   d[3] = 10;
/* 15 */}
     ⋮
```

Compiling this source file with the following switches on the command line yields the following diagnostics:

```
=> icl -QxP -Qvec_report1 main.c
...
main.c(6)  : (col. 11) remark: LOOP WAS VECTORIZED.
main.c(7)  : (col. 11) remark: PARTIAL LOOP WAS VECTORIZED.
main.c(11) : (col. 11) remark: BLOCK WAS VECTORIZED.
```

The diagnostics report vectorization of the loop at line 6, partial vectorization of the loop (after loop distribution) at line 7, and vectorization of the straightline code (after loop materialization) starting at line 11. The format is compatible with the Microsoft Visual C++ environment (Microsoft 2003), where double-clicking on one of the diagnostics in the output window moves the focus of the editor window to the corresponding source file and position.

Switches -Qvec_report2 and -Qvec_report3 provide feedback for the loops in a program that were not vectorized, which may be useful while trying to make the program more amenable to intra-register vectorization. Compiling the previous source file on the command line as follows, for example, yields the more verbose output:

```
=> icl -QxP -Qvec_report3 main.c
...
main.c(6)  : (col. 11) remark: LOOP WAS VECTORIZED.
main.c(7)  : (col. 11) remark: vector dependence:
   proven FLOW dependence between b line 8, and b line 8.
main.c(7)  : (col. 11) remark: loop was not vectorized:
   existence of vector dependence.
main.c(7)  : (col. 11) remark: PARTIAL LOOP WAS VECTORIZED.
main.c(11) : (col. 11) remark: BLOCK WAS VECTORIZED.
```

Feedback generated by these switches may become rather verbose, since diagnostics are given for every loop in the program, even for loops that are unlikely candidates for vectorization. Therefore, using these diagnostics to compare the number of vectorized loops against the number of loops that are not vectorized generally provides a very poor measure of the quality of vectorization. The diagnostics merely serve the purpose of guiding the task of rewriting important code fragments into a form that can be effectively vectorized, as illustrated in the section "Diagnostics-Guided Optimization" later in this chapter.

Table 9.2 lists a number of other useful compiler switches that are not directly related to intra-register vectorization. Switches -Od and -O1 through -O3 control different levels of generic optimizations for code size and code speed. The switch -Fa generates an assembly file, which can then be inspected to determine the quality of the generated instructions. This process is illustrated in the following for the source file main.c shown earlier. Note that only the vector instructions for the statement at line 9 after applying loop distribution and peeling to the loop at line 7 are shown. For ease of reference, the Intel compiler annotates each assembly instruction with the line and column number of the original statement in the source file (;line.col).

```
=> icl -QxP -Fa main.c
...
=> type main.asm
         ⋮
.B1.2: movaps    XMMWORD PTR _c[eax+4], xmm0      ;9.12
       add       eax, 16                          ;7.16
       cmp       eax, 124                         ;7.11
       jb        .B1.2                            ;7.11
         ⋮
       END
```

Table 9.2 Other Useful Compiler Switches

Windows Switch	Semantics
-Od -O1 -O2 -O3	disable optimizations enable optimizations for code size enable default optimizations for speed enable all optimizations for speed
-Fa	generate assembly file
-Qunroll0 -Qprefetch-	disable loop unrolling disable software prefetching
-Qip -Qipo	enable interprocedural optimizations in a single source file enable interprocedural optimizations among source files
-fast	enable best switch combination for speed
-Op	restrict floating-point optimizations
-Qrestrict	enable use of restrict keyword
-Qparallel -Qopenmp	enable automatic parallelization enable parallelization with OpenMP extensions
-Qc99	enable C99 extensions

Switch -Qunroll0 disables loop unrolling in general and, hence, unrolling vector loops in particular. Loop unrolling that supports cache line split or prefetch instructions cannot be overridden by this switch.

The compiler insertion of prefetch instructions is disabled with the switch -Qprefetch-. Switches -Qip and -Qipo enable interprocedural optimizations within a single source file and among multiple source files of a program, respectively. Among a wide variety of interprocedural optimizations, these switches enable interprocedural alignment analysis for formal pointer arguments. The switch -fast enables the best possible generic switch combination to optimize for speed. Switch -Op restricts the compiler to optimizations that preserve floating-point precision and changes the default fp:performance mode into the fp:precision mode, as discussed in Chapter 5. Switch `-Qrestrict` enables the use of the keyword `restrict` that conveys non-aliasing properties to the compiler.

Switches `-Qparallel` and `-Qopenmp` instruct the compiler to exploit, respectively, implicit parallelism—detected by means of compiler analysis—and explicit parallelism—expressed in the program text by means of the OpenMP extensions (OpenMP 1998). When combined with intra-register vectorization, these switches enable exploiting multilevel parallelism—both fine-grained and coarse-grained control parallelism—on a multimedia-extended multiprocessor or processor that supports Hyper-Threading Technology (Bik et al. 2001a, Tian et al. 2002).

Finally, switch `-Qc99` enables features of the C99 standard (ISO 1999).

Profile-Guided Optimization

In a traditional static compilation model, the compiler must necessarily base all optimization decisions on only an estimate of important execution characteristics. Branch probabilities, for example, are estimated by assuming that a controlling condition that tests for equality is less likely to succeed than a condition testing for inequality. Relative execution counts are based on static properties such as nesting depth. Such estimated execution characteristics are later used to make optimization decisions such as selecting an appropriate instruction layout, function inlining (Muchnick 1997), or generating a sequential or vector version of a loop. The quality of these optimization decisions can substantially improve if more accurate execution characteristics are available, which becomes possible under *profile-guided optimization*. Table 9.3 shows the compiler switches that enable the following three-step compilation session for profile-guided optimization.

Table 9.3 Compiler Switches for Profile-Guided Optimization

Windows Switch	Semantics
`-Qprof_gen` `-Qprof_use`	generate instrumented executable use profile summary to optimize program

1. Generate an instrumented executable with `-Qprof_gen`.
2. Apply this executable to one (or several) representative dataset(s).
3. Generate an optimized executable with `-Qprof_use`.

When the instrumented executable generated in the first step is applied to a representative dataset in the second step, important execution characteristics are gathered in a profile summary. Optimization decisions are subsequently based on this profile summary during the third step rather than on a static estimate of execution characteristics. Profile-guided optimization is most effective when a few small, but representative, training datasets are used in the second step and the third step is combined with other optimizations such as interprocedural optimizations or vectorization. A typical command-line session to compile the source file `program.c` into a profile-guided optimized executable for a Pentium 4 processor with HT Technology is shown here:

```
=> icl -Qprof_gen program.c
...
=> program.exe < train_dataset.txt
...
=> icl -Qprof_use -QxP -Qipo -O3 program.c
...
```

The new executable is now optimized according to the execution characteristics that were observed while running the training data set.

Compiler Hints

Table 9.4 summarizes all the compiler hints that are relevant to automatic intra-register vectorization. The pragmas must be inserted before a loop to convey certain information about this loop to the compiler. As explained at the end of Chapter 5, any vectorization-enabling pragma also instructs the compiler to proceed with vectorization of `if` statements without explicitly testing whether bit masking could introduce guarded errors into the execution path.

Table 9.4 Compiler Hints for Intra-Register Vectorization

Syntax of Hint	Semantics
#pragma ivdep	discard assumed data dependences
#pragma vector always #pragma vector nontemporal #pragma vector [un]aligned	override efficiency heuristics enable streaming stores assert [un]aligned property
#pragma novector	disable vectorization
#pragma distribute point #pragma loop count (<int>)	suggest point for loop distribution estimate trip count
restrict	assert exclusive access through pointer
_declspec(align(<int>,<int>)) __assume_aligned(<var>,<int>)	suggest memory alignment assert alignment property

Inserting `#pragma ivdep` before a loop asserts that none of the conservatively *assumed* data dependences that prohibit vectorization of the loop actually occur. This pragma is useful in cases where data dependence analysis fails to detect a vector loop that is obvious to a programmer with more knowledge of the application domain. In the following loop, for example, if variable k is always non-negative, the programmer can use `#pragma ivdep` to inform the compiler that the assumed flow dependence $S_1\delta^f_{(<)}S_1$ can safely be discarded:

```
        #pragma ivdep
        for (i = 0; i < N; i++) {
S₁:        a[2+i] = a[2+i+k] + 1;
        }
```

If the compiler cannot prove data independence statically, but is able to vectorize the loop with run-time data dependence testing, this pragma is still useful for avoiding this testing overhead altogether. The pragma cannot be used, however, to override *proven* data dependences. In the example above, if variable k statically evaluates to the value −1, the `#pragma ivdep` is simply ignored by the compiler, and the loop remains sequential due to the now-proven flow dependence.

In situations where vectorization of a loop is valid, but built-in efficiency heuristics of the compiler deem vectorization unprofitable, `#pragma vector always` can be used to override this decision. This pragma suggests vectorization of the loop regardless of the outcome of efficiency heuristics. Validity considerations other than guarded errors cannot, however, be overridden with this pragma. The pragma in the following fragment has no impact, because the compiler is unable to vectorize the output statement in the loop:

```
#pragma vector always
for (i = 0; i < 100; i++) {
  printf("i=%d\n", i);
}
```

Conversely, `#pragma novector` disables vectorization of a loop, which is useful to prevent vectorization of a loop that seems profitable to the compiler, but actually exhibits a slowdown at run time.

Inserting `#pragma nontemporal` before a loop instructs the compiler to handle all 16-byte aligned memory references as streaming data to minimize cache pollution. The programmer can use `#pragma unaligned` and `#pragma aligned` to instruct the compiler to assume that all memory references in the loop are either unaligned or 16-byte aligned, respectively. Both pragmas must be used with care because incorrect usage can result in performance degradation or, worse, a program fault.

The loop-oriented pragmas explained above could even be inserted directly before straightline code from which a loop may materialize, as illustrated by the following example:

```
float a[4];
#pragma vector nontemporal        translates
a[0] = 0;                             →      xorps    xmm0, xmm0
a[1] = 0;                          into      movntps a,      xmm0
a[2] = 0;
a[3] = 0;
```

Since loop materialization is not guaranteed, however, the compiler is also free to ignore such pragmas altogether.

Suitable points for loop distribution can be suggested to the compiler without actually performing the source code modifications with one or several #pragma distribute point hints in the loop body, as illustrated by the following. Suggestions that violate data dependences are always ignored, however.

```
for (i = 0; i < N; i++) {                for (i = 0; i < N; i++) {
  a[i] = 0;                suggests          a[i] = 0;
#pragma distribute point         →         }
  b[i] = 0;                                 for (i = 0; i < N; i++) {
}                                             b[i] = 0;
                                           }
```

An estimated trip count can be conveyed to the compiler as shown in the following, where the programmer has indicated that the i-loop typically iterates only seven times. This estimate is subsequently used by the compiler to determine whether vectorization of the loop seems profitable.

```
#pragma loop count (7)
for (i = 0; i < n; i++) {
  a[i] = 0;
}
```

The keyword restrict asserts that a pointer variable provides exclusive access to its associated memory region. If the following function add() is only applied to distinct arrays, for example, the non-aliasing information of the formal pointer arguments p and q can be conveyed to the compiler as follows:

```
void add(char * restrict p, char * restrict q, int n) {
  int i;
  for (i = 0; i < n; i++) {
    p[i] = q[i] + 1;
  }
}
```

This keyword provides a convenient method to assert the exclusive access property for pointer variables that are used in many different loops, because it avoids the tedious task of inserting a #pragma ivdep before every potential vector loop. In contrast with pragmas, which are typically ignored by other compilers, this language extension requires the compiler switch -Qrestrict to compile with the Intel C/C++ Compiler, and may cause syntax errors for other compilers. The program can still be kept portable, however, with the following macro mechanism, where the default compilation with any compiler simply discards all the restrict hints, now spelled in capitals, while the hints are conveyed to the compiler with the switch combination -D__RESTRICT -Qrestrict to define the macro name.

```
#ifdef __RESTRICT
#define RESTRICT restrict
#else
#define RESTRICT
#endif

void add(char * RESTRICT p, char * RESTRICT q, int n) {
  ...
}
```

The programmer can use _declspec(align(base,off)) in a declaration, where $0 \leq$ off $<$ base $= 2^n$, to suggest allocating the declared entity at an address a that satisfies the equality a mod base $=$ off. Suppose, as an example, that most of the execution time of a program is spent in a loop of the following form:

```
double a[N], b[N];
...
for (i = 0; i < N; i++) a[i+1] = b[i] * 3;
```

Since the compiler most likely selects a 16-byte alignment for both arrays, either an unaligned load or an unaligned store must be used after vectorization. The programmer can suggest the alternative alignment shown in the following, which results in two aligned access patterns after vectorization:

```
_declspec(align(16, 8)) double a[N];
_declspec(align(16, 0)) double b[N]; /* or: align(16) */
```

If program analysis has failed to determine an appropriate alignment for the memory regions that may be associated with a particular pointer variable p, the programmer can insert the hint __assume_aligned(p, base); where base = 2^n, to convey that all memory regions that are associated with the pointer variable p are guaranteed to satisfy at least the given alignment. Consider, for example, the following function:

```
void fill(char *x) {
  int i;
  for (i = 0; i < 1024; i++) x[i] = 1;
}
```

If interprocedural alignment analysis, enabled under -Qip or -Qipo, has failed to derive any useful conclusion on the alignment of the memory regions associated with the formal pointer argument x, the compiler resorts to dynamic loop peeling to enforce an aligned access pattern in the i-loop. Refer to Chapter 6 for more information. This method provides a generally effective way to obtain aligned access patterns at the expense of a slight increase in code size and testing overhead. If incoming access patterns are guaranteed to be 16-byte aligned, however, the programmer can avoid this testing overhead altogether by conveying the alignment information to the compiler as follows:

```
void fill(char *x) {
  int i;
  __assume_aligned(x, 16);
  for (i = 0; i < 1024; i++) x[i] = 1;
}
```

Like all other alignment hints, this hint must be used with care because incorrect usage can result in a program fault.

Vectorization Guidelines

To obtain high software performance, one must carefully select the proper algorithms and then implement them efficiently. Even though an expert programmer usually excels in both areas, the size of most applications renders hand optimizing all parts impossible. A more practical approach to improving software performance, therefore, is to let a compiler optimize the program as a whole and then to run a performance analysis to determine where additional optimization is required. This subsequent optimization may simply consist of rewriting the source into a form that is more amenable to optimization or, as a last resort, hand optimizing the code with intrinsics or inline assembly. This section provides some guidelines that may help the Intel C++ and Fortran compilers exploit multimedia extensions.

Design and Implementation Considerations

Decisions made during both the design and implementation phase of an application can ultimately have a profound impact on resulting performance. While optimizing an existing application, time or resource constraints usually prohibit reversing decisions that turn out to affect performance adversely. Therefore, selecting appropriate algorithms and data structures during the design and early implementation phase of an application is probably the most critical step toward high software performance.

Topics related to algorithm selection are clearly outside the scope of this book (Garey and Johnson 1999; Hopcroft and Ullman 1979; Knuth 1997a, 1997b, and 1997c; Sedgewick 1988). The only guideline that can be given in this context is that it may be worthwhile to take amenability to vectorization into consideration while deciding among several, equally suited algorithms. However, one algorithm should not be favored over another that has lower computational complexity, merely because the former is more amenable to vectorization. To take this argument to the extreme, given a choice between the following two ways to compute

$$\sum_{i=1}^{n} i$$

favoring the $O(n)$ function `fn()` over the $O(1)$ function `f1()` simply because the reduction can be vectorized seems rather senseless.

```
int fn(short n) {
  int r = 0, i;
  for (i = 1; i <= n; i++) {          int f1(short n) {
    r += i;                             return (n > 0)
  }                      which one?      ? (n*(n+1))/2
  return r;                 ↔            : 0;
}                                      }
```

On the other hand, given the choice between two algorithms with identical computational complexity, secondary considerations such as being more amenable to vectorization may become a deciding factor.

Selecting appropriate data structures can also make vectorization of the resulting code more effective. To illustrate this point, compare the traditional array-of-structures (AoS) arrangement for storing the x_1, x_2, x_3, and x_4 components of a set of four-dimensional points with the alternative structure-of-arrays (SoA) arrangement for storing this set.

```
/* AoS */                         /* SoA */
struct {                          struct {
  double x1;                        double x1[N];
  double x2;          ↔             double x2[N];
  double x3;                        double x3[N];
  double x4;                        double x4[N];
} points[N];                      } pointset;
```

With the AoS arrangement, a loop that visits all components of a point before moving to the next point exhibits a good locality of reference because all elements in fetched cache lines are utilized.

```
/* AoS */
for (i = 0; i < N; i++) {
  points[i].x1 *= scale1;
  points[i].x2 += trans2;
  points[i].x3 += trans3;
  points[i].x4 = 0;
}
```

The disadvantage of the AoS arrangement, however, is that each individual memory reference in such a loop exhibits a non-unit stride, which, in general, adversely affects vector performance. Furthermore, a loop that visits only one component of all points exhibits less satisfactory locality of reference because many of the elements in the fetched cache lines remain unused. In contrast, with the SoA arrangement, the loop shown above is expressed as follows:

```
/* SoA */
for (i = 0; i < N; i++) {
  pointset.x1[i] *= scale1;
  pointset.x2[i] += trans2;
  pointset.x3[i] += trans3;
  pointset.x4[i] = 0;
}
```

These unit-stride memory references are more amenable to effective vectorization and still exhibit good locality of reference within each of the four data streams. Note that cache anomalies that may reduce the memory performance of such separate streams can be avoided by applying loop distribution before vectorization. Additionally, loops that visit only one component of all points still exhibit the same favorable characteristics. Consequently, an application that uses the SoA arrangement may ultimately outperform an application based on the AoS arrangement when compiled with a vectorizing compiler, even if this performance difference is not directly apparent during the early implementation phase.

In other situations, the AoS arrangement may be the data structure of choice, as illustrated by the following operation, which adds all components of one point to another point:

```
/* AoS */
points[0].x1 += points[1].x1;
points[0].x2 += points[1].x2;
points[0].x3 += points[1].x3;
points[0].x4 += points[1].x4;
```

The loop materialization method presented in Chapter 8 maps this operation into only a few two-way SIMD parallel instructions. In contrast, the SoA arrangement now provides no opportunities for vectorization.

```
/* SoA */
pointset.x1[0] += pointsset.x1[1];
pointset.x2[0] += pointsset.x2[1];
pointset.x3[0] += pointsset.x3[1];
pointset.x4[0] += pointsset.x4[1];
```

This example illustrates the importance of selecting a data structure that effectively accommodates all frequently occurring operations. In some cases, hybrid data structures or even run-time conversions between two different formats may be required to expose the most available parallelism to a vectorizing compiler.

To illustrate another important consideration while selecting appropriate data structures, consider the following function to sum all elements in an array with data type short:

```
int add(short *a, int n) {
  int r = 0;
  while (--n >= 0) r += *a++;
  return r;
}
```

The Intel C/C++ Compiler is able to recognize a well-behaved loop in the while statement, which is subsequently vectorized, as can be seen in the following command line session on a source file add.c, which contains this function starting at line 10:

```
=> icl -Fa -QxP add.c
...
add.c(12) : (col. 3) remark: LOOP WAS VECTORIZED.
...
=> type add.asm
      ⋮
.B1.9:
```

```
movq        xmm1, QWORD PTR [esi+ecx*2] ;12.26
punpcklwd xmm1, xmm1                    ;12.26
psrad       xmm1, 16                    ;12.26
paddd       xmm0, xmm1                  ;12.20
add         ecx, 4                      ;12.3
cmp         ecx, eax                    ;12.3
jb          .B1.9                       ;12.3
    ⋮
```

The accumulation of words into a doubleword accumulator is recognized as one of the idioms discussed in Chapter 7. The vector loop exploits four-way SIMD parallelism while computing partial sums, which are subsequently added into one final scalar value in a postlude. Now suppose that the programmer knows that either only the lower 16-bits of the sum are eventually used at all call sites, or the nature of all arrays passed to this function is such that the sum never exceeds a 16-bit precision. In that case, simply changing the data type of the accumulator into short enables the compiler to generate more efficient vector code, as follows:

```
=> icl -Fa -QxP add.c
...
add.c(12) : (col. 3) remark: LOOP WAS VECTORIZED.
...
=> type add.asm
        ⋮
.B1.9:
        paddw   xmm0, XMMWORD PTR [esi+ecx*2] ;12.20
        add     ecx, 8                        ;12.3
        cmp     ecx, eax                      ;12.3
        jb      .B1.9                         ;12.3
        ⋮
```

Inspecting the generated assembly file reveals that the vector loop now exploits eight-way SIMD parallelism while computing partial sums.

This example clearly shows that a relatively simple source code modification makes the difference between four-way or eight-way SIMD parallelism in the generated vector code. Because a compiler is usually not able to make such modifications, the data type of even a simple accumulator should be carefully selected to maximize the amount of available parallelism in the program. A general guideline in the context of intra-register vectorization, therefore, is to use the smallest data type possible for each data structure, since this ultimately enables the most parallelism in the resulting code.

Focus of Optimization

A generally useful optimization guideline is a result of Amdahl's law (Amdahl 1967), which states that if ρ denotes the fraction of dynamically executed instructions that inherently cannot exploit any parallelism in a program, then the maximum obtainable speedup S for this program with w-way parallelism is bounded by the following formula:

$$S \leq \frac{1}{\rho + \frac{(1-\rho)}{w}} \leq \frac{1}{\rho}(\text{for } w \to \infty)$$

As an example, if 80 percent of the execution time of a program is spent in inherently sequential code ($\rho = 0.8$), then the best speedup that can be obtained by vectorizing the remaining code is bounded by $S \leq 1.25$. This implies that, before optimizing a program with multimedia extensions, the maximum obtainable speedup should first be estimated because the program may reap little benefit from SIMD parallelism, no matter how much effort is put into the optimization.

If vectorization seems profitable, Amdahl's law also reveals what parts of a program benefit the most from using multimedia extensions. For example, suppose a program spends 2 percent of its execution time in initialization code and the remaining 98 percent in a computational kernel, and both code regions can be vectorized. If time constraints allow for the optimization of *only one* code region ($\rho_1 = 0.98$ and $\rho_2 = 0.02$), then clearly the most benefits can be expected from vectorizing the kernel ($S_1 \leq 1.02$ versus $S_2 \leq 50$). As a result, when optimizing a program, the first focus should be on the hot spots—the parts of the program with intense activity (Gerber 2002). A software profiler like the Intel VTune™ Performance Analyzer (Intel 1998–2004b) is an essential tool to detect such regions. Due to diminishing returns for less frequently executed regions of a program, these colder regions should be optimized only after all other means of improvement have been exhausted.

Diagnostics-Guided Optimization

Vectorization diagnostics are useful to determine where automatic vectorization has been successful and where it has failed. Based on this information, the programmer can apply code restructuring or insert compiler hints to make important hot spots that remain sequential more amenable to vectorization or to disable the vectorization of every code fragment that adversely affects performance.

Table 9.5 shows common vectorization diagnostics. Compiler switch `-Qvec_report1` provides feedback on successful vectorization of loops, distributed loops, and straightline code fragments. In addition, switch `-Qvec_report2` provides feedback on loops that fail to vectorize, followed by a short description of the reason for failure. The table shows only a few examples. Note that, as compiler capabilities improve, later versions of the compiler may provide more detailed failure descriptions or even report success where former versions reported failure. The message `vectorization possible but seems inefficient`, for example, indicates that the efficiency heuristics of the compiler deem vectorization unprofitable, even though vector code could potentially be generated. As explained earlier, this decision is simply overridden with a compiler hint `#pragma vector always` before the loop. Not all vectorization failures are easily remedied, however. Data dependences, for example, may reflect execution order constraints that prevent vectorization altogether. In such cases, `-Qvec_report3` may provide more insights on whether any of the data dependence eliminating techniques described in the literature (Padua and Wolfe 1986, Polychronopoulos 1988, Wolfe 1996, Zima and Chapman 1990) may help to enable vectorization.

Table 9.5   Common Vectorization Diagnostics

Windows Switch	Diagnostic

`-Qvec_report1`
(and higher)
	`LOOP WAS VECTORIZED`
	`PARTIAL LOOP WAS VECTORIZED`
	`BLOCK LOOP WAS VECTORIZED`

`-Qvec_report2`
(and higher)
	`loop was not vectorized:`
	
	  `existence of vector dependence`
	  `low trip count`
	  `mixed data types`
	  `not inner loop`
	  `operator unsuited for vectorization`
	  `subscript too complex`
	  `statement cannot be vectorized`
	  `unsupported loop structure`
	  `vectorization possible but seems inefficient`
	  `#pragma novector used`
	  ⋮

`-Qvec_report2`	`vector dependence:`
	
	  `proven  [FLOW/ANTI/OUTPUT] dependence between ...`
	  `assumed [FLOW/ANTI/OUTPUT] dependence between ...`

To illustrate diagnostics-guided optimization, suppose that most of the execution time of an application is spent in the following function, which computes the product of a matrix and a vector:

```
int size1, size2;

void matvec(double a[][N], double b[], double x[]) {
  int i, j;
  for (i = 0; i < size1; i++) {        /* line 14 */
    b[i] = 0;
    for (j = 0; j < size2; j++) {      /* line 16 */
      b[i] += a[i][j] * x[j];
    }
  }
}
```

If this function is defined at line 12 in source file ax.c, the following vectorization diagnostics result when the program is compiled on the command line as follows:

```
=> icl -Fa -QxN -Qvec_report2 ax.c
...
ax.c(14) : (col. 3) remark: loop was not vectorized:
                           not inner loop.
ax.c(16) : (col. 5) remark: loop was not vectorized:
                           unsupported loop structure.
...
```

Although failure to vectorize the outer loop is expected, the diagnostic on an unsupported loop structure at line 16 comes somewhat as a surprise. This complication arises from using a global variable size2 as upper bound, because type-unaware aliasing assumptions prevent the compiler from proving loop invariance of this variable and, hence, detecting a well-behaved inner loop. Even though interprocedural aliasing analysis—enabled with either -Qip or -Qipo—eliminates most of such false aliasing assumptions, this particular complication is also easily remedied while compiling the function in isolation by means of the following source code modification:

```
void matvec(double a[][N], double b[], double x[]) {
  int i, j, sz2 = size2;
  for (i = 0; i < size1; i++) {      /* line 14 */
    b[i] = 0;
    for (j = 0; j < sz2; j++) {      /* line 16 */
      b[i] += a[i][j] * x[j];
    }
  }
}
```

Vectorization diagnostics now report successful vectorization:

```
=> icl -Fa -QxN -Qvec_report2 ax.c
...
ax.c(14) : (col. 3) remark: loop was not vectorized:
                    not inner loop.
ax.c(16) : (col. 5) remark: LOOP WAS VECTORIZED.
...
```

At this point, programmers can typically start focusing on the next hot spot in the program. Inspection of the corresponding assembly file, however, would reveal that the compiler resorted to dynamic data dependence testing and loop peeling to handle the possibility of overlap between the left-hand and right-hand side expressions and misalignment, respectively. Although these dynamic methods provide a convenient way to improve performance of the function when no further information is available, in some cases the associated run-time overhead can be avoided altogether. Suppose, for example, that a programmer with some knowledge of the application domain realizes that this function is exclusively applied to disjoint memory regions that are 16-byte aligned. This additional information is easily conveyed to the compiler by means of the following compiler hints:

```
void matvec(double a[][N], double b[], double x[]) {
  int i, j, loc_size = size;
__assume_aligned(a, 16);
__assume_aligned(b, 16);
__assume_aligned(x, 16);
  for (i = 0; i < loc_size; i++) {
    b[i] = 0;
#pragma ivdep
    for (j = 0; j < loc_size; j++) {
      b[i] += a[i][j] * x[j];
    }
  }
}
```

The alignment pragmas together with the statically known value of N enable the compiler to determine the alignment of all access patterns in the innermost loop. The other pragma enables the compiler to discard all assumed data dependences. Figure 9.1 shows performance results on a 3-gigahertz Pentium 4 processor for varying matrix sizes. These results are based on execution times that were obtained by running the function matvec() repeatedly and dividing the total run time accordingly. Speed-ups are shown for vector versions that use the default dynamic optimizations (S-vec), the alignment pragmas (S-align), the data dependence pragma (`S-ivdep`), or both sets of pragmas (`S-both`). These results show that, although the performance improvements obtained with fully automatic vectorization are already quite satisfactory—speedups in the range 1.4 to 2.7 for the given matrix sizes, compiler hints can help to squeeze more performance out of this fragment—speedups in the range 2.3 to 3.1. For an application that spends most of its execution time computing the product of a matrix and a vector, this extra improvement can be quite noticeable in the performance of the application as a whole.

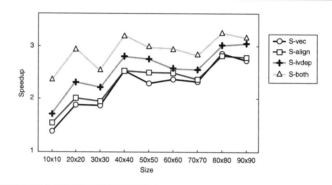

Figure 9.1   Matrix x Vector Speedup—3-Gigahertz Pentium® 4 Processor

Fully automatic vectorization, possibly assisted by minor source code modifications and compiler hints, is clearly the preferred way to exploit multimedia extensions. The approach preserves portability of the program, simplifies maintenance, and allows future releases of the vectorizing compiler to take advantage of the latest multimedia extensions. Despite ongoing efforts to improve compiler technology, however, hand optimizing a fragment with intrinsics or inline assembly is sometimes the only viable way to exploit multimedia extensions. Even with this last resort, preserving the original source code by means of a macro mechanism similar to the one following is highly recommended:

```
#ifdef __HANDOPT
   /* hand optimized implementation */
   _asm {
      ...
   }
#else
   /* original source code */
   ...
#endif
```

The original source code typically reflects the functionality of the code fragment more clearly, which simplifies maintenance and even enables an occasional comparison of the quality of the hand-optimized implementation with code that is generated by different or newly released compilers. The hand-optimized implementation is simply integrated into the executable by compiling the program with the additional switch -D__HANDOPT to define the macro name. For a detailed description of intrinsics and inline assembly, refer to the Intel documentation (Intel 1998-2004a, 2003a, 2003b, 2003c, 2003d).

Final Remarks

This book concludes with some remarks on the current intra-register vectorization capabilities of the Intel C++ and Fortran compilers and an outlook on possible future trends in multimedia extensions.

Some More Experiments

The Callahan-Dongarra-Levine Fortran benchmark (Callahan, Dongarra, and Levine 1988; Levine, Callahan, and Dongarra 1991) consists of a variety of numeric kernels that are intended to test the analysis and code generation capabilities of vectorizing compilers. The Intel Fortran Compiler can currently vectorize about 60 percent of the kernels, although this percentage drops to 40 percent under the default efficiency heuristics used by the compiler. As a rough comparison, the percentage of vectorized kernels reported in the literature for a variety of vectorizing compilers falls in the range 25 percent to 80 percent with earlier versions of the benchmark (Allen and Kennedy 2002, Chapter 5; Callahan, Dongarra, and Levine 1988; Levine, Callahan, and Dongarra 1991). These results qualitatively place the loop-oriented vectorizing capabilities of the Intel Fortran Compiler somewhere in the middle when compared with vectorizing compilers for the more traditional vector processors.

Figure 9.2 summarizes performance results of this benchmark on a 3-gigahertz Pentium 4 processor when all trip counts are set to 1,000. Speedups observed for all kernels when comparing the execution times under the switch -O2 with the execution times under the switches -O2 -QxN -Qip are sorted in increasing order for the single-precision and double-precision floating-point versions of this benchmark. The resulting graph illustrates the typical performance behavior of automatically optimized code. Although performance degradation can be avoided altogether when optimizing each kernel individually, choosing efficiency heuristics that are beneficial for a wide range of applications almost inevitably results in a slight slowdown for a few cases. On average, however, loops benefit from automatic intra-register vectorization, which becomes the most apparent for the single-precision floating-point version of the benchmark.

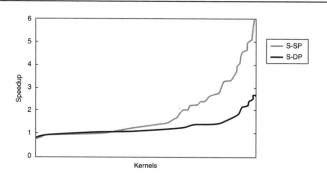

Figure 9.2   Fortran Benchmark Speedup—3-Gigahertz Pentium® 4 Processor

To give another flavor of speedups that can be obtained for a numeric application as a whole, performance results are reported for a short-term regional weather-forecasting Fortran program that was developed at the Hydrometeorological Center of Russia (http://hmc.hydromet.ru/). Table 9.6 shows the execution times in seconds on a 2.2-gigahertz Pentium 4 processor and 2.8-gigahertz Pentium 4 processor with HT Technology for one hour of weather forecast under generic optimization as well as Pentium 4 processor-specific optimization with and without intra-register vectorization. Without vectorization, other processor-specific optimizations yield a speedup in the range 1.18 to 1.27. With vectorization, the total speedup falls in the range 1.50 to 1.78.

Table 9.6   Weather Forecast Performance

Execution Time	-O2	-O2 -QxN (novec)	-O2 -QxN (vec)	*S* (novec)	*S* (vec)
2.2GHz P4	66.8s.	56.8s.	44.5s.	1.18	1.50
2.8GHz P4 with HT	50.8s.	40.1s.	28.5s.	1.27	1.78

Finally, to illustrate the impact of intra-register vectorization on a variety of applications in general-purpose computing, performance results are given for SPEC CPU2000 (Henning 2000, SPEC 2000). This industry-standardized benchmark suite consists of 14 floating-point and 12 integer C/C++ and Fortran benchmarks. These benchmarks are derived from real-world applications. Speedups are computed for these benchmarks using the Intel C++ and Fortran compilers on a 2.8-gigahertz Pentium 4 processor with HT Technology by comparing the execution times under default generic optimizations (-O2) with the execution times under high-level, interprocedural, profile-guided, and processor-specific optimizations -O3 -Qipo -Qprof_use -QxP after a training run. The speedups are sorted in increasing order in Figure 9.3. The contributions of exploiting SIMD parallelism are shown separately in black. Although the figure reveals definite advantages of advanced and processor-specific optimizations up to $S = 2$, only moderate performance improvements can be attributed to intra-register vectorization.

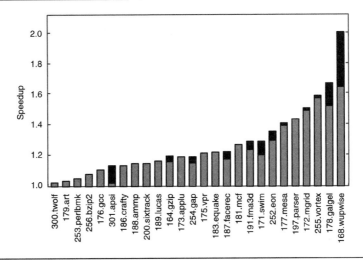

Figure 9.3   SPEC CPU2000 Speedup—2.8-Gigahertz Pentium® 4 with HT Technology

Several reasons can be given to explain the moderate impact of intra-register vectorization on this wider variety of applications. Most importantly, many benchmarks spend a significant part of their execution time in hot spots that simply cannot be optimized with the current vectorization methodology or multimedia extensions, so that Amdahl's law restricts the best obtainable speedup. In other cases, vectorization is possible but exhibits a slowdown due to the performance penalties of data rearranging instructions, misaligned memory references, failure of store-to-load forwarding, or the additional overhead of run-time optimizations to enable vectorization. Finally, for a few applications, memory hierarchy performance restricts improvements that can be obtained with computational optimizations. Future trends in multimedia extensions may resolve some of these complications, which will, in turn, increase the importance of multimedia vectorization in general-purpose computing as well, as explained in the next section.

Future Trends in Multimedia Extensions

Multimedia extensions have also made their entry in the domains of embedded and mobile computing. Intel Wireless MMX technology (Paver, Aldrich, and Kahn 2004), for example, provides high-performance, low-power multimedia extensions to Intel XScale® microarchitecture, which can help to improve software performance on Intel mobile devices. The vectorization methodology described in this book has also been employed in Intel C++ and Fortran compilers for Intel XScale microarchitecture, which provides programmers a similar look and feel in exploiting these multimedia extensions. Consider, for example, the following contents of a source file `bsat.c`:

```
#define N 128
unsigned char x[N], y[N], z[N];

void sat(int n) {
  int i;
  for (i = 0; i < n; i++) {
    int t = x[i] + y[i];
    z[i] = (t <= 255) ? t : 255;
  }
}
```

This source file is optimized for Intel Wireless MMX technology by the Intel XScale compiler `ccxsc` by means of following command line session, which contains a few familiar elements:

```
=> ccxsc -QTPxsc3 -Qvec_report1 bsat.c

bsat.c(6) : (col. 3) remark: LOOP WAS VECTORIZED
```

The resulting assembly is as follows. Figure 9.4 shows the speedup of exploiting Intel Wireless MMX technology when compared with a sequential implementation of function `sat()` on a 377-megahertz Intel® PXA27x processor.

```
L:  ...                    ;
    wldrd   wR0, [r1, #0]  ; load  8 bytes from x
    wldrd   wR1, [r2, #0]  ; load  8 bytes from y
    waddbus wR0, wR0, wR1  ; add   8 bytes and saturate
    wstrd   wR0, [r3, #0]  ; store 8 bytes into z
    ...                    ;
    bcc     L              ; looping logic
```

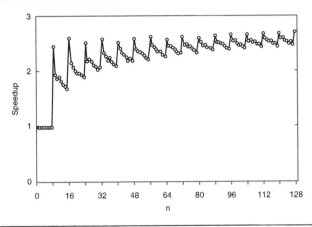

Figure 9.4   Saturation Speedup—377-Megahertz Intel® PXA27x Processor

Because short lifecycles and the wide diversity of supported hardware features in the domains of embedded and mobile computing make hand optimizing applications for each next generation of multimedia extensions virtually impossible, retargetable compilation systems that can be easily modified to support new multimedia extensions can be expected to become essential tools in these domains (Pokam, Simonnet, and Bodin 2001).

The importance of automatic vectorization for multimedia extensions is likely to increase in the domain of general-purpose computing as well. At the architectural level, further replicating execution units to support the full 128-bit data format, rather than just half the data format that is currently supported, or even wider multimedia data formats, generalized support for store-to-load forwarding, and reduced performance penalties for misaligned memory references can all be expected to improve the effectiveness and applicability of multimedia extensions in the near future. At the programming level, an increased awareness of the capabilities of vectorizing compilers for multimedia extensions could even change common programming practices to make code more amenable to effective automatic vectorization, much like the Fortran coding styles that evolved during the time of vector processors. Finally, multimedia extensions and compiler technology can be expected to mature beyond today's capabilities (Ren, Wu, and Padua 2003; Talla, John, and Burger 2003; Zhou and Ross 2002).

References

Abrosimov, D., V. Zelenogorsky, and M. Kryukov. 1999. Computer simulation of water surface view. In *Graphicon'99: The Ninth International Conference on Computer Graphics and Vision*, Moscow, Russia (August).

Aburto, Alfred. 1992. *Flops Benchmark,* (aburto@sbcglobal.net).

Aho, Alfred V., Ravi Sethi, and Jeffrey D. Ullman. 1986. *Compilers: Principles, Techniques and Tools.* Addison-Wesley, Reading, Massachusetts.

Allen, Randy and Ken Kennedy. 1987. Automatic translation of FORTRAN programs to vector form. *ACM Transactions on Programming Languages and Systems,* 9: 491–542.

Allen, Randy and Ken Kennedy. 2002. *Optimizing Compilers for Modern Architectures.* Morgan Kaufmann Publishers, San Francisco, California.

Amdahl, G.M. 1967. Validity of the single processor approach to achieving large scale computing capabilities. In *AFIPS Conference Proceedings,* 30: 483–485.

Ancourt, Corinne and Francois Irigoin. 1991. Scanning polyhedra with DO loops. In *Proceedings of Third ACM SIGPLAN Symposium on Principles and Practice of Parallel Programming,* pages 39–50.

Antonakos, James L. 1997. *The Pentium Microprocessor.* Prentice Hall, Upper Saddle River, New Jersey.

Appel, Andrew W. and Maia Ginsburg. 1998. *Modern Compiler Implementation in C.* Cambridge University Press, Cambridge, UK.

Ayguadé, Eduard and Jordi Torres. 1993. Partitioning the statement per iteration space using non-singular matrices. In *Proceedings of the International Conference on Supercomputing,* pages 407–415.

Banerjee, Utpal. 1988. *Dependence Analysis for Supercomputing.* Kluwer Academic Publishers, Boston, Massachusetts.

———. 1990. Unimodular transformations of double loops. In *Proceedings of Third Workshop on Languages and Compilers for Parallel Computing.*

———. 1993. *Loop Transformations for Restructuring Compilers: The Foundations.* A Book Series on Loop Transformations for Restructuring Compilers. Kluwer Academic Publishers, Boston, Massachusetts.

———. 1994. *Loop Parallelization.* A Book Series on Loop Transformations for Restructuring Compilers. Kluwer Academic Publishers, Boston, Massachusetts.

———. 1997. *Dependence Analysis.* A Book Series on Loop Transformations for Restructuring Compilers. Kluwer Academic Publishers, Boston, Massachusetts.

Barnett, Michael and Christian Lengauer. 1992. Unimodularity considered non-essential. In *Proceedings of the Second Joint International Conference on Vector and Parallel Processing.*

Bhargava, Ravi, Lizy K. John, Brian L. Evans, and Ramesh Radhakrishnan. 1998. Evaluating MMX technology using DSP and multimedia applications. In *International Symposium on Microarchitecture,* pages 37–46.

Bik, Aart J.C., Milind Girkar, Paul M Grey, and Xinmin Tian. 2001. Efficient exploitation of parallelism on Pentium® III and Pentium® 4 Processor-based systems. *Intel Technology Journal* (February). This paper is available at http://www.intel.com/technology/itj/.

———. 2001. Experiments with automatic vectorization for the Pentium 4 Processor. In *Proceedings of the 9th Workshop on Compilers for Parallel Computers*, pages 1–10, Edinburgh, Scotland, UK (June).

———. 2002. Automatic detection of saturation and clipping idioms. In *Proceedings of the 15th International Workshop on Languages and Compilers for Parallel Computing*, pages 75–88, College Park, Maryland (July).

———. 2002. Automatic intra-register vectorization for the Intel architecture. *International Journal on Parallel Processing*, 30(2):65–98.

Bik, Aart J.C., Milind Girkar, and Mohammad R. Haghighat. 1999. Incorporating Intel® MMX™ Technology into a Java† JIT compiler. *Scientific Programming*, 7(2):167–184.

Bistry, David et al. 1997. *The complete guide to the MMX™ technology*. McGraw-Hill, New York, NY.

Blank, T. 1990. The Maspar MP-1 architecture. In *Proceedings of the IEEE Compcon*.

Booth, Rick. 1997. *Inner Loops: A Sourcebook for Fast 32-Bit Software Development*. Addison-Wesley, Boston, Massachusetts, Pearson Education.

Brainerd, W.S., C.H. Goldberg, and J.C. Adams. 1990. *FORTRAN 90*. Academic Service.

Burke, Michael and Ron Cytron. 1986. Interprocedural dependence analysis and parallelization. In *Proceedings of the Symposium on Compiler Construction*, pages 162–175.

Callahan, D., K.D. Cooper, K. Kennedy, and L.M. Torczon. 1986. Interprocedural constant propagation. In *Proceedings of the SIGPLAN Symposium on Compiler Construction*, New York, NY.

Callahan, D., J. Dongarra, and D. Levine. 1988. Vectorizing compilers: A test suite and results. In *Proceedings of Supercomputing*, pages 98–105. The latest version of the Fortran benchmark is available at http://www.netlib.org/benchmark/.

Callahan, D., K. Kennedy, and A. Porterfield. 1991. Software prefetching. In *Proceedings of the Fourth International Conference on Architectural Support for Programming Languages and Operating Systems*, 26: 40–52, SIGPLAN Notices.

Cockshott, Paul and Ken Renfrew. 2002. *SIMD Programming with Vector Pascal*. University of Glasgow. Vector Pascal is available at http://www.dcs.gla.ac.uk/~wpc/.

Cooper, Keith D., Mary W. Hall, and Ken Kennedy. 1992. Procedure cloning. In *Proceedings of the IEEE International Conference on Computer Languages*, pages 96–105.

Cooper, Keith D., Ken Kennedy, and Linda Torczon. 1986. The impact of interprocedural analysis and optimization in the R^n programming environment. *ACM Transactions on Programming Languages and Systems*, 8(4):491–523.

Dantzig, George B. 1963. *Linear Programming and Extensions*. Princeton University Press, Princeton, New Jersey.

Dantzig, George B. and B. Curtis Eaves. 1973. Fourier-Motzkin elimination and its dual. *Journal of Combinatorial Theory*, 14:288–297.

DeVries, Derek J. and Corinna G. Lee. 1995. A vectorizing SUIF compiler. In *Proceedings of the First SUIF Compiler Workshop*, pages 59–67.

Dongarra, Jack J., Jeremy Du Croz, Sven Hammarling, and Iain Duff. 1990. A set of level 3 basic linear algebra subprograms. *ACM Transactions on Mathematical Software*, 16:1–17.

———. 1990. A set of level 3 basic linear algebra subprograms: Model implementation and test programs. *ACM Transactions on Mathematical Software*, 16:18–28.

Dongarra, Jack J., Jeremy Du Croz, Sven Hammarling, and Richard J. Hanson. 1988. An extended set of FORTRAN basic linear algebra subprograms. *ACM Transactions on Mathematical Software*, 14: 1–17.

———. 1988. An extended set of FORTRAN basic linear algebra subprograms: Model implementation and test programs. *ACM Transactions on Mathematical Software*, 14: 18–32.

Dongarra, Jack J., Iain S. Duff, Danny C. Sorensen, and Henk A. van der Vorst. 1991. *Solving Linear Systems on Vector and Shared Memory Computers*. Society for Industrial and Applied Mathematics.

Dongarra, Jack J. and Stanley C. Eisenstat. 1984. Squeezing the most out of an algorithm in CRAY FORTRAN. *ACM Transactions on Mathematical Software*, 10: 219–230.

Dongarra, Jack J. et al. 1994. *Linpack Benchmark*. This benchmark is available at http://www.netlib.org/benchmark/.

Dowd, Kevin and Charles Severance. 1998. *High Performance Computing*. O'Reilly & Associates, Sebastopol, California.

Dowling, Michael L. 1990. Optimal code parallelization using unimodular transformations. *Parallel Computing*, 16: 157–171.

Fischer, Charles N. and Richard J. LeBlanc Jr. 1991. *Crafting a Compiler with C*. Benjamin-Cummings, Menlo Park, California.

Fisher, Randall J. and Henry G. Dietz. 1998. Compiling for SIMD within a register. In *Proceedings of the 1998 Workshop on Languages and Compilers for Parallel Computing*.

Flynn, M.J. Very high-speed computing systems. 1966. *Proceedings of the IEEE*, 54(12): 1901–1909.

——. 1995. *Computer Architecture*. Jones and Bartlett Publishers, Boston, Massachusetts.

Gallivan, Kyle, William Jalby, and Dennis Gannon. 1988. On the problem of optimizing data transfers for complex memory systems. In *Proceedings of the International Conference on Supercomputing*, pages 238–253.

Garey, Michael R. and David S. Johnson. 1999. *Computers and Intractability—A guide to the theory of NP-completeness*. W.H. Freeman and Company, New York, NY.

Gerber, Richard. 2002. *The Software Optimization Cookbook*. Intel Press, Hillsboro, OR.

Gilbert, William J. 1976. *Modern Algebra with Applications*. John Wiley and Sons, New York, NY.

Gosling, James, Bill Joy, and Guy Steele. 1996. *The Java™ Language Specfication*. The Java Series. Addison-Wesley, Reading, Massachusetts.

Greene, Michael A. 1997. Pentium processor with MMX technology performance. In *Proceedings of the IEEE Compcon*, pages 263–267.

Guthaus, Matthew R., Jeffrey S. Ringenberg, Dan Ernst, Todd M. Austin, Trevor Mudge, and Richard B. Brown. 2001. MiBench: A free, commercially representative embedded benchmark suite. In *IEEE 4th Annual Workshop on Workload Characterization*, Austin, Texas (December).

Hennessy, John L. and David A. Patterson. 1990. *Computer Architecture: A Quantitative Approach*. Morgan Kaufmann Publishers, San Mateo, California.

Henning, John L. 2000. SPEC CPU2000: Measuring CPU performance in the new millennium. *IEEE Computer*, 33(7): 28–35.

Hinton, Glenn, Dave Sager, Mike Upton, Darrell Boggs, Doug Carmean, Alan Kyker, and Patrice Roussel. 2001. The microarchitecture of the Pentium 4 Processor. *Intel Technology Journal*. This paper is made available at http://www.intel.com/technology/itj/.

Hockney, R.W. and C.R. Jesshope. 1981. *Parallel Computers: Architecture, Programming and Algorithms*. Adam Hilger, Bristol, England.

Hopcroft, John E. and Jeffrey D. Ullman. 1979. *Introduction to Automata Theory, Languages, and Computation*. Addison-Wesley, Reading, Massachusetts.

Intel Corporation. 1997. *Intel Architecture MMX™ Technology— Programmer's Reference Manual*. This manual is made available at http://developer.intel.com/

———. 1998-2004. *The high-performance Intel® C++ and Fortran Compilers*. More information on the compilers can be found at http://developer.intel.com/software/products/compilers/.

———. 1998-2004. *The Intel VTune™ Performance Analyzers*. More information on the performance analyzers can be found at http://developer.intel.com/software/products/vtune/.

———. 2003. *IA-32 Intel® Architecture Optimization Reference Manual*. This manual is made available at http://developer.intel.com/.

———. 2003. *IA-32 Intel® Architecture Software Developer's Manual, Volume 1: Basic Architecture*. This manual is made available at http://developer.intel.com/.

———. 2003. *IA-32 Intel® Architecture Software Developer's Manual, Volume 2: Instruction Set Reference*. This manual is made available at http://developer.intel.com/.

———. 2003. *IA-32 Intel® Architecture Software Developer's Manual, Volume 3: System Programming Guide*. This manual is made available at http://developer.intel.com/.

International Organization for Standardization. 1999. *ISO/IEC 9899:1999*. The standard can be obtained at http://www.iso.org/.

Jordan, Harry F. and Gita Alaghband. 2003. *Fundamentals of Parallel Processing*. Prentice Hall, Upper Saddle River, NJ, Pearson Education.

Kernighan, Brian W. and Dennis M. Ritchie. 1988. *The C Programming Language*. Prentice Hall, Englewood Cliffs, New Jersey.

Knuth, Donald E. 1997. *The Art of Computer Programming*, vol. 1: Fundamental Algorithms. Addison Wesley, Boston, Massachusetts, third edition.

———. 1997. *The Art of Computer Programming*, vol. 2: Semi-numerical Algorithms. Addison Wesley, Boston, Massachusetts, third edition.

———. 1997. *The Art of Computer Programming*, vol. 3: Sorting and Searching. Addison Wesley, Boston, Massachusetts, third edition.

Koffman, Elliot B. and Frank L. Friedman. 1990. *Problem Solving and Structured Programming in FORTRAN 77*. Addison-Wesley, Reading, Massachusetts, fourth edition. Temple University.

Krall, Andreas and Sylvain Lelait. 2000. Compilation techniques for multimedia processors. *International Journal of Parallel Programming*, 28(4): 347-361.

Kuck, David J. 1978. *The Structure of Computers and Computations*. John Wiley and Sons, New York, NY. vol. 1.

Kumar, Vipin, Ananth Grama, Anshul Gupta, and George Karypis. 1994. *Introduction to Parallel Programming*. The Benjamin/Cummings Publishing Company, Redwood City, California.

Lamport, Leslie. 1974. The parallel execution of DO loops. *Communications of the ACM*, pages 83-93.

Larsen, Samuel. 2000. Exploiting superword level parallelism with multimedia instruction sets. Master's thesis, Massachusetts Institute of Technology.

Larsen, Samuel and Saman Amarasinghe. 2000. Exploiting superword level parallelism with multimedia instruction sets. In *Proceedings ACM SIGPLAN Conference on Programming Languages Design and Implementation*.

Larsen, Samuel, Emmett Witchel, and Saman Amarasinghe. 2002. Increasing and detecting memory address congruence. In *Proceedings of the 11th International Conference on Parallel Architectures and Compilation Techniques*. Charlottesville, VA.

Lawson, C.L., R.J. Hanson, D.R. Kincaid, and F.T. Krogh. 1979. Algorithm 539: Basic linear algebra subprograms for FORTRAN usage. *ACM Transactions on Mathematical Software*, 5: 324–325.

———. 1979. Basic linear algebra subprograms for FORTRAN usage. *ACM Transactions on Mathematical Software*, 5: 308–323.

Lee, Chunho, Miodrag Potkonjak, and William H. Mangione-Smith. 1997. MediaBench: A tool for evaluating and synthesizing multimedia and communication systems. *IEEE Micro*, 30.

Lee, Ruby B. Subword parallelism with MAX-2. 1996. *IEEE Micro*, 16(4): 52–59.

Lempel, Oded, Alex Peleg, and Uri Weiser. 1997. Intel's MMX technology: A new instruction set extension. In *Proceedings of the IEEE Compcon*, pages 255–259.

Levesque, John M. and Joel W. Williamson. 1991. *A Guidebook to FORTRAN on Supercomputers*. Academic Press, San Diego.

Levine, D., D. Callahan, and J. Dongarra. 1991. A comparative study of automatic vectorizing compilers. *Parallel Computing*, 17(10–11):1223–1244. The latest version of the Fortran benchmark is made available at http://www.netlib.org/benchmark/.

Lewis, John G. and Horst D. Simon. 1988. The impact of hardware gather/scatter on sparse Gaussian elimination. *SIAM J. Sci. Stat. Comput.*, 9: 304–311.

Lewis, Ted G. 1994. *Foundations of Parallel Programming*. IEEE Computer Society Press, Washington.

Li, Wei and Keshav Pingali. 1992. Access normalization: Loop restructuring for NUMA compilers. In *Proceedings of the Fifth International Conference on Architectural Support for Programming Languages and Operating Systems*, pages 285–295.

———. 1992. A singular loop transformation framework based on non-singular matrices. In *Proceedings of the Fifth Workshop on Languages and Compilers for Parallel Computing*.

Loveman, David B. 1977. Program improvement by source-to-source transformations. *Journal of the ACM*, 24: 121–145.

Mano, M. Morris. 1993. *Computer System Architecture*. Prentice Hall, Englewood Cliffs, New Jersey, third edition.

McCalpin, John D. 1991. *STREAM Benchmark*. University of Virginia. More information can be found at http://www.cs.virginia.edu/stream/.

Microsoft. 2003. Microsoft® Visual C++® Developer Center. More information can be found at http://msdn.microsoft.com/visualc/.

Muchnick, Steven S. 1997. *Advanced Compiler Design and Implementation*. Morgan Kaufmann Publishers, San Francisco, California.

Neves, Kenneth W. 1984. Vectorization of scientific software. In J.S. Kowalik, editor, *High-Speed Computing*, pages 277-291. Springer-Verlag, Berlin, NATO ASI Series, vol. F7.

OpenMP. 1998. *Simple, Portable, Scalable SMP Programming*. More information can be found at http://www.openmp.org/.

Padua, David A. and Michael J. Wolfe. 1986. Advanced compiler optimizations for supercomputers. *Communications of the ACM*, 29: 1184-1201.

Parsons, Thomas W. 1992. *Introduction to Compiler Construction*. Computer Science Press, New York, NY.

Paver, Nigel, Bradley Aldrich, and Moinul Khan. 2004. *Programming with Intel Wireless MMX Technology: A Developer's Guide to Mobile Multimedia Applications*. Intel Press, Hillsboro, OR.

Peleg, Alex and Uri Weiser. 1996. MMX technology extension to the Intel Architecture. *IEEE Micro*, 16(4): 42-50.

Plauger, P.J. 1992. *The Standard C Library*. Prentice Hall, Englewood Cliffs, New Jersey.

Pokam, Gilles, Julien Simonnet, and François Bodin. 2001. A retargetable preprocessor for multimedia instructions. In *Proceedings of the Ninth Workshop on Compilers for Parallel Computers*, pages 291-301, Edinburgh, Scotland, UK.

Polychronopoulos, Constantine D. 1988. *Parallel Programming and Compilers*. Kluwer Academic Publishers, Boston, Massachusetts.

Pryanishnikov, Ivan, Andreas Krall, and Nigel Horspool. 2003. Pointer alignment analysis for processors with SIMD instructions. In *Proceedings of the 5th Workshop on Media and Streaming Processors*, pages 50-57, San Diego, California (December).

Quinn, Michael J. 1987. *Designing Efficient Algorithms for Parallel Computers*. McGraw-Hill, New York, NY.

Quinn, Michael J. 1994. *Parallel Computing: Theory and Practice*. McGraw-Hill, New York, NY.

Raman, Srinivas K., Vladimir Pentkovski, and Jagannath Keshava. 2000. Implementing Streaming SIMD Extensions on the Pentium III Processor. *IEEE Micro*, 20(4): 47–57.

Ren, Gang, Peng Wu, and David A. Padua. 2003. A preliminary study on the vectorization of multimedia applications for multimedia extensions. In *Proceedings of the 16th International Workshop on Languages and Compilers for Parallel Computing*, College Station, Texas.

Russel, R.M. 1978. The CRAY-1 processor system. *Communications of the ACM*, 21(1): 63–72.

Ryder, Barbara G. 1979. Constructing the call graph of a program. *IEEE Transactions on Software Engineering*, SE-5: 216–226.

Schmit, Michael L. 1995. *Pentium™ Processor Optimization Tools*. Academic Press Professional, Boston, Massachusetts.

Schrijver, Alexander. 1986. *Theory of Linear and Integer Programming*. John Wiley and Sons, Chichester, England.

Sedgewick, Robert. 1988. *Algorithms*. Addison-Wesley, Reading, Massachusetts, second edition.

Shin, Jaewook, Jacqueline Chame, and Mary W. Hall. 2003. Exploiting superword-level locality in multimedia extension architectures. *Journal of Instruction-Level Parallelism*, 5: 1–28.

Sima, Dezső, Terence Fountain, and Péter Kacsuk. 1997. *Advanced Computer Architectures: A Design Space Approach*. Addison-Wesley, Harlow, England.

Skadron, Kevin, Marty Humphrey, Bin Huang, Edgar Hilton, Jihao Luo, and Paul Allaire. 2001. The use of mini-vector instructions for implementing high-speed feedback controllers on general-purpose computers. In *Proceedings of the Third Workshop on Media and Stream Processors* (December).

Slingerland, Nathan T. and Alan Jay Smith. 2000. Multimedia instruction sets for general purpose microprocessors: A survey. Technical Report CSD-00-1124, University of California, Berkeley.

Smith, Kevin B., Aart J.C. Bik, and Xinmin Tian. 2004. Support for the Intel® Pentium® 4 Processor with Hyper-Threading Technology in Intel® 8.0 Compilers. *Intel Technology Journal*, 8(1). This paper is available at http://www.intel.com/technology/itj/.

Sreraman, N. and R. Govindarajan. 2000. A vectorizing compiler for multimedia extensions. *International Journal on Parallel Processing*.

Standard Performance Evaluation Corporation. 2000. *SPEC CPU2000*. More information can be found at http://www.spec.org/.

Stroustrup, Bjarne. 1991. *The C++ Programming Language*. Addison-Wesley, Reading, Massachusetts, second edition.

Talla, Deepu, Lizy K. John, and Doug Burger. 2003. Bottlenecks in multimedia processing with SIMD style extensions and architectural enhancements. *IEEE Transactions on Computers*, 52(8):1015–1031.

Tarjan, R. 1972. Depth-first search and linear graph algorithms. *SIAM J. Computing*, pages 146–160.

Thakkar, Shreekant and Tom Huff. 1999. Internet streaming SIMD extensions. *IEEE Computer*, 32(12): 26–34.

Tian, Xinmin, Aart J.C. Bik, Milind Girkar, Paul M Grey, Hideki Saito, and Ernesto Su. 2002. Intel OpenMP C++/Fortran compiler for Hyper-Threading technology: Implementation and performance. *Intel Technology Journal*. This paper is available at http://www.intel.com/technology/itj/.

van de Goor, A.J. 1989. *Computer Architecture*. Delftse Uitgevers Maatschappij, Delft.

van Engelen, Robert A. and Kyle A. Gallivan. 2001. An efficient algorithm for pointer-to-array access conversion for compiling and optimizing DSP applications. In *Proceedings of the International Workshop on Innovative Architectures for Future Generation High-Performance Processors and Systems*, pages 80–89, Maui, Hawaii (January).

Wolf, Michael E. and Monica S. Lam. 1991. A data locality optimizing algorithm. In *Proceedings ACM SIGPLAN Conference on Programming Languages Design and Implementation*, pages 30–44.

———. 1991. A loop transformation theory and an algorithm to maximize parallelism. *IEEE Transactions on Parallel and Distributed Algorithms*, pages 452–471.

Wolfe, Michael J. 1986. Loop skewing: The wavefront method revisited. *International Journal of Parallel Programming*, 15: 279-293.

――――. 1988. Vector optimization vs. vectorization. *Journal of Parallel and Distributed Computing*, 5: 551-567.

――――. 1989. *Optimizing Supercompilers for Supercomputers*. The MIT Press, Cambridge, Massachusetts.

――――. 1996. *High Performance Compilers for Parallel Computing*. Addison-Wesley, Redwood City, California.

Xue, Jingling. 1994. Automating non-unimodular loop transformations for massive parallelism. *Parallel Computing*, 20: 711-728.

Zhou, Jingren and Kenneth A. Ross. 2002. Implementing database operations using SIMD instructions. In *Proceedings of the ACM SIGMOD Conference*, pages 145-156, Madison, Wisconsin (June 4-6).

Zima, Hans and Barbara Chapman. 1990. *Supercompilers for Parallel and Vector Computers*. ACM Press, New York, NY.

Index

T

throughput, *See* bandwidth

topological sorting, 71

triplet notation, 70, 77

type conversions, *See* data types, conversions

U

unimodular transformation, 171

V

vector processors, 5, 13, 213, 218

vector registers, reusing, 173

vectorization, 5, 13
  arithmetic operators, 97
  intra-register, 13, 15, 69, 76, 119, 145, 158, 188, 194, 196, 199, 207
  outer loop, 172
  validity, 69

vectorizing compilers, 6, 193, 218

vectors
  data type, 149
  length, 5, 18, 59, 70, 71, 77, 79, 81, 155, 165
  vector data type, 79

VLIW (very long instruction word) architectures, 7

W

while statements, 47, 48, 206

wrap-around arithmetic, 10, 14, 25, 45, 75, 86, 87, 89, 150

Z

zero extensions, 44, 100, 103, 146

About the Author

Aart J.C. Bik (a.k.a. Arjan Bik) was born in 1969 in Gouda, the Netherlands. In 1988, he passed the propaedeutic exam in computer science cum laude. He received his M.S. in computer science cum laude from Utrecht University in 1992. He received his Ph.D. from Leiden University in 1996. His Ph.D. research under supervision of Professor Harry A.G. Wijshoff resulted in the implementation of a *sparse compiler,* a compiler that transforms a program that uses a two-dimensional array as implementation for every matrix into a semantically equivalent program that operates on complicated compact data structures for matrices that are sparse. His Ph.D. thesis received the C.J. Kok Award (outstanding thesis award) from Leiden University. In 1996–1997, Aart was a postdoctoral researcher at Indiana University, Bloomington, where he conducted research in high performance compilers for the Java programming language under supervision of Professor Dennis B. Gannon. In 1998, Aart began work on Java JIT compilation as a Senior Software Engineer at the Microcomputer Research Laboratories of Intel Corporation in Santa Clara, California. In 1999, he moved to what is now the Software Solutions Group of Intel Corporation, where he is currently working as a Senior Staff Engineer on the high performance Intel® C++ and Fortran compilers. In March 2002, Aart received the Intel Achievement Award—the highest company award—for making SSE2 easier to use through automatic vectorization and thereby increasing Intel NetBurst® microarchitecture usage.

66 *As the pace of technology introduction increases, it's difficult to keep up. Intel Press has established an impressive portfolio. The breadth of topics is a reflection of both Intel's diversity as well as our commitment to serve a broad technical community.*

I hope you will take advantage of these products to further your technical education. **99**

Patrick Gelsinger
Senior Vice President and Chief Technology Officer
Intel Corporation

Turn the page to learn about titles from Intel Press for system developers

Practical Advice for Writing Faster, More Efficient Code

Intel® Integrated Performance Primitives
How to Optimize Software Applications Using Intel® IPP
By Stewart Taylor
ISBN 0-9717861-3-5

Intel® Integrated Performance Primitives (Intel® IPP) is a software library for application developers that increases performance from Intel's latest microprocessors. Incorporating these functions into your code provides time-to-market advantages while reducing the overall cost of development. The lead developer of Intel IPP explains how this library gives you access to advanced processor features without having to write processor-specific code.

Introducing the many uses of Intel IPP, this book explores the range of possible applications, from audio processing to graphics and video. Extensive examples written in C++ show you how to solve common imaging, audio/video, and graphics problems.

You will learn how to:
- Become proficient using the Intel IPP library and application programming interface
- Apply Intel IPP to improve performance and speed up the development of your applications
- Solve common application problems using Intel IPP

❝ Filled with comprehensive real-world examples. I'm recommending this book to my entire software team.❞

*Davis W. Frank,
Software Program Manager,
palmOne, Inc.*

● *The Software Optimization Cookbook*
High-performance Recipes for the Intel® Architecture
By Richard Gerber
ISBN 0-9712887-1-2

Through simple explanations and C/C++ code samples, a former Intel trainer explains the techniques and tools you can use to improve the performance of applications for Intel® Pentium® III and Pentium 4 processors. This book also includes tested food recipes for those long nights of coding and testing.

Use performance tools and tested concepts to improve applications

● *Programming with Hyper-Threading Technology*
How to Write Multithreaded Software for Intel® IA-32 Processors
By Richard Gerber and Andrew Binstock
ISBN 0-9717861-4-3

For software developers who are accustomed to single-threaded programs, this book helps you to make a seamless transition to multithreaded code. You will learn how to use Hyper-Threading Technology to maximize processor throughput, efficiency, and parallelism. It is a practical, hands-on volume with immediately usable code examples that enable readers to quickly master the necessary building blocks.

❝ ...comprehensive and filled with illustrative examples about parallel programming.❞

Oleksiy Danikhno,
Development Director,
A4Vision, Inc.

Please go to this Web site

www.intel.com/intelpress/bookbundles.htm

for complete information about
our popular book bundles.
Each bundle is designed to
ensure that you read important
complementary topics together,
while enjoying a total purchase
price that is far less than the
combined prices of the
individual books.

About Intel Press

Intel Press is the authoritative source of timely, highly relevant, and innovative books to help software and hardware developers speed up their development process. We collaborate only with leading industry experts to deliver reliable, first-to-market information about the latest technologies, processes, and strategies.

Our products are planned with the help of many people in the developer community and we encourage you to consider becoming a customer advisor. If you would like to help us and gain additional advance insight to the latest technologies, we encourage you to consider the Intel Press Customer Advisor Program. You can **register** here:

www.intel.com/intelpress/register.htm

For information about bulk orders or corporate sales, please send email to
bulkbooksales@intel.com

Other Developer Resources from Intel

At these Web sites you can also find valuable technical information and resources for developers:

developer.intel.com	general information for developers
www.intel.com/IDS	content, tools, training, and the Early Access Program for software developers
www.intel.com/software/products	programming tools to help you develop high-performance applications
www.intel.com/idf	world-wide technical conference, the Intel Developer Forum

INTEL
PRESS